# Ramona's

# Angel

## By

## P L Jenkinson

# Ramona's Angel

## By P L Jenkinson

This story is a work of fiction.  All aspects of this work; whether invented by the author or any real places which are mentioned within, have been used fictitiously.

Dedicated to Liam,

with much love and pride

Much gratitude goes to Nicky Wilkinson for all of her hard work in helping me edit this, my debut novel.  Your input has been invaluable and very much appreciated.

Also, many thanks to Ray Graham, The Cloud Whisperer, for your amazing artistic, technical and photographic expertise in helping me to create the cover.

Last but not least.  Thank you to my amazing friends and colleagues, who inspire me on a daily basis.

# Prologue

## South-West coast of Scotland, 1977

The sad faced little boy was sitting on the window sill looking out across the harbour towards The Queens Arms pub on the other side; that tight, familiar fear beginning to build within his chest. Daddy would be heading home soon, from over there. It was starting to get dark and the wind was intensifying, a storm was brewing sure enough. Today was the last day of the Tattie holiday, the name given to the October half term in that part of Scotland, due to the local children historically being given the time off school to help the farmers with the last of the potato harvest. Back to school tomorrow though.

He'd make sure he was tucked up in bed before his dad got in; he should be okay then but he really wished he still had his mammy to look after him. He shifted his gaze to a photograph of her that was sitting on the mantel-piece. He missed her, yet without her picture to remind him he found it so difficult to recall her face in his mind's eye. "Poor wee laddie," he remembered overhearing Mr McStay saying to his wife at Mam's wake.

Looking across the street the boy noticed the lights in the Isle Kirk switching off one by one as evening fell. Mrs McGuffie exited the building with her usual shuffling gait. She did the flowers in the Kirk and helped his daddy, Reverend Eban Whithorn, keep the place in order after service. Or rather, Mrs McGuffie kept the Kirk in order after service as his dad was far more likely to be found propping up the bar at The Queen's Arms. Sometimes she'd call over and collect his school clothes for washing or fix him some tea, but not today. Instead she raised her hand in a brief wave in his direction and shuffled off past the McWilliam's shop towards her own cottage at the end of the row.

He heard the hinges of the back door creak as it opened slowly. His heart began to pound and he couldn't stop panting as the panic set in. He'd not been watching out properly; it must be daddy back from the pub early. He wanted to run upstairs but found himself frozen to the spot in fear; it was as if all the muscles of his body were ignoring him. He held his breath to try and stem the panic though all he could hear was the pounding of his heart as the throbbing in his chest worsened.

"It's alright wee man." It was Mr McStay. What was he doing there? Through the frosted glass of the door there looked to be others too. Mrs McStay, she was the school teacher, and he'd be seeing her in the morning...wouldn't he? And Jock Maguire, the Harbour Master. Why were they here? They must be looking for the Reverend.

"My da's no' here," the boy said. "I think he'll be home soon though."

"Your daddy's still in the pub laddie," Jock said. "He'll be a while yet, yae mark my words, I've just put another pint and a dram or two in front o' him. I reckon that gives us about a half o'the hour." He indicated to the others.

Mrs McStay smiled. "Now ye neednae' worry Michael. Ye neednae be scared o'the man no more. We promised your good mother we'd look out for ye, save yae from him if it came ta it. And God rest her sweet soul but wae' intend tae keep our word tae' her."

Tears began to well up in the boy's eyes, a mixture of fear and relief, if there could be such a thing. "My ma?" he asked. "My mammy?"

Mr McStay rested a huge hand to the boy's shoulder. "Och laddie," he said softly, "yae didnae think that fine woman would've left yae alone wi' a man like that if she'd o' had anything tae do wi' it do yae? A man o' his standing too. He shames us all so he does..."

"That'll do now Joe, he's just a child." Mrs McStay stemmed her husband's rant. "Now, Michael, where's your shoes laddie? And your coat? Yae'll need tae wrap up tonight, yae've a journey ahead o' ya."

"Where ma' going?" Michael was worried.

Mrs McStay bent down to his level as she helped him on with his coat. She gently wiped a tear from his cheek as one broke free from her eye and rolled down her own. She smiled but a gentle quiver of her chin gave away her distress. "Now Michael, yer tae be a brave wee man now. Yer lovely mammy was my very best friend, yae know that don't yae?" He nodded. "Well before she died son, she made me promise tae look out for yae. She had a plan yae see. She was goin'ae take yae away from here, from him. The both o' yae were going tae get away from him. But before she got the chance tae..." She stopped herself, tears rolling freely now. "Well now, it's just you Michael, and we need ta keep our promise t'yer mammy, we need ta make sure yae're safe laddie. It's what she wanted son, d'ya understand?"

It was very dark outside now and the rain was pounding so hard it looked like rods of glass shattering on impact with the stone cobbles. It made visibility poor to the point where you could barely make out the lights of the buildings on the other side of the harbour, including The Queens Arms. Jock Maguire threw a blanket around the boy's shoulders as added protection from the weather. Though in reality it was drenched in minutes and became an added soggy weight for his small frame to carry.

They made their way down the back alley to the end of Main Street and rounded the corner of Mrs McGuffie's cottage and onto Harbour Row.

"Where we going?" Michael asked.

"Tae the Cairn, tae where the old life boat used tae launch back in the day," Jock said. "The Charlie Peake's there, waiting for us laddie."

*The Charlie Peake?* Michael puzzled. That was Jock's own fishing boat; it was sturdy enough alright, but on a night like this? In a storm like this? The odd fork of lightening hit the surface of the water out to sea, a closer one lit up the whole harbour briefly. Michael was afraid that any minute the Reverend would appear, furious at his deceit and drag him home kicking and begging for mercy. He was so afraid in fact that the poor child wet himself right there in the street but said nothing.

As they passed The Solway Harvester Inn the door blew open a little and he could hear the radio playing inside. It was "Thunder in my Heart" by Leo Sayer, *number twenty-four in this week's hit-parade* it said. His mammy would've liked that; she liked Leo Sayer. The Reverend didn't allow the radio on anymore though, Michael wasn't sure why.

"We have tae hurry," Mr McStay said. "They'll be waiting for them at Ku-koo-bree (Kirkcudbright)."

They headed down the slope to the old launch. The Charlie Peake was about twenty-five yards out, it was too shallow for her to get any closer, but it meant that they should be able to clear the harbour without being seen from the main street. Mrs McStay kept a tight hold of the boy's hand all the way to the water's edge, where she bent down and hugged him hard. "This is as far as me and Joe are going Michael. I'm going tae miss yae so much laddie. Our wee classroom'll no' be the same without yae, but I'll be sleeping easier in ma bed knowing yer safe, knowing that yae'll be happy an' cared for wi' yer auntie, an' knowing that I didnae let yer mammy down. She wanted this for yae Michael, this was always her plan. I just wish she could've been here for yae still." She was all but sobbing as Jock Maguire swept Michael up onto his broad shoulders and waded out into the freezing water.

The launch was dug into the side of the Cairn and the waters there were sheltered from the rest of the harbour, which was a good thing, as Jock was almost chest deep by the time they'd made it to the portside of the boat. The boy looked up to see Jamie McGuffie, Mrs McGuffie's eldest son, reach over and lift him from the shoulders of Jock, before reaching back down to help Jock aboard too. "Welcome aboard tae the two o' yae." He grinned, his features all but distorted by the rain and the howling wind.

"Feels like a south-easterly Jamie," Jock stated.

"Aye, 'tis that," Jamie winced. "An' it's going tae make getting outta here a wee bit tricky." A south-easterly wind was the worst wind direction for any vessel attempting to navigate its way out of the Isle harbour. The lay of the land meant that a strong south-easterly damn near trapped everything in there. A sail boat wouldn't have a hope in hell of getting out. A small fisher like the Charlie Peake would seriously struggle too, but these were experienced seamen; no-one knew these waters like the Harbour Master and the local fishermen. If anyone could challenge nature, then these men could.

The door of the pilot's hut opened and a woman held on to the handle for dear life as the raging wind tried to tear it out of her hand. She looked at the boy. "Oh Michael," she called over the sound of the gale. "Oh you've grown so. D'ya remember me son?"

There was the muffled sound of the wireless playing from where she stood. *"And reaching number twenty – it's the delightful Elkie Brooks with Sunshine after the Rain,"* the DJ said.

The lady did look a little familiar, but the boy couldn't quite place the face. Her voice sounded familiar too, though there seemed

11

to be the hint of an English accent to it, a bit like the sound of those folks on the tele, on Emmerdale Farm. It was still Scottish, but a bit not Scottish too and he couldn't remember where Emmerdale Farm was meant to be, in England somewhere maybe?

She wrapped a waterproof sheet around them both and pulled him in to sit beside her at the back of the boat, while Jock manned the pilot's hut and Jamie weighed anchor. "I'm your Auntie," she said. "Your mam's sister. D'ya remember me Michael?"

"I think so," he said, though he wasn't really sure. "Yae look quite like my mammy's photograph on the mantle."

His Aunt smiled. "Aye, we were two peas in a pod yer mam an' me. We were sometimes mistaken for twins when we were girls, we were so alike. But we're not. I'm just over two years older than your mam love." Her smile faded a little and she looked out to sea. "Well, than your mammy would'ae been." She tightened her arm around him. "Yae must miss her son?"

"Aye," was all he could manage without bursting into tears.

"Yae know love, your mammy was planning to fetch yae both tae live wi' me. Did yae know that Michael?" He bowed his head. "She wanted ta protect yae. Eban, yae're dad, was always a harsh man, but now the drink's taken him...well, he's a dangerous man now. Man o'God or not, he cannae be trusted sweetheart. An' before she died, your mam wanted tae make sure you'd be safe, even if she couldnae take care o' ya herself. We promised her son."

"Aye, I know. Mrs McStay said." Even as he said the words, he couldn't fathom the mixture of emotions battling through his very being. He was terrified that his daddy would catch up with him and about what would happen if he did. Would he be alright without the Reverend? He felt nothing at the thought of not seeing him again; not fearful nor regretful. Yet he was fearful of where he might end up. Ku-koo-bree? That's what the grown-ups had said. He'd been there before and so had the Reverend; he'd find him there and then what? He had a real sense of foreboding now, so much so that it was making him feel sick. The rocking and rolling of the boat as it fought its way around the Perch, at the harbour mouth, against the violence of the south-easterly wind that was pushing them back wasn't helping.

His auntie clung hard to him as the boat lurched first this way, then that. She held onto a rope with her other hand, all the time the rain pounding them all like they were nothing but blades of grass or the like. It felt never ending and it was impossible to see where they were through the torrent from above. They could've been heading out to Man, or Ireland for all Michael knew. There was no sense of direction to be had at all, no land to be spied.

"We'll no' be long now!" Jamie shouted. "There's the mouth of the harbour we're rounding now laddie. Once we're tae' open sea the wind'll be for us, help us on our way. You'll see soon enough."

The boy could just make out the bent iron marker of the perch, put there as a warning of the rocks beneath; but the iron rod had long since been bent further and further over by numerous bufferings over the years, as many a boat had skimmed it on their way in or out of the small harbour mouth. It was behind them now, which meant they were finally free of the harbour and out into the Solway Firth. Open sea. It was only then that Jock lit up the boat. Michael hadn't noticed before; they'd been sailing blind, and Jock Maguire the Harbour Master too. He'd have put a rocket up anyone else for being so foolish Jock would. Michael had heard him shouting at folk before for it. He'd called them *foolhardy* and sworn a lot.

Jamie had been right, the wind was for them and they seemed to be making progress, though it was impossible to tell how long they'd been at sea and he'd lost all track of time. It felt like forever and each lurch of the boat felt never ending. The boy felt exhausted by all of the events the evening had brought and he still felt quite sick as the boat rolled around on the hostile sea. His auntie kept a tight hold of him, but that and the intense nausea were beginning to make him feel claustrophobic, daft as that might sound out in the open Solway. Jock poked his head out of the pilot's hut window and shouted above the noise of the wind and the waves. "There! D'ya see those lights ov'r there? That's the White Bay Isle. Once we round that, we'll no' be far tae Ku-koo-bree. We'll no' be long now laddie, soon be there."

It was no good, he was going to vomit and he knew it. "I'm going tae be sick!" he shouted to his auntie, but she couldn't make out his feeble child's voice properly above the sound of the storm and he didn't have time to repeat himself. He fought his way out of her grasp despite her best efforts and lunged for the side of the boat just as the contents of his stomach parted company with him.

The rail was wet and he couldn't keep a proper grip of it as the boat listed to one side. He felt his auntie desperately trying to grab at him as she screamed for help from Jamie. The sound of the storm drowned out both of their voices as the boy's body hit the icy water. He went under, then surfaced again briefly, long enough to gasp for air. The undercurrent pulled at him hard as he reached his hand out of the water in a desperate attempt to grasp onto something, anything. The Solway Firth closed in around him and he felt himself drifting away into an icy, muffled darkness until there was nothing.

# Chapter One

Present day.

The bright red telephone burst into life again just as Liam, the junior doctor who was sitting beside it; was about to take a sip of coffee from his machine vended plastic cup. It startled him, but he didn't quite spill anything. He shuffled forward to allow the woman in dark blue scrubs to reach in behind him for the receiver. "Accident and emergency; Sister Miller speaking."

The young Doctor passed her a pen and she scribbled something rapidly onto a corner of the A4 pad she had in front of her, and then tapped at it with her index finger to attract his attention to it, while continuing her brief conversation. The junior Doctor looked at the two words she had written "trauma call", and he felt himself begin to breathe just that little bit faster in nervous anticipation. This was only the beginning of his career; he'd only been in A&E for around two months and he was going through one of the many phases well known to newly qualified Doctors the world over: self-doubt, massive self-doubt. The reality that he quite literally had people's lives in his hands was starting to seriously overwhelm him in a way he'd been warned about in Med School, but never truly understood until now. He'd hit the ground running, but felt that he just didn't have the wear-with-all to keep up the pace.

During his first week in A&E he'd got off on the wrong foot. Like a lot of new Doctors before him, he was factory-fresh, thinking he knew everything and could conquer the world. He'd made the mistake of thinking that the Nurse's role was only to assist the doctor and that Paramedics were nothing more than glorified taxi drivers with a few first aid skills. He had no real concept of the dedication and seriously life-saving skills that these people possessed between them. He cringed as he thought back to his third shift where he'd taken the handover of a patient along with Sister Miller in the absence of the Registrar who was with another patient at the time.

As the stretcher was being wheeled into Resus, the Paramedic had been explaining that she queried an LVF, heart failure in effect. Instead of actually listening to what she had to say, he'd jumped in. Knowing that he was at that moment the only Doctor there, he'd made the grave error of thinking he was in charge of the situation until the Senior Reg arrived. He'd sarcastically asked the Paramedic just when it was that she'd gained her medical degree, then went on to order a Staff Nurse to *go and find the Reg*. Sister Miller had shot him a look that damn near turned him to stone, just as one of the Consultants walked in.

The Paramedic had begun her handover again for the Consultant and nursing staff. He'd heard the words 'IV access, GTN, furosemide' and at first he thought that Dr King was instructing the Nurse in the course of treatment, before realising that he was repeating, for clarification, what the Paramedic had just told him.

Once the initial furore had subsided and the Paramedic was to one end of the Resus room completing paperwork, Sister Miller had pulled him to one side, literally, by the elbow. "Don't you *ever* let me catch you speaking to any of my Nurses like that again," she growled in a lowered tone, "and as for the way you spoke to that Paramedic! Just who the fuck d'ya think *you* are?" He'd stood wide eyed, feeling like he'd been hauled into the lion's den and desperately searching for an exit, but there were none as the tirade had continued. "The reason that patient is still breathing is purely down to the actions of that Paramedic! How dare you speak to her like that? Kath's got more experience in her little finger than you've had in your whole, entire, sorry little life! *Do you understand*?"

It seemed more a statement than a question, but he'd nodded anyway before attempting a feeble explanation. "I'm er, sorry. It's just that erm, well in the scenarios in med school we...."

She cut him dead. "Well you're not in med school now are you? You're in fucking A&E and you'll learn to do it our way or you'll learn how hard your life becomes without the help and support of the staff here, many of whom were saving lives while you were still shitting in yer nappies!" With that she'd walked away, leaving him both stunned at what had just happened, but also relieved that it was over. He'd felt very alone.

***

The Trauma Team had congregated just outside Resus only about thirty seconds before the buzzer at the Ambulance entrance went off. Sister Miller called out, "They're here! Somebody buzz 'em through please." The double doors opened up and six people walked through. Four of them were uniformed Police officers, one of whom was guiding the bottom end of the stretcher, with a Paramedic at the top. Another Police officer was trotting alongside, holding aloft a bag of fluid. The other two brought up the rear while the second Paramedic carried a mobile suction device, the end tubing of which she repeatedly pushed under the oxygen mask and placed into the mouth of the bloodied, groaning wreck of a man, immobilised on the stretcher, bright orange head-blocks holding his head in place while a neck-collar forced his chin up into position to keep his airway open.

"Ok, what have we got?" Mr Rhodes, one of the A&E Consultants directed at the Paramedic.

"Unknown male, mid-thirties at a guess, unknown history. Currently GCS five; won't tolerate an airway. Found collapsed on the canal tow-path at the foot of twelve stone steps, looks like a possible assault but unwitnessed so unclear if he collapsed where he fell or actually fell down the steps, though that appears to be more likely." She continued, "He's got a head injury, query basal skull fracture," pointing towards the tell-tale battle signs on his face, "with a haematoma above the right brow line and a two inch laceration behind the left ear. I'm not certain, but I think that's blood stained

CSF leaking from his left ear. Other injuries top-to-toe include; a query right shoulder luxation and a potential fracture around the elbow area of the same arm." She indicated towards the man's massively swollen upper arm and elbow. Mr Rhodes sucked in air through pursed lips in acknowledgement of the battered looking arm. The Paramedic continued, "There's a lot of thoracic bruising with reduced air entry, right side. Bruising down both legs and an open fracture to the left ankle though circulation appears intact."

Mr Rhodes nodded once. "Thank you," he said. "How've his obs been?"

"Heart rate around one-thirty, sats were ninety-six on air, now ninety-nine on a hundred percent oxygen, but his systolic BP was only seventy-seven on scene. Access is left ACF and he's now halfway through his second bag of fluid, but I've not managed to raise it beyond ninety-two I'm afraid. I didn't get a temp Doc, but he feels very cold to the touch; it's unknown how long he was there before he was found though."

Liam stood in awe of how easily the Consultant seemed to be processing this cascade of apparently varied information and wondered if he could ever get to be so calm and accepting of such situations. He doubted it. He doubted his own abilities so much so, that he'd recently begun talking to friends about a career change. *How could he ever have imagined himself to have had what it takes to be a doctor?* And yet, here stood Mr Rhodes making the whole process look like water off a duck's back.

He remembered med school and how 'distracting injuries' were something that was rammed down a student's proverbial throat when assessing trauma patients. Would he have kept all of that in mind without Rhodes and Sister Miller being there? Or would he have panicked, lost focus and honed in on the most obvious injury? The honest answer was that he didn't know, maybe, maybe not. Yet it appeared to be second nature to the two of them and to the Paramedics too, his opinion of whom had changed radically since that false start two months previously, more especially since Sister Miller had arranged for him to go out with a crew as an observer for the day.

He had witnessed his Paramedic lying on his belly, legs wrapped awkwardly around the base of a bed in order to successfully intubate a rather obese lady in cardiac arrest on the floor of a cluttered bedroom, while the Technician performed chest compressions from above the lady with one leg knelt on the bottom of the bed and the other reaching over her, wedging his foot in position on the radiator pipes just above the skirting board. He looked more like a fourteen stone acrobat, contorted into the most uncomfortable looking position, than he did the skilled clinician that he actually was. Liam had felt helpless, he'd wanted to assist in some way but there just wasn't the room for any more bodies in that all too diminutive space which was filled predominantly by the patient who was anything but petite.

They had somehow managed to defibrillate her twice, maintaining her airway and keeping up chest compressions between them for nearly twenty-five minutes before the arrival of a second crew and a rapid responder to assist with moving her. They looked so knackered, but it had certainly been an education to Liam on thinking outside of the box.

The next job had been a teenager having a panic attack, convincing herself she was about to die. The crew dealt with her sympathetically, talked her down and calmed her, when all Liam could think to himself was '*for God's sake, get a grip!*' The Technician had told him afterwards how important it was that each job didn't bleed into the next, that it wasn't fair on a patient if you still had your last job in mind while dealing with them, that your next patient was not responsible for what you might have just had to do before you'd got to them. It had sounded very cold at the time, but having pondered it, Liam understood that if you couldn't disconnect in that way, then you couldn't and shouldn't be doing that kind of job. Emotional involvement would breed error.

He'd noticed that A&E staff, both pre-hospital on the ambulances and within the department itself, had a weird, almost warped sense of humour that outsiders might find sick or offensive. But that was how they coped with the daily dramas they were faced with. They would be clinical and efficient in their task, but they were still fallible human beings, just like everyone else. They would still be caught hiding round quiet corners in the sluice room crying, after having just dealt with the death of a child in Resus, before rallying themselves and moving onto the next sorry soul. They were each other's counsellors because there was no-one else who could understand, and that wicked sense of humour was just part of the process.

***

The man on the stretcher groaned again; his eyes flickered though there didn't appear to be any focus in them and he began to gently strain his right leg against the straps of the scoop-stretcher that was encompassing his broken form.

"Has he been like this throughout?" Rhodes asked.

"Yeah, pretty much," came the reply from the Paramedic. "He seems to have moments of quietness then the agitation starts up again. We were in two minds about immobilising on scene cos of it, but he seemed to settle enough so we risked it. He's made a fair bit o' noise at points but nothing we can understand; he keeps moving his mouth occasionally as if he's trying to talk, but it just comes out as groans."

Rhodes thanked the ambulance crew and took over care of the bloodied, unknown patient. Once the patient had been transferred to the Resus trolley he became more agitated, there was blood in his mouth, but he clenched his teeth each time the Nurse had tried to suction him, and when Sister Miller had attempted to get an oral pharyngeal airway in to aid his breathing, he just resisted with his tongue in the same way he'd done in the ambulance.

Mr Rhodes needed to get x-rays of his injury sites and more especially a CT scan of the head, but in this agitated state it would prove impossible and the patient's condition was deteriorating by the second. "Lisa! Would you page the on call anaesthetist please? I think it's Gabriel Marsh on today. Tell him we need him to RSI as soon as poss' please."

A Rapid Sequence Induction could be dangerous, but without being anaesthetised it would be damn near impossible to assess further and Rhodes knew the chances of survival for this pathetic looking creature here would be slim to zero.

"Is there anything I can do?" Liam asked Mr Rhodes.

"You can check again for pupillary response before the anaesthetist arrives please. Talk to him, see if he makes any kind of intelligent response, that sort of thing," Rhodes instructed. Liam wasn't so sure that Rhodes wasn't just giving him something to do rather than contributing anything of real value. Either way, he was grateful to not just be a spare part in proceedings.

Liam took his pen torch from his pocket and leant over the patient's head, shining it first into one of his partially opened eyes and then the other, though it was more difficult on the right side due to swelling around that eye in particular. "Pupils equal and reactive," he called out. He looked back into the eyes of this sorry being, and for the briefest of moments he thought that the man was looking back at him.

"Hello," he said to him, "my name's Liam, I'm one of the doctors looking after you today." The patient's eyes appeared to flit briefly in Liam's direction as he spoke. He couldn't be sure if it had been conscious effort or coincidence. He tried again. "I don't know if you can hear me sir, but if you can I want you to know that you're in the very best hands and that we'll take good care of you." Rhodes and Lisa Miller looked at each other with a knowing smile. *We'll make a good doctor out of him yet*, Miller had thought.

One of the Police officers finished speaking into his Airwaves radio, listening to the reply in his ear piece. He approached the bay, tapping Liam on the shoulder. "Is it gonna prove?" He asked. "Only CID need ta know if possible."

"Is it gonna what?" Liam was mystified.

"Fatal," the officer said. "Is it gonna prove fatal?"

"For Christ's sake!" Sister Miller interrupted. "If ya want to ask those kind o' questions you ask ta speak to someone outside and

25

never in front of the patient.  Can this poor man hear what you just said?" Having been on the wrong end of Lisa Miller himself, Liam almost pitied the careless Policeman.

The officer was taken aback.  "Erm, I don't know Sister. Can he?"

"We don't know the answer to that question either," she countered.  "Which is *why* we choose our words very carefully in such situations.  You'll do well to remember that." Having accepted his nervous apology, she directed him outside to the nurse's station where she explained what was known so far.

The door to Resus burst open and a tall, middle aged man with dark, greying hair tied back in a short pony tail walked in, wearing pale blue theatre scrubs and a red bandana with pictures of Homer Simpson on it.  "Good morning Martin," he directed at Rhodes with a distinct South African twang.

"Gabe," Rhodes smiled, "thank you for coming.  I believe we'll be needing your particular skills in this case."

The anaesthetist looked across at the patient.  "Agitated head injury eh?"  He asked the attending Staff Nurse for the patient's current obs, all of which he listened to while washing his hands in preparation.  "I take it we've got venous access?" he queried.

"We do, courtesy of the Ambulance Service," Rhodes confirmed.

"God bless those boys and girls." Gabe quipped rhetorically. "Makes our lives so much easier when all the prep's done before we get there don't ya think? Nurse, if you'd be good enough to draw me up five-hundred milligrams of Propofol/Diprivan into a fifty mil syringe please and all the usual standbys." He turned his attention to Rhodes. "So, wadda ya reckon this fella weighs then? 'About eighty-five, ninety kilo?"

Gabe Marsh grabbed a stool and positioned himself at the head of the broken man. He pushed the syringe into Liam's hand. "You'll do young man," he exclaimed. After asking for the patient's obs again, he sat ready with a bag and mask in hand. "Now then young doctor wad'eva yer name is."

"Erm, Drake, Liam Drake."

"Really? Well quack, quack Doctor Drake you're now my stand in Reg okay? When I tell ya and not before, I want you to start pushing the loopy juice through alright? Leave the Saline running to keep the vein open; an' Nurse," he directed towards the Staff Nurse just behind Liam, "get ready to change it, that one looks all but done and can we have plenty standing by please? Something tells me we're gonna need to push a fair bit o' the stuff through this fella. Right, off ya go Drakey."

Liam nervously began to slowly push down on the plunger of the syringe, stopping and starting again on the anaesthetist's instruction. Within what seemed like no time at all, Dr Marsh took over breathing for the patient using the bag and mask plus oxygen. "Can I have a Mach four blade on the laryngoscope please? And I think we'll go with a size eight tube. What's his obs looking like?"

"He's stable," Rhodes replied as the Staff nurse wheeled the sterile equipment tray around to within reach of the big man, who set to work with experienced precision.

# Chapter Two

Something woke the old man from his slumber, sweaty and feeling himself panting a little. He was anxious; was he dreaming? He wasn't sure. It was still dark and a sense of strange unease had crept over him as he reached for the bed control with his good hand. It felt like someone was there in the room with him. Nervously feeling for the control pads, he pressed the wrong one at first and the bottom half of his bed began to raise. Correcting his error quickly, he reversed his action before finding the correct pad with his feeble thumb and raising himself to a sitting position.

He tapped hard on his bedside table and the sensor detected the movement switching on his lamp which took a few seconds to warm up to full strength. A glance at the clock told him that it was morning already, but not quite daylight yet. Scanning the room with his dark, watery eyes, he swallowed hard all the saliva that'd built up in his throat.

He wanted to call out but couldn't; it'd been years since his voice worked on anything more than a cough or a grunt. Pressing the call button round his neck, he waited impatiently for someone to come.

There was no-one in the room that he could see, but that unease wasn't dissipating at all and he felt the need to not be alone, even if only for a few minutes.

After a couple of minutes his door opened and a tall, slim, middle-aged man, the German, filled its frame before making his way round to the side of the bed, taking his hand. "Reverend what is it? What on earth's wrong? Are you alright, are you ill?"

The old man exhaled a long sigh of relief as he shook his head in response.

"You're dripping wet Reverend; are you sure you're alright? I'm going to take your temperature and let's get you into some fresh pyjamas shall we?"

*** 

Doctor Drake went up to theatre, he was nearly half way through his shift anyway and it was almost five hours since the unknown trauma patient had been wheeled out of A&E to be scanned. From there he'd been taken upstairs to the Acutes theatre, but nothing had filtered back down to the A&E staff since then, so they didn't know if he was still in there or not, or even if he was still alive.

"You looking for someone Doc?" The voice startled him a little, he looked behind himself to see an Operating Department Practitioner (ODP) standing behind him.

"Oh, erm hi, yeah." Liam stumbled. "I'm Dr Drake from A&E. There was a man brought in this morning; multiple traumatic injuries…"

"Oh yeah, the guy with the head injury? Marsh RSI'd him; that who ya mean?"

Liam felt a little uneasy at how apparently flippant clinical staff could come across sometimes. He hoped he'd be the same one day, but for now he was still suffering with a little *stuffed-shirt syndrome.* Clearly not a real occurrence, but something the A&E nurses had told him he'd need to abandon in favour of a more approachable stance if he was to get on in his chosen profession; he was trying.

"Yes, that's him." Liam replied. "Is he still in theatre do you know?"

"Nah mate," the ODP replied. "Went up to Neuro about an hour ago. He didn't look too cracking either. Not sure what his prognosis is though; they'll be able to tell ya more over there to be honest."

Liam nodded his acknowledgement. "Ok, thanks. I'll call up later then."

The ODP smiled and nodded as he walked past him and rounded a corner to the left, leaving the young Doctor wondering if he should have a quick look for Gabriel Marsh, if he'd know any more. He decided that if Marsh was still in the department, that he was most likely in theatre and otherwise occupied, so he only hovered a few moments before making his way off the corridor and back towards the stairwell.

It could wait, it wasn't like the patient was in any fit state to get up and walk away. So unless he went to the mortuary overnight, he'd still be there in the morning. Maybe they'd know who he was by then too.

***

The Reverend's late wife stared out at him from a framed photograph that was sitting on the cabinet at the far side of his room. He kept feeling drawn into looking at her. Occupying himself with the daily newspaper instead, he sat in his wheelchair by the bay window, occasionally staring out to sea. It was almost a clear day, though he couldn't quite make out the Northern Irish coast on the horizon yet. Maybe he would once the haze had cleared later in the afternoon.

That damn picture kept distracting him; he didn't want to look at her. These god-awful people that controlled his life thought he'd like to have photos of his family around him. Bloody idiots! What did they know? He couldn't speak to tell them though and his one good arm was no longer strong enough to hold a spoon properly, let alone control a pen.

He could hook his thumb through the handle of a half-filled cup and manage to get it up to his mouth, and he could just about manage to turn the pages of the newspaper by sliding the side of his hand across it while hooking his thumb under the next page. It didn't always work though and there was many a day when his frustration took over and he'd sweep that and everything else from the table onto the floor in anger, only to have some well-meaning, overly sympathetic pleb cleaning up the mess whilst talking to him like he was a child. Idiots! He hated the lot of them and if he could muster the strength to do it, he'd throw something at that bloody woman smirking at him from the confines of that picture frame. Bitch!

# Chapter Three

It was the following morning when Liam stopped off at the Neurology Intensive Care ward, using his swipe card to gain access. He'd only just made it through the doors when he was challenged by the ward Sister. "I'm a Doctor," he smiled.

Sister Butterfield glanced at his ID badge. "I can see that," she said, "but you're not one of the ICU doctors. Can I help you? Did you take a wrong turn? Only it says A&E on your badge."

"Drakey isn't it?" The gruff South African accent was unmistakable. It was Dr Marsh. "It's okay Sister, ya can leave the fella alone, I'll vouch for him." Sister Butterfield nodded her compliance and returned to her rounds. "So young Drakey, ya came to check on your patient have you? Very commendable."

Liam didn't quite know how to respond to a senior consultant who appeared to be treating him as an equal; it almost felt like some kind of a trick. "I, erm...well, I..."

"You were just wondering how he was doing right? If he made it through the night? What his chances are? That sort of thing eh?"

Liam nodded.

"Yeah, me too," Dr Marsh continued. "They still don't know who the hell he is though. Come on then, let's have a look at the fella." They made their way together to the man's bedside.

"What's happening with him then?" Liam asked. "Has he improved at all since yesterday?"

Gabe Marsh waved to the ICU duty Registrar before picking up the patient's notes from the end of his bed. "He's heavily sedated at the minute Drakey. There's no knowing how he'll be until they're able to start bringing him out of it."

"What were the results of the scan? A cerebral haemorrhage?"

"Nah, no bleed, just swelling. Though to be honest young doc, a swelling on the brain is often far worse than a bleed, you ask any self-respecting Neuro nerd. That's why they'll keep him like he is for now an' hopefully it'll reduce on its own. Keeping him sedated will help avoid raises in intracranial pressure. It takes away any external stimuli, it's more comfortable for the patient and it reduces his metabolic requirements. Gives his brain a break so to speak. Apparently, bad as they are, it seems all of the other injuries will fix in time."

"He's still ventilated," Liam noted. "Is he unable to breathe without help?"

Gabe pulled his mouth down at both corners and shrugged his shoulders. "Don't know, maybe, maybe not. But it's more likely that they wanted to control it for him. If they keep him under and tubed, then there's no gag-reflex, no urge to cough or swallow. Little things like that can have a dire effect on intracranial pressure; plus, the Neuro geeks can control his rate and blood gasses, that sort of thing. They know what they're doing young fella. They're the dog's bollocks you know; the Neuros at this hospital. Transfer patients from all over to be treated here." With that he replaced the patient's notes, nodded once to Liam and left like the whirlwind he was, larger than life, then gone in a breath.

It was only as Liam watched Gabe Marsh disappear down the corridor that he noticed the two police officers standing by the door. One of them was in uniform, the other plain clothes, but a copper none the less.

Sister Butterfield approached him. "I'm Debbie," she said, "you were there when he was brought in weren't ya?"

Liam nodded.

Debbie looked towards the policemen. "They're here because no-one knows who he is, or why he was attacked. I mean, they're kinda here to protect him I suppose, in case anyone comes looking to finish him off." She winked sarcastically. "Or maybe they're just hoping he'll wake up an' tell 'em who did it, save 'em an investigation eh?" She wrote something in the patient's notes as

Liam stood by the foot of the bed, mystified by the swollen and bruised face of the man lying there helpless.

His whole head appeared to be twice the size it had been the previous day, the skin around his eyes was so swollen it shone. He was battered and bruised right enough. Both his eyes were blackened and it was hard to make out how he should look. At the moment he'd have guessed he was round-faced just because of the swelling, though to be honest it was anyone's guess. That poor man. He'd probably begun the previous day just like anyone else, with no sense or reason of what would befall him once he left home. Looked like he'd been to the gym, or jogging or something by the way he'd been dressed when he was brought in, which probably didn't help when it came down to identifying him. He'd nothing on him. Well Liam didn't suppose he would have done, not if he'd been jogging, why would he? It wasn't the sort of activity a person might take any personal belongings along with them. Liam certainly wouldn't. Where would you put a wallet, credit cards, mobile? He'd be sure to lose them if he tried it.

Sandy red hair, Liam noticed. He's got sandy red hair. It hadn't been possible to tell the previous morning, but it was as plain as day now. There looked to be the slightest smattering of grey around the temples too.

Liam knew it wasn't really his business anymore; this wasn't his patient anymore after all, but he wanted to know. It was the first time he'd dealt with this kind of thing and he was nothing if not intrigued. He took a breath and approached the policemen. "Any joy finding out who he is?" he chanced.

The plain clothed CID officer bent forward slightly as he examined Liam's hospital ID. "Dr Drake." He raised his gaze to meet Liam's eye. "We're currently looking into any missing person reports that may have landed over the past forty-eight hours. If that doesn't raise anything we'll look at widening the parameters. There's nothing coming back so far, but we have to give it time."

Liam was dumbfounded. "Surely someone would've noticed him missing by now, be getting worried at least?"

"Not necessarily," the uniformed officer replied. "He might be out of town, visiting. His friends or family might be away. If he lives alone, it just depends how often he'd normally have contact with someone. There's no real way of telling these things. However, if there's a family missing a husband and dad, it'd certainly make things easier for us." It sounded cold, but Liam knew he was right. If this guy did turn out to be a loner who worked from home maybe, well, God knows how long it could be before he was claimed by someone. "What about a picture in the paper?" he asked.

"Oh we'll be doing that if we really have to, but only as a last resort. For one thing, until we get our hands on who did this, or he wakes up, we can't say for certain that it wasn't personal. We could be placing him in more danger by going public. Besides, at the moment we wouldn't be able to get an accurate photo, not until his face settles at least. An' hopefully he'll have woken by then sir."

Liam looked back at the sorry state of the unknown man. "Thank you," he said to the officers, before vacating the ward himself.

***

Three ear-shattering beeps in a row brought the Registrar, Sister Butterfield and two nurses hastily to the unknown man's bedside. "SVT," the Reg said. "I wonder what's brought that on? Can someone get another set of baselines please? And Debbie, could you page Mr Kane; it's possible he might want to scan him again. There might be increasing pressure on the Medulla. What's his current rate please nurse?"

"Two-twenty-seven," he replied promptly.

"Okay; wow." The Reg seemed surprised but kept his cool. "Let's keep him stable please guys. He took his pen torch from his shirt pocket and proceeded to pull up the lid of the man's right eye, but the muscles of the eye resisted. He looked like he was experiencing rapid eye movement, a kind of dream state. The ventilator was still pacing his breathing rate, yet his heart was racing. Why?

"Two-forty-two." The nurse stated, trying to keep a lid on his growing anxiety at the situation.

Mr Kane, the senior Neurological Consultant Surgeon walked in, rubbing alco-gel into his hands as he approached. "Any pre-cursor to this?" he asked.

"Nothing at all we can think of" replied the Reg. "It's got us all flummoxed. He was maintaining...then this."

"Well he can't maintain at this rate, he'll arrest if it goes on much longer. Can we prep him for scan please? Now!" He strode purposefully to the desk and lifted the phone to call radiology.

"Wait!" the Reg called after him.

Mr Kane looked over his shoulder to his subordinate who was in turn staring at the monitor and feeling for a radial pulse at the same time.

"One-fifty-eight...One-thirty-four...One-sixteen...eighty-nine...eighty-two. It's settling. He's haemodynamically stable again. I'm not sure what happened there, but he seems to have settled again."

"For now maybe," Mr Kane added, "but something caused that. I'd still like him re-scanned please, and can we have another ECG? In fact, leave the twelve lead in situ when you've done, if it happens again I want it recording immediately." He addressed his

Reg. "Simon, take some bloods. Let's check his troponin levels, just in case. Anything changes, page me. I'm on site in meetings all afternoon so I'll not be far away."

## Chapter Four

Platform six at Norwich railway station looked busy to say the least, as Lynsey pushed her way through the turnstile and headed for the waiting train. She could hear her phone ringing in her handbag but didn't want to delay getting on the train before answering. She'd been trying to get hold of Robbie since late afternoon the previous day, in between meetings and business dinners that is. It would do him good to bloody wait, serve him right for taking this long to return her calls. He could at least wait until she'd got herself planted in a seat, forward facing of course, as travelling backwards always made Lynsey feel ill.

By the time she'd found herself an appropriate seat and having deposited her overnight bag in the overhead shelf, the damn phone had stopped ringing. Typical. She made herself comfortable by the window before fishing around in her bag for it. The missed call icon was flashing, but no message. Lynsey pressed the button to select the '*view missed call*' option, but she didn't recognise the number. It was a landline with the 0113 prefix, so it was definitely a Leeds number which meant that it was more than likely Robbie, calling from one of the work phones; it wouldn't be the first time, the cheeky sod. She could almost picture him sitting at a desk, allegedly rectifying some IT glitch somewhere in the building, which knowing Robbie he'd have fixed in approximately thirty seconds flat, then wasted time on Ebay or Amazon buying computer parts while making personal calls. *Great work if you can get it,* she'd thought to herself. She pressed *call*, assuming that she'd only just missed him and he'd therefore be likely to still be at the desk.

"Mark Pallister," the voice at the other end answered.

Lynsey was taken aback. "Oh, sorry. I think I've returned a call that wasn't meant for me."

"Is that Lynsey?" the man asked. "Lynsey Lewis?"

Lynsey was puzzled, but couldn't be bothered with time wasters. "Yes it is, but if this is a marketing call, then I'm sorry but I'm really not interested."

She'd been about to hang up but for the pleading tone in his voice. "No, no Lynsey it's not. It's Mark, remember? I work at Fletcher Dean's with Robbie. We met at the Christmas do a couple of months back. I was a bit worse for wear I think. Sorry."

Memories of the Fletcher Dean Christmas Party came flooding back to Lynsey's mind. "Oh, right. Were you the guy that Robbie was piggy-backing over the seats? You both fell onto the pool table and then..."

"...I threw up all over it. Yeah, that's me." Mark was glad this was a phone call and she couldn't see how red his face had turned.

Lynsey smiled to herself briefly before wondering why this man would be calling her. Was something wrong? Robbie, was it Robbie? "Is everything alright? Is Robbie okay?" she queried.

"Well that's why I'm calling *you* t' be honest," Mark said. "I was gonna ask you the same thing. He's not tipped up for work today. There was a meeting this morning with Project Development an' he was meant t' be heading it, but no-one's seen him. I've tried his mobile but that just goes straight t' voice-mail and he hasn't got back to any of the messages I've left on your land-line either. He's not been ill has he?"

Lynsey felt a god-awful sinking sensation in the pit of her stomach. "Shit!" she said, before realising that she could be overheard in the train carriage. "No, not that I know of. Oh God, I've been trying t' get hold of him too. I've been away since the day before yesterday with work. I'm in Norwich, well just leaving actually. Was he at work yesterday?"

"No," Mark said, "but he was planning on working from home yesterday anyway. He was prepping for this project we've been working on, ya know, this morning's meeting."

Lynsey began to feel sick and a little faint. "Oh yeah, that's right. He told me he'd be working from home. Said he needed t' get all the loose ends tied up ready for today," she paused. "Mark, I haven't spoken to him since Monday evening. I called t' let him know I'd arrived safe, whinged about the hotel, ya know, that sort of thing. An' yesterday; I just thought he was busy. When his phone kept going t' voice-mail, I just assumed he'd run the battery down an' forgot t' charge it. I'm sure ya know what he's like? An' he's a typical bloke, can't multitask, sorry, no disrespect, but he can't. If he's busy with work he won't notice the answer phone flashing."

"Sounds like the Robbie I know," Mark quipped. "It's just not like him t' miss this project presentation, it's our baby. We've been on it six months nearly."

"Mark, I won't be home for hours yet. Do ya know where we live?"

Mark tried to sound reassuring. "Yeah, I've picked him up from home a few times. D'ya want me t' call round? See if he's under the poorly blanket?"

Lynsey felt so helpless being so far away. She was a self-admitted self-control freak who hated not being able to do something about things there and then. "Would you mind Mark? Only, I have t' be honest, I'm worried. This isn't like him; he'd still answer the phone if he were ill, surely."

"Not a problem. And don't worry too much at the moment Lynsey. We don't know if there's anything t' worry about yet do we hun?"

She hated being called 'hun'. That particular term of endearment really ground on her, but under these circumstances she could live with it. "Can I take your mobile number please Mark? I'll give his mum a ring, an' his brother. See if they've heard anything. Will you ring me back when you get to the flat?"

She scribbled Mark's number onto the back of her hand before saving it into her phonebook. She then proceeded to psych herself up to call his mum. She needed to think about how to word things in such a way that wouldn't cause panic. She couldn't think straight and she didn't think she'd be able to hide the concern in her own voice. His mum was knocking on a bit, but she wasn't stupid. She decided to call Richard instead, Robbie's brother, she could explain the situation to him, that way he could call their mum and just ask in conversation if she'd heard from him recently. Richard might have heard from him anyway. Yes, that was a much better idea. At least it was for the time being.

\*\*\*

It was just short of an hour before Mark's number appeared on Lynsey's screen. She'd barely allowed it to ring once before answering. "Mark," she jumped to answer. "Anything? Have you been t' the flat yet?"

"I'm here now," he replied. "I've been knocking for over five minutes, even shouted through the letterbox but there's no reply. I can't hear a TV on or anything. He's probably not here."

46

"But what if he is, what if he's....something might have happened to him Mark."

"Listen hun; don't go letting your imagination go mad. The chances are he's fine and there'll be some perfectly logical explanation for this. C'mon, you know him better than anyone. He can look after himself, he'll be fine, you'll see."

Lynsey felt herself grasp at his words. Something was wrong and she knew it. Her eyes were welling up and it took everything she had to stop herself from breaking down. Staring out of the window she tried to distract herself with the view of the open countryside racing past. "Listen. Richard's on his way over; he's got a key."

"D'ya mean Robbie's kid brother? The Tattooist? I've met him a couple o' times on nights out. What d'ya want me t' do?" Mark was beginning to fight his rising anxiety now too.

"If you stay, you won't be in trouble at work will ya Mark?"

"Haha, no, not at all." She could hear him pacing around while he was talking to her.

"Then would ya mind? Staying I mean. It's just that...well if Rich gets there he can let himself in an'..." She couldn't finish the sentence.

"...you don't want him going in on his own. Just in case," Mark finished for her. He heard a soft sniffle at the other end of the line. "Of course I'll stay. I know it's a ridiculous thing for me t' say, but please try not t' worry too much at this stage. We don't know what's happened yet, so let's wait until we do before we get upset love, eh?"

Lynsey knew she wouldn't be able to hold in her tears if she tried to speak. Mark seemed to sense it. "I'll call ya back as soon as his brother gets here hun, I promise. That way we can all go in together so to speak."

"Thank you," was all Lynsey could manage. Even those two short words were enough to instigate a cascade from her eyes. She turned towards the window, hoping that no-one else on the train had seen her crying. Even if they had, no-one appeared to care, and thankfully she was left alone.

It had seemed like an absolute age before Lynsey's phone rang again, but in fact it was around twenty-five minutes and she'd just disembarked at Peterborough and was scanning the information board for her connecting train to Leeds.

It was Richard's number this time. "Rich. You heard anything? You been in the flat yet?"

"I've just got 'ere Lyns. Mark said you wanted us t' call before we go in. Where are you?"

"Peterborough. I'm just heading for my connection but it doesn't leave for another fifteen or twenty minutes or so. Oh shit Rich, where the fuck is he?" An overwhelming sense of doom washed over her. "I need ya t' go in now Rich. I need t' know if he's in there. I don't think I can get on the Leeds train 'til I know." Lynsey quickly glanced around for somewhere relatively quiet among the hustle and bustle that was going on all around her. She spotted a cold, mesh, metal bench just near the entrance to the gents' toilets; it was the best she could come up with. "Is Mark still there? Ya won't go in on your own will you?"

"He's here yeah," Richard said. "Look Lyns ya need t' chill out a bit. I know you're worried, but you're starting to freak me out a bit now."

"I know, I'm sorry. I can't help it. Something's not right. Don't ask me how I know, I just do."

"I'm gonna put Mark on Lynsey. My heart's pounding enough as it is." *"Here,"* she heard him talking to Mark, *"If I unlock it will you go in first?"* *"Yeah, sure mate,"* came Mark's reply.

She could hear them talking as they went in. Mark updated her as they went right through the flat from the front door onwards. *Nothing in the living room. Nothing in the bedroom, the bathroom, the kitchen.* In fact, there was no sign of Robbie anywhere in the flat at all, not in their study or even out on the balcony. Lynsey felt a massive weight lift from her chest as she got up and headed for the

49

Leeds train. It still didn't explain where the hell he was, but at least he wasn't dead on the floor in there, which is what she'd been terrified was going to be the case.

"There's just one thing that's a bit odd," Mark stated. "It's just that all the blinds are still closed an' the lights in your bedroom, kitchen an' living room are all on."

Lynsey puzzled momentarily. "So it must've been dark when he went out then? He'd have opened 'em otherwise wouldn't he?"

"Well you'd know the answer to that one I think," he said. "Hang on, Richard wants a word."

"Hiya, what time d'ya get into Leeds Lyns?" he asked.

"Train's due in at about quarter past five Rich. Why?"

Richard looked at his watch. "It's nearly ten t' four now. I'll pick you up from the station. We need t' wrack our brains, see if there's anywhere else he could be, okay?

# Chapter Five

Richard's Mitzubishi Warrior was parked just to the right of the station entrance, engine running and headlights dipped. Lynsey spotted him almost immediately. Not because he was in her eye-line but because, as was typical of him, he'd taken up a designated taxi space and an irate taxi driver was blasting his horn and gesticulating at him. The commotion is what had attracted Lynsey's attention and that of several dozen others too. However, completely oblivious to it, Rich waved the minute he saw her. The unforgiving taxi driver didn't appear to be quite so amiable though, as his clenched teeth and middle finger bore witness to as they'd pulled away.

"Well, Nice as it is t' see ya Lyns, any more thoughts?"

"On where he could be? No. Nothing. I've rung round a few mates but no-one's any the wiser. I just don't get it Rich; he can't have just vanished. Don't suppose you knocked at any of my neighbours did ya? See if they'd seen him?"

"Yeah, well Mark did. He'd already tried that before I got there. The old guy next door didn't know anything, just told Mark that Robbie would be at work at that time of day. Number six opposite wasn't in and number seven said she hadn't seen either of ya for over a fortnight."

"No help there then," Lynsey sighed. "Where's Mark now? Still at the flat?"

Richard shook his head. "No, he said he'd have t' check back in at work. Was gonna ask a few more people while he was there. Check his emails an' stuff. He's gonna come back tonight, 'bout half seven though." He glanced at her briefly. "Unless...sorry, didn't think t' check that wi' you. I can give him a ring an' tell him t' leave it for tonight if it's too much?"

"No it's fine. I'm running out of ideas on my own. It'll be good t' go through it with you both. You can stay can't you Rich? Jodie's okay with it? Have ya told her what's going on?"

"Yeah, she's offered t' get her mum t' babysit an' come over if you want a bit of girlie moral support."

Lynsey smiled. "Yeah maybe. Let's see where we're at first. What does your mum know?"

"Nowt, last time she spoke to him wa' Saturday. I haven't told her we can't find him though...*yet*," Richard emphasised the last word. "We *are* gonna have t' tell her though Lyns, ya do know that love?"

"Yeah." She felt exhausted, ill, washed out, and almost detached somehow, as if the day's events were going on around her, like she was watching them unfold through a window or something.

It was the most 'unreal' feeling she'd experienced. Like she was teetering on the edge of a massive precipice, unable to control which way she was about to fall. Back to earth and normality? Or into the abyss, where nothing would ever be the same again?

***

Walking into the flat somehow felt very strange to Lynsey. It was her flat, hers and Robbie's, yet she felt as though she were intruding. Mark and Rich had left everything as they'd found it. She'd asked them to because she imagined that she might be able to make sense of it better if she actually, physically laid eyes on it herself. She'd know if anything was out of place or missing.

In the kitchen she noticed a few unwashed pots in the sink. "He'd never do that," she told Rich. "Ya know what he's like about going out and leaving things in the sink like that. He'd have rinsed 'em out at least. If he went out leaving them there, then he must've planned coming back fairly soon. Went to the shop or something maybe."

"Or for a run?" Rich added. A sudden realisation hit home for Lynsey after that. She rushed past Richard and into the bedroom, where she began to haphazardly rifle through drawers.

"Lyns? What is it? What ya looking for?" Richard was puzzled at this sudden bursting into life she'd displayed.

Lynsey flopped herself down on the edge of the bed, disheartened. "Nothing," she said, "I don't know. It just suddenly dawned on me that he may well have gone for a run like ya said. But if he did, then he would've gone in the morning. If he ever went for a run, it was always in the morning. He says it wakes his brain up. An' him and Mark've been working on this project ya see, they were meant t' do a presentation on it today..."

"What're ya gettin' at Lyns?" Rich wasn't quite following her lead.

"What I mean is that it's only just dawned on me that we've absolutely no idea how long he's been gone. I last spoke to him on Monday evening from my hotel; nobody seems to know anything after that. So...did he go that evening after speaking to me or the next morning, out running or something? Last night? Or this morning? All I can tell with any real kind of certainty is that whenever he went, it must've been dark, so it must've been early morning or tea-time onwards. Otherwise, why else leave all the lights on an' blinds closed?" She began to cry. "Oh Christ Rich, where is he? He wouldn't do this t' me, to any of us. *You* know that. Something bad's happened, I just know it has," she sobbed.

Richard sat beside her resting a heavily tattooed arm around her shoulder. "Come on lass," he tried to reassure. "What we need is a plan of action. Number one; I'll stick the kettle on 'cos my mouth feels like the bottom of a budgie's sodding' cage." He smiled as he stood up again.

"An' number two?" Lynsey asked, resting her head on his shoulder.

Rich pondered for a moment before replying, "Well; number two is...look, there's two bloody hospitals in this city. We could start there."

Sitting bolt upright and drying off her tears, Lynsey looked him dead in the eye. "Shit, of course there is...oh I hadn't even thought of that."

Lynsey was scribbling down the numbers of St Jerome's' and the Leeds District Infirmary from the yellow pages when Richard placed a mug of tea beside her. She took a moment and looked at the cup, *'when you're awesome and you know it'* was written around it with a smiley face picture. Robbie had brought it home from the market one day last summer, *a present to himself,* he'd joked.

She lifted the cup, clinging onto it with both hands and blew steam away from the top before looking up at Richard. "I've got the numbers," she said. "But, what do I say? Who do I ask to speak to?"

"Accident and Emergency I would o' thought. D'ya want me t' do it Lyns?"

She ripped the top sheet from the pad of paper and held it up for Richard to take from her. "Would you?" she sounded relieved. "I mean, if you're sure."

He took the small square of paper from her; "He's my brother Lynsey, of course I'm sure."

***

Lynsey jumped to her feet as she heard the door open, *it might be Robbie* she'd thought, but only for the briefest of moments as she recognised Mark's voice as he called through to let them know he was back. Lynsey's pleading eyes followed him across the room to the sofa. He read her expression.

"I'm sorry Lynsey, I haven't heard any more. No-one I've spoken to at work's heard from him. He hasn't emailed, rung in, nothing I'm afraid."

"Rich's just rung the hospitals; he's not there either. Nobody matching his description has been admitted. They suggested contacting the police, which is pretty much the conclusion we'd come to anyway. We've run out of other options."

Mark looked a little uneasy. "It's just a thought, an' I know it's probably completely wrong an' everything. But it'd occurred to me that...well..."

"He's not seeing anyone else Mark, that crossed my mind too, but he's not." Lynsey was adamant.

Mark was a little embarrassed. "I'm sorry. It's just...well...it's one of those elephants in the room isn't it?"

"We need to tell my mum Lyns," Rich interrupted. "We can't put it off any longer." She nodded her agreement as Richard paced the room nervously. "I'm not sure how t' tell her though," he continued. "The last thing I want is her going off on one. She's bound t' flap though isn't she?" He looked to the others for reassurance. There was none.

"I dunno Rich. I can't say it's a predicament I've ever been in before." Mark answered. "Just be honest with her and calm. Make sure you don't sound like the prophet of doom an' gloom. He's her son an' she's gonna be worried, bound t' be."

It was agreed that Lynsey should be the one to phone the police, as she'd been the last person to speak to Robbie as far as anyone was aware. She would probably be able to tell them more. Rich would be the one to phone his mum. They were both trembling as they picked up their respective mobiles. Rich took his into the kitchen for some privacy and Mark stayed in the living room with Lynsey while she made the most nerve racking call of her life. "Hello, I...er...I think I need to report a missing person."

# Chapter Six

He can see the woman standing in the doorway of that cottage. She's smiling at him and she looks so familiar, but he can't think why. She makes him feel warm and comforted. Maybe that's what's familiar about her, he's not sure.

He starts to become aware of the sound of a bell ringing somewhere. It's not a buzzer like a fire alarm, or the heavy *ding dong* of a Church bell. It sounds a lighter ringing of some kind, but where's it coming from? There's a woman's voice calling "Michael". He turns round to look in the direction of the voice. He hears her again, is she calling him? "Michael!" There's no-one there, but he seems to be in a yard of some kind. He thinks it looks like a school yard. *Don't ask me how I know that, I just do,* he thinks to himself. Is that the smell of the sea, or is it just that he can hear gulls and it's making him think of the sea? He looks back around for the cottage and the smiling woman, but can't see them.

It starts to feel cold now and the ground looks wet, cold and wet. Over by the railings there looks to be the outline of a man. He's heading purposefully towards him; he's in silhouette until he's really close. *Fuck, he looks big, much bigger than me*, he thinks. *I don't like the look of this.* He doesn't want to stick around but he can't bring himself to move. He's shouting but it's all muffled and he can't make out what's being said, *I don't understand him. Jeez he looks mad.* His face is all contorted in anger and to be honest he's more than a little bit scary. As the angry man lunges his face closer to him, he lunges backwards away from the vile freak causing himself to gasp hard.

Then just as suddenly, the angry man's gone and it's dark for a moment. Then out of the nothingness he hears another voice, in the distance somewhere but it's getting closer. "Hello," he calls. "Can you hear me?"

*Yes, yes I can but I don't know where you are, I can't see you.*

"Can you open your eyes for me?" he asks.

He feels his eyes spring open and his whole body feels stunned, like that feeling you get when you're just about to fall but you manage to stop yourself in the nick of time. What fills his eyes makes him realise where he is: in hospital. It's not where he expected to be when he opened his eyes. He's unsure of exactly where he thought he'd be, he just didn't expect it to be here. There's a man standing over him with a stethoscope hung loosely around his neck, a doctor. Then he kind of remembers something but when he tries to speak his throat feels dry and weird and he just coughs instead. He winces in discomfort; his bloody chest kills when he coughs. He's gradually becoming more aware of the rest of his body, which is feeling stiff and achy. "Take it steady," the doctor says. "Don't try to rush things. I know you must have a million questions but let's just go easy, okay."

He tries to talk again, slower this time, testing his voice. It's somewhere between a whisper and a croak, but it's working. "Are you that doctor Liam? Drakey?"

Simon looks confused until Sister Butterfield clarifies things for him. "He's a junior in A&E," she explains. "He was working when this chap was brought in."

Simon raises his eyebrows in surprise as he turns back to his patient. "Really?" He looks impressed. "You've had a reduced level of consciousness ever since you were found, sir. Are you saying you remember the doctor from when you were in A&E?"

"I just remember him," he croaks. "I don't know where he was from."

Mr Kane, the consultant joins them. "Welcome back." He smiles. "How are you feeling?"

"I'm sure I've had better days."

"I'm sure you have. Do you remember what happened at all? Why you're here?"

He gently shakes his head. "Okay," Mr Kane continues, "well not to worry. A certain amount of amnesia can be normal following a head injury. It's very rare that it would be ongoing though, so I'm sure things will start to come back in their own time. Tell me, do you know who you are? Your name?"

He wrinkles his forehead in concentrated effort for a moment. "I'm...er...I'm not sure...I...erm...think I must be Michael," he finally says.

"Do you have a surname Michael? A date of birth? Only we haven't been able to get any medical history on you. You've been our mystery patient since your arrival," Mr Kane explained.

A look between frustration and confusion washed over Michael's swollen face as he struggled to draw up the information, but it was futile. "No," he said finally. "I don't know. Sorry."

"That's alright Michael," Mr Kane consoled. "There's no panic at the moment. Is there anything you're able to recall? Do you have a wife? Kids? Do you remember your address at all?"

"Leeds," Michael said. "I live in Leeds I think, yeah Leeds. With...I don't know, Mortimer? I'm sorry, I'm just not sure." Michael felt exhausted; he closed his eyes again. "I'm so tired, sorry."

"That's fine. Maybe Mortimer's your last name or the name of someone close. It's something to go on at any rate. At least now

we have something to call you rather than 'unknown patient' don't
we Michael?"

# Chapter Seven

The incessant sound of the vacuum cleaner was irritating the old man to the point of distraction, not to mention the god-awful, irksome warbling of the moronic imbecile who was pushing it round his room. He'd already had to tolerate the pathetic chattering of her and the other one who helps dress him on a morning; idiots the pair of them. He'd seen off more fools than this lot could imagine in his time. If only his body could still follow the commands of his mind, he'd put one or two in their places.

He'd lashed out at the other one on more than one occasion, tried to hit her with his grabbing stick, but he just didn't have enough grip to maintain it. So as it'd made contact with her back, it just fell out of his hand. She'd looked a bit uneasy, but definitely unhurt, more's the pity. The German fellow in charge had a word with him about it, wittering on about how it wasn't acceptable behaviour etcetera. How he wished he could just tell them all to *fuck right off,* how he wished he could tell them a lot of things and just leave, but his legs didn't work anymore than his voice did these days. Instead, all his sorry days were spent going through the same old routines, groundhog days with no escape.

Days spent sitting in that sodding window, staring out to the sea and wishing the time away while having to stomach the fucking do-gooders talking to him in those patronising ways they had, like he was a child. Who the hell did they think they were? Much of his time was consumed by his bitterness towards them. All the ways he'd imagined he could hurt them if his body hadn't let him down. He'd sometimes see them walking across the grounds outside and envisage a tree branch crashing down on them, or a local farmer's tractor, out of control and careering towards them.

One of them had even brought a dog in once, said it was known to help people feel better, but the animal wouldn't go near him; it clearly had more bloody sense than the troop of idiots that worked there did. Not a clue; none of them.

***

By the time a police officer arrived, Lynsey, Richard and Mark had been joined by Richard's wife, Jodie, Annie, the boys' mother, and her husband, Clive. It was late but none of them cared. Knowing Robbie as they did, they knew that something dire must have happened to him. He would never go this long without speaking to any of them, one of them at least. Usually Lynsey, but certainly his mother or Rich, he would never deliberately allow them to worry like this; it'd be just so totally alien to his nature.

"Hello everyone," the uniformed sergeant addressed the six anguished faces. "My name's Sajid Bashir, but please call me Bash, everyone else does, apart from my mother of course who's had a few choice names for me over the years, just not Bash." He was well aware of the gravity of the situation for the people in the room, but experience had taught him well. He knew it would help to break the ice between them and it would help them to see past his uniform, to see that he was part of someone's family too and that he understood.

"Did you deserve them?" Annie asked with a forced smile. "The names I mean."

"Oh yes madam, I'm afraid I did. I was a bit of a tearaway as a child."

"I bet she's proud of you now though, eh?"

"I'm sure she is madam. I hope so," Bash added. "Now, I've already met Lynsey who I believe made the call, is that right?" He looked to Lynsey for confirmation. "Could I now please take the names of everyone else here if that's okay?" He opened his notebook and began to write. "Lynsey Lewis wasn't it? And you're Robert's wife. Is that correct?"

"No," she began, "we're not married. I'm his girlfriend, partner, whatever ya wanna call it. We live together."

"Right, sorry," Bash said. "and how long have you been living together?"

"Eight years, three of them here in this flat." *Eight years* she thought, bloody hell, *eight years*. She hadn't really given it much thought before. *Where had all the time gone?*

Turning one by one to the others, Bash continued to scribble down the information he needed while confirming it out loud. "Richard McAndrew, Robert's brother. Jodie McAndrew, you're Richard's wife. That's right isn't it? And Annie, you're his mum. That'll be Annie McAndrew at a guess?" he queried.

"Annie Wilkinson," she corrected. "This is my second husband, Clive. The boys' stepdad."

Bash continued. "Okay." Then, turning to Mark. "And you are...?"

"Mark Pallister, Robbie's a friend and colleague o' mine."

"A colleague where, sir?" Bash asked.

"Fletcher Dean's. It's an IT company. We're based in Leeds. In the Omega buildings, just off The Headrow."

"Oh yeah, I know where ya mean. Thank you." Bash finished writing for the moment. "Right, just to clarify events. Lynsey, you left for a business trip this Monday gone. Was Robert, Robbie here when you left?"

"No he was at work. I left at three-ish. I spoke to him from the hotel I was staying at in Norwich though. That would've been about...eight-thirty, nine-ish."

"And he didn't mention any plans to go out that evening?"

"No. Quite the opposite in fact, he said he was gonna have an early night. That he planned working from home the next day, Tuesday, cos he needed t' put the finishing touches t' some presentation he was meant t' be doing for work on Wednesday morning."

"That's right," Mark interrupted, "but I don't think he finished." He looked a little sheepish before continuing. "I've...er...been into his laptop. Lynsey said it'd be okay. So I've hacked in, t' see how far he got with the project."

Bash raised his eyebrows. "And...?"

"Well, it doesn't look as though he'd got much further than the last time I saw it. Monday, at work. It's definitely not presentation ready."

Lynsey explained the relevance to Bash. "He would've worked on that all day Tuesday. Which, from what we've been able to work out, that and the fact that the blinds were all closed and the lights all on, would indicate that he went out on either Monday night some time or else Tuesday morning, early. Ya see, if he'd have gone out for the day, he would've turned everything off an' opened the blinds. He always did, he's nothing if not consistent."

Bash nodded as he listened and once he was satisfied he began to go through what would happen next. "Okay, thank you. Right, what would be really helpful now would be a list of any other friends or relatives that Robbie could have called on. Even if it seems unlikely t' you at the moment, it's worth us having them. Apart from work and home, where would he be likely t' visit on a regular or semi-regular basis? Pubs, coffee shops, that sort of thing. Might be, if we show his picture around at some of those places where his face'd be known, someone may remember seeing him." He turned to Lynsey. "So any recent photos you've got would be helpful. Could we just have a word in private please Lynsey?"

She got up and led him through to the kitchen, pushing the door to behind him. He continued. "Sorry, there's just some things that I need to ask you in private really. Things you might not want t' share, or things that Robbie might have hidden from other people, family, ya know." Lynsey nodded, though she kind of guessed what Bash's next question would be.

"Lynsey," he paused, "I know it's difficult, but was everything okay between you and Robbie?"

"You want t' know if he was seeing anyone else don't you?"

"Well...yes. Or, were you? Had there been any kind of argument at all? Any reason for him to just up an' go?"

Lynsey felt almost sullied by the question, but she knew that he'd had to ask it. "No, he wasn't, I wasn't, an' we hadn't fallen out about anything."

"Okay, thank you. And I am sorry, but we have to ask. Also what are his finances like? There are no money worries at the moment?"

Again she shook her head. "No, nothing. He's well paid; we both are I s'pose. Everything goes out on direct debit."

"I'll need his bank details if that's okay? And are you able to say if anything like that's missing from here: bank cards etcetera?"

"It's not, I've already checked," she confirmed.

Bash nodded then went towards the door. "Okay, we can go back through now if that's alright." He held the door for her as they made their way back into the living room.

"Can I just ask about Robbie's general health? I mean, he's not diabetic or anything an' gone off without his medication has he?"

"No, he's fit as a flee. He looks after himself," Lynsey said.

"And on the days he goes for a run, does he have a usual route he follows?"

"I don't think so. It depends on how much time he's got really. If he just feels like waking himself up before work he might only be out twenty minutes or so."

"But if it was a day when he's gonna be working from home?" Bash pushed.

"Well yeah, he can be out well over an hour on occasion. He runs on the towpath sometimes..." She stopped herself. The sudden realisation that he might have fallen into the canal. Hit his head and drowned, or twisted his ankle, fallen in and been unable to get himself out...She suddenly felt sick again, if not a little light-headed, especially when she noticed the look on Robbie's mother's face. She was imagining the worse too, that much was obvious.

"One more thing," Bash asked. "I might actually need to ask you Mrs Wilkinson. As Robbie an' Lynsey aren't actually married, I'm afraid in the eyes of the law that makes you his next of kin rather than Lynsey here. It's just that if it comes to it we like to use the local press, but we'll need your permission t' do that."

"Of course. Anything," Annie said. She hadn't moved from the sofa with her husband beside her the whole time, sandwiching her hand between both of his and softly stroking her wrist with his thumb. She looked pale and quietly terrified.

Lynsey led Bash around the flat so that he could get a feel of Robbie's normal routine. Plus, it gave him chance to go through things with her again and to double check if anything was missing. Being a police officer, he was of course also subtly looking out for any signs that things might not be as they seemed, any signs of violence, spots of blood and the like. In the bathroom, he'd asked her if he could take Robbie's toothbrush with him, for DNA comparisons should any articles of clothing be found, that sort of thing, though Lynsey knew full well that what he really meant was should a body be found. She knew it but she didn't say anything; she simply complied by dropping Robbie's toothbrush into the small plastic bag he'd pulled from his breast pocket and opened in front of her.

"So what now?" she asked.

"Now I go back to the station and get someone to enter all this on the police national database, while I set to, seeing if anyone has seen him, checking for movement on his bank account and following up everything else. I'll recheck the hospitals. One thing I do have to inform you of Lynsey is that should Robbie be found, if he's done this deliberately an' so doesn't want any contact with you or the family, then I'm afraid we are duty bound to respect his wishes. We'll let you know that he's safe of course, but we won't be able to divulge his whereabouts. You understand don't you?"

Lynsey sighed. "Yes, I understand but he wouldn't do that. He's really not like that."

He handed her a card with his contact details on telling her to contact him at any time and to inform him should anything come to light or should Robbie turn up or get in touch at all, and another card with details of the National Missing Persons website. "Just in case.

They deal with this all the time.  Ya' never know they might have something constructive, or just someone t' talk things through with."

"Thanks, but I'm really tired of talking now.  I just want him back."

# Chapter Eight

Arriving home later that evening, Clive and Annie pulled into their driveway. Clive had been trying to keep things light the whole way back, chatting about things Robbie had done in the past, the scrapes he'd got into as a child, the time the police had brought him home drunk when he was fifteen and how he'd fallen out of their car when the Policewoman had opened the door and she'd had to jump backwards out of the way just in time to avoid him throwing up copious amounts of Christ knows what all over her boots. "The point I'm making love, is that he's always been alright. No matter what he's got himself into, he's always been okay hasn't he?"

Annie didn't answer; she merely continued staring out of the passenger window, trancelike. Clive gently bit down on his bottom lip, unsure of how to handle things, of what to say. He and Annie had been like soul mates ever since they'd met. This was the first time he'd felt in a position where he couldn't reach her and he didn't like it.

As they entered the house, Clive went on ahead to put the kettle on. He'd told Annie to just take it easy and that he'd make them both a hot drink, but then he'd heard a thud behind him as he was just going into the kitchen. Looking round, he realised it was Annie falling back against the front door causing it to slam shut as she collapsed against it and began to slither to the floor in a fit of uncontrollable sobbing. He rushed to her aid, hot, sharp pain in his bad knee as he got to the floor to be with her. He clung tightly to her, tears rolling down his face at the distress of his beautiful wife of thirty years, the strongest, most caring woman he'd ever known reduced to this wreckage before him. She was beside herself and nothing he could do was helping. She wasn't even looking at him, but beyond him, lost somewhere within her own despair.

***

Mark had gone home but Lynsey's sister Natalie had arrived from her home in Middlesbrough to offer support and to see if there was anything she could do. Rich and Jodie were still there too. They'd all agreed to stay together, at least for the time being. Jodie was on the phone to her mother, checking on the kids and going through what the eldest would need for school in the morning. Lynsey had always admired what great parents Jodie and Richard were, if less than conventional. Rich had his own tattoo business, and was covered in them himself. Jodie had several too, dyed black hair with copper tips, a pierced nose, eyebrow and ears, one of which was pierced all the way round finishing off the look. Lynsey could just picture the raised eyebrows at school parents' evenings. Jodie looked like a less severe version of Lizbeth, the character in 'Girl with the Dragon Tattoo', though she was a much warmer, friendlier person. If she could help someone, she would. She was brilliant with the kids and Rich adored her.

Lynsey couldn't bring herself to sit down. If she sat down she felt as though the whole world might come to a stop somehow. Instead she paced the floor of the flat, all around really, but mostly from the balcony window to the phone and back again. Waiting for news, anything, just waiting.

She felt drained, a mountain of emotion was crushing her yet she was too exhausted to react, to release it. It was the kind of crippling oppressive feeling the likes of which she'd never before encountered. She knew she hadn't eaten anything since the two slices of toast she'd had in the hotel in Norwich that morning. Not enough to sustain, but she'd no appetite and had all but bitten her sister's head off when she'd kept going on about it. She'd apologised immediately, but she just didn't have the energy for explanations. She was close to her sister and knew she'd understand. She hated this lack of control and this helplessness was a most uncomfortable anguish.

\*\*\*

Sergeant Sajid Bashir was sitting at his desk inputting data onto the system to do with Robbie's disappearance and updating a couple of other cases he was working on while he had the chance. It was just turned four in the morning when one of his constables interrupted him. "Sarg, there's a call on line three for ya. It's Bradford Met to do wi' one o' yer miss-per's. Oh an' Pete's got the kettle on, you want a brew sir?"

Bash nodded his acknowledgement and grateful acceptance of the offer of a well overdue coffee as he picked up the telephone. "Sergeant Bashir," he said. "Yes Sir, that's right."…"Oh, I see, bit odd but okay. Well that certainly appears to fit in with the info we've got."…"Yes."…"Yes Sir that's fine by me."…"Do you have any further details on roughly what time this would've been?"…"Right, I see, we can't afford t' rule anything out at this stage. Could be very relevant by the sound of it."…"Yes Sir, got it. Well I'll just make a couple of calls, get things organised then I'll get onto the next of kin. Thank you for the call Sir. Hopefully we'll be able t' get one ticked off the books eh?" He relaxed back into his chair as he picked up the coffee that Pete had put on one side of his desk mid-call. He glanced at the time display at the bottom right of his computer screen, *04:26,* it read. Was it too early to start ringing people? Should he think about leaving it a couple of hours? Then he thought about his own mum, his wife, the rest of the family. *They'd want to know,* he thought to himself. The time of day would be irrelevant; they wouldn't be likely to care.

He finished his coffee, then getting up from his desk he paced the area around it for a few moments as he yawned and stretched his arms out. *Night shifts; it didn't matter how many years under your belt you had, you never got used to them.* This was his fifth in a row and it was taking its toll. Then, sitting back down he picked up the telephone receiver and began to dial.

\*\*\*

Annie was standing in the bay window, watching for headlights to turn into the cul-de-sac where she lived. Her heart was pounding so hard and fast that she was finding it difficult to keep a check on her breathing. She looked at the clock: five-eleven. "What's taking so long?" she asked Clive.

"He's on his way love, give him chance. He did say he had t' contact the hospital t' find out a bit more first. It's the middle o' the night Annie; well it is for most people anyway. These things take a bit o' time. And I don't want t' sound like the devil's advocate, but he did say that it might not be him didn't he? Just try not t' work yerself up too much is all I'm saying. Are Lynsey an' our Richard coming here?"

"Yes they are. They'll be here any minute too. Lynsey wanted tae go straight tae the hospital like I did. But I told her what Bash'd said about 'em no' letting any of us in 'til a more reasonable hour...Oh Clive, I just need tae know if it's him or not. I can't stand this. I feel all...I've let him down, oh I don't know how I feel. I just need to know."

"Let him down?" Clive didn't understand. "How've ya let him down love? You've been a wonderful mother t' them two boys. How could you have possibly let him down? Either of 'em?"

"Oh never mind." Annie snapped. "It doesn't matter. Oh..." She stopped short as she noticed a car turning into the cul-de-sac. "Someone's here," she announced.

"You sure it's not just the milkman?" Clive asked.

"No, no, it's definitely no' the milkman," Annie claimed. "I think it's our Richard's car, that truck thing. It is isn't it Clive?"

After confirming it was, Clive went to meet them at the door. Everyone hugged as they entered the house, Lynsey and Annie more especially so, each of them knowing the other's pain.

"I know he said not t' get too excited just yet, 'til we know for definite, but I can't help it Annie, it's driving me mad is this. Why can't we just go straight there? I don't understand. If it's Robbie we can confirm it the minute we see him." Lynsey had wound herself up.

"Bash told ya why not Lyns," Rich interrupted, an air of frustration in his voice. "If it's not him, it'd be dead inappropriate t' be wheeling random people past some sick bloke's hospital bed, just on the off chance."

Natalie put a hand on her sister's arm. "C'mon Lyns, ya know they're right. Imagine how you'd feel if it wasn't Robbie after all this. Imagine being whoever it is, having t' put up with a trail of strangers staring' at ya just in case you're *their* missing person. I'm sure they understand what everyone's going through, but from the hospital's point o' view, they're bound t' put the patient's welfare first."

"And quite right too." Annie stepped in to try and help ground them all.

"Someone's here," Jodie announced. "It's a police car; it's him."

She rushed out of the living room door and went to let Bash in. Annie turned to Clive for support; Rich held her hand while Lynsey and Natalie linked arms closely.

As he entered the living room, Bash smiled cautiously at the anxious, eager faces. "Hello again everyone. Right, I'll get t' the point as I'm sure you're wanting t' know about the development I mentioned over the phone; about the man in Bradford City hospital."

Annie sat in stunned silence while Lynsey couldn't contain her need to know. "Is it him?" she demanded. "Please just say it's him."

"It *would* seem that there's a strong possibility that it's Robbie," Bash began, "but...and I must stress the 'but' here…there's something that doesn't fit. The man at Bradford was found unconscious early on Tuesday morning as I've already explained. He was wearing joggers, trainers an' a tee-shirt, which ties in with Lynsey's theory that he might have gone for a run. He didn't have any form of identification on him, so the Bradford police among other things, were scouring for missing person reports. They got back to me a couple of hours ago once Robbie's information had been entered into our system. The problem we have at the moment, is that though this man *has* now regained consciousness, he is still very poorly and," he paused for a moment, "because of the head injury he sustained, he's currently having some memory problems. The bottom line is that he's not sure of who he is himself and this is the inconsistency…he told the doctor that his name's Michael."

Annie felt the blood drain from her head and her whole body went limp in Clive's arms.

"Annie?" Clive turned towards her causing everyone else to look too.

"I'm okay," Annie sighed. "Can we please just get on with this?"

Bash looked concerned but he understood her need for urgency. "Okay, apparently he's quite adamant that he lives in Leeds, though he's currently unable to elaborate on that. His last name could be Mortimer. He didn't call himself Michael Mortimer, just Michael, but he apparently mentioned the name Mortimer when he was asked if he could remember anything about where he lived."

Lynsey began sobbing and laughing at the same time; everyone else stopped and looked. She'd pulled away from her sister and was contorted in this strange outburst, her hand over her mouth. She managed to fight for some composure briefly. "It's him," she stated. "It's the Mortimer Project. That's what he was working on, the presentation him an' Mark were meant t' be doing on Wednesday morning." She turned to Annie. "It's him Annie. I just know it's him."

Annie had a torrent of silent tears cascading down her pale cheeks. "I think so too love." She whispered, a weakened smile gently growing on her lips.

# Chapter Nine

It was just turned eight-fifteen on the Thursday morning when Bash walked onto the neurology ICU ward; he was suffering the strain of having done his fifth nightshift in a row. He should've been home in his bed by now, but he felt it only fair that he be the one who dealt with the Michael/Robbie situation himself, for continuity, for the sake of Lynsey and the family really. He'd be going straight home once he'd spoken to Michael, and it had been his last shift, so he didn't mind the end of shift overtime on this occasion.

The first person he spoke to was his colleague from the Bradford Met division. The sole uniformed officer had been there for a couple of hours having taken over duty from the night officer. It had been decided that someone should watch over Michael at all times for two reasons, one being that they still hadn't apprehended the perpetrator and couldn't rule out that this had been a targeted attack, attempted murder maybe, and secondly, in case Michael remembered anything that could be helpful, especially about the attack.

"Morning," Bash addressed the police constable who was sitting at the nurses' station idly reading a newspaper.

Noting the three stripes on Bash's uniform, the young officer jumped to his feet. "Morning sir," he spurted his embarrassed reply.

Bash smiled at the memory of his own early days in the force, and how he'd been in awe of, if not a little intimidated by, anyone who ranked above him. He introduced himself and asked the young officer if there was anything further to report. The young neophyte went over the handover he'd had from the officer he'd taken over from, adding nothing new to what was already known. Bash then went on to ask if he could speak to a doctor regarding Michael's general state, if he'd be up to a few more questions as it might now be the case that his identity had been established, though it was important that he be spoken to in order to try and clarify one or two facts first.

Mr Kane had just arrived ready to do his ward round. He gave his permission, but wanted to assess Michael first himself before letting Bash near his patient. Once satisfied, he nodded his approval.

Looking down upon the pitiful man from his bedside, Bash smiled. "Hello." He began. "I'm Sergeant Sajid Bashir. If it's okay with you, I'd like to go over one or two things, but only if y' feel you're up to it sir?"

Michael looked at him for a moment, unsure of what it was about and assuming that yet another person was going to try and pump him for information that he just couldn't come up with. He felt weary and in pain, and frustrated at his own inability to remember. "Yeah, sure," he relented.

"I realise you're probably sick t' death of hearing this from everyone, but I have to ask...have you remembered anything more sir?" Bash asked. Michael sighed and very carefully shook his head.

Bash knew he must be in pain and hated the thought of making him more uncomfortable. He just hoped that this didn't turn out to be a complete waste of time. "What I'd like t' do, is run some names past ya, see if it jogs your memory at all. It's just that we've had a missing person's report which appears on the face of it t' match up with you sir."

Michael's eyes lit up and his fading interest was suddenly reignited. "Really? Who is it? Who am I? I mean...what's my last name? I know they think it's Mortimer cos I remembered that name, but it doesn't feel like mine."

"It's not; at least we don't think it is," Bash confirmed. "Problem is...if you are who we now think ya might be, then your name isn't Michael either."

That wasn't what he'd been expecting. Michael felt a sudden sinking feeling, as if it had all been a mistake and he wasn't the man that Bash was talking about at all. He closed his eyes.

Bash continued with his theory. "If I said the name Annie to you, would that conjure anything up?"

"I think I've got an auntie Annie somewhere," Michael strained to recall.

Bash was a little puzzled, but put it down to amnesia. "Annie Wilkinson? Clive Wilkinson?"

As soon as Michael heard the name Clive Wilkinson, he knew immediately that he was his stepfather. This caused the penny to drop with 'Annie' too. 'Clive and Annie', 'mum and Clive', of course. He said as much to Bash, who asked him if he knew who Rich was, and Jodie. He did, he knew straight away that Rich was his younger brother, and Jodie was Rich's wife. He couldn't remember that they had kids though when Bash asked him, but it didn't matter at that precise point because he was remembering.

"Can ya tell me who Lynsey is?" Bash asked him.

*Oh my God, Lynsey.* Oh Lynsey. How could he have forgotten about her? He felt tears begin to well up in his eyes. "I'm Robbie aren't I? Robbie McAndrew?"

Bash smiled with a warm, satisfied feeling in the pit of his stomach. "Yep, I do believe that you are indeed Robbie McAndrew."

"Then why did I think I was called Michael?" Robbie asked. "Who's Michael?"

Shaking his head in casual negation, Bash replied. "Dunno. I've spoken t' yer family an' they couldn't shed any light on that one either. Maybe we'll never know or maybe it's just some random memory. Who knows? Probably just how yer mind decided t' process things after what happened." He couldn't possibly have known then, just how close to the bone that statement would turn out to be. "Anyway, there are some rather emotional an' very relieved people who'd love t' see *you* Robbie."

Dr Liam approached the bedside as this was going on. He'd been back up to visit the previous day after Sister Butterfield had informed him of developments. He could see that Robbie looked to be crying, that he was upset. "Michael?" He puzzled. "What is it? What's wrong?"

Debbie Butterfield grinned, having overheard everything. "Who's Michael?" she said to Liam with a twinkle in her eye. "There's no Michael here, but allow me to introduce you to Robbie, Robbie McAndrew."

"Oh?" Liam was surprised. "In that case, congratulations on your newly regained identity Robbie McAndrew!"

Robbie was exhausted, but feeling very, very happy. "Sergeant, this is Drakey; he was one of the doctors who looked after me when I first came in." He looked at Bash. "Where are they? My family an' Lyns? Where's Lyns? Shit, she must've been so worried, they all must."

"Yeah they were, very much so," Bash said. "They won't let more than two visitors at a time in here though Robbie. So how about Lynsey an' your mum for starters? They can swap round later. I'll send a car for them..."

"They're not here?" Robbie asked.

"No. They wanted t' come here with me, but I didn't think it wise 'til we knew for definite, which I think it's safe t' say we do now."

Robbie was trying hard not to cry. Not because he felt himself too macho to be displaying that kind of emotion, but because it bloody well hurt. Each sniffle was causing him pain, but he couldn't help it.

## Chapter Ten

It was coming up for lunchtime before Mr Kane would allow
any family in to see Robbie. They'd been waiting in the relatives'
room together all morning, but the consultant had made them wait as
he'd wanted Robbie to be taken down for another scan and ECG.
They'd felt it a little harsh at the time, as they'd been so desperate to
see him with their own eyes, but they understood the reasoning. Dr
Simon had been in to explain that it was just the way things worked
in the hospital environment. Robbie needed another scan but the
radiology department would only do it as it fit in with them. There
was a backlog in that department, which was normal, therefore if Mr
Kane had missed a slot, it could be hours before Robbie was seen.
There were only the emergency admissions which could supersede
this order of things and of course, Robbie had been one of those
emergency admissions only a couple of days previously himself.
They knew that, and they understood that too, but it didn't stop them
almost bursting with a mixture of excitement and anxiety.

The young policeman, Kim Bennett, had been sitting with
them all morning. He'd explained everything that was known so far
with regard to what had happened to Robbie. "As you know, he was
found by members of the public in a collapsed stated, quite clearly
the victim of an assault of some kind."

Rich wanted to know more. "I don't get why he ended up here. In Bradford I mean. Him an' Lyns live in a city centre apartment block in Leeds. Why wasn't he taken there?"

Bennett looked around at the puzzled faces. "Oh, right," he said. "Sorry I just assumed ya'd know. He was found near Apperley Bridge. Bradford woulda been the closest hospital from there an' of course the Paramedics wouldn't have had any idea where he was from. Not that it woulda made a difference at that point, they just got him t' the nearest A&E."

"I know Apperley Bridge," Clive said. "I used t' do footy training there in me younger days. What the 'ell was he doing there?"

Rich wasn't surprised. "It's the canal Clive. I've run that far with him before. If ya jog along the tow path ya can go miles in no time at all."

"Anyway," Bennett continued, "we're still not entirely sure of what occurred an' for the moment at least, Robbie can't help wi' that. We've got some officers trawling through CCTV footage from a couple o' shops nearby an' the entrance to a farm that's got a camera too. Sadly there weren't any cameras covering the bridge or the access to the tow path, where the incident happened. But we think it'd be safe to assume that whoever was responsible woulda had t' go in one direction or the other. The only problem is, that it's possible that person or persons unknown used the tow path themselves t' make their escape."

Lynsey's initial distress had begun to morph into anger. "How could they? How could one human being do something like that to another? An' for what? Cos all that he'da had on him would've been his mobile phone. He never takes anything when he goes for a run, just that so he can listen to music while he's out."

"What sort o' phone does he have Lynsey?" Bennett asked. "Only he wasn't found wi' one."

"It's a Nokia I think, one o' them Smartphones. He's not had it long."

"It's a Nokia Lumia 920," Rich explained.

Bennett nodded his head by way of understanding. "Right, so it's worth about five-hundred then? Expensive."

"An' it's missing?" Lynsey queried before answering her own question. "Well it's not at home anyway. So if it's not with Robbie, then it's missing."

Annie had barely spoken all morning. She'd been polite, she'd answered any questions that were asked of her, politely declining all offers of a cup of tea that were made. But she hadn't maintained a conversation with anyone. She still felt sick with it all, still had that God-awful sensation in the pit of her gut. He was alive, battered but safe and alive, yet she couldn't shake this feeling.

Just then the door opened and Mr Kane walked into the room with Dr Simon close at heel. "Hello," he announced in that confident '*I'm only one step away from being God*' way that some consultants have about them. "I'm Mr Kane. Myself and my team have been looking after Robert. Firstly, let me apologise for the delay in you seeing him, I'm sure my colleague here has explained why. And secondly, I've got the results of Robert's latest scan and from what I can tell; the swelling to his brain has all but subsided. I'd be happier to keep him here in ICU for another night, but should he continue to improve then I'll have him moved to the neurology ward where he can continue to recover at some point tomorrow."

"Can we see him now?" Annie pleaded.

"Yes, I don't see why not. Sister Butterfield only allows two visitors at a time around a patient's bed," he explained. "It's all the equipment and the seriousness of patient conditions you see, but there's no reason why you can't swap and change about. May I just ask that you *do* leave when required to though? We do have to put our patients first, and certainly in Robert's case, he does tire very easily."

They all agreed to do as they were asked. Though it was clearly no contest when it came down to who would be first in to see Robbie, as Annie and Lynsey were heading out of the room almost on Mr Kane's shirt tails. Sister Butterfield met them at the door to ICU.

"Now," she said, "ya have been warned about the bruising haven't ya?" They both nodded. "His face is all the colours of the rainbow at the moment an' I don't want ya t' be frightened by that. He is getting better. The bruising's normal considering what's happened but he is healing. Just try not to react to it too much when ya see him. We don't want him being upset or distressed because he's worried about you now do we?"

Annie took a deep breath and followed Lynsey in through the double doors. As soon as she laid eyes on him, Lynsey burst into tears. He looked at her, tears in his own eyes. "Hey you," he said as she stood over him, desperate to touch him yet fearful of hurting him. He sensed her anguish. "You can hold my hand." Slowly moving his left hand out towards her. "It's okay, don't get upset. I'm okay." His voice was still a little croaky from when he'd been intubated. He saw over Lynsey's shoulder that his mum was standing in silent shock, not crying, but pale and quivering slightly as if she might faint in a heartbeat.

A nurse brought two chairs to the bedside for them. Lynsey immediately pulled hers up and sat beside him but Annie remained standing for the moment, putting her hands on the chair back to rest her weight. "Oh Robbie," she said faintly. "Oh my sweet boy. I thought...we thought..." She stopped herself briefly. "I didn't think I was going tae see you again son. I've been so scared."

"I'm okay mum." Robbie tried to reassure her. "It looks worse than it is. I'm fine mum, honest."

She smiled as she remembered the family joke. *"Honest? Now I know you're lying."* He blew her a small kiss as she sat down.

She felt herself to be in the middle of a dream as she sat there listening to Lynsey explaining to Robbie what had happened. How they'd all realised he was missing, the fear, the dread and ultimately the relief at finding him to be alive after all. Though he knew immediately who they were, it was obvious that there was still a lot that he either didn't remember at all or else had somehow mis-remembered in his confusion.

It took a good fifteen or twenty minutes before Lynsey realised that she'd been hogging him. She kissed the fingers of his left hand and offered to go back to the relative's room for a bit, to give Rich or Clive a chance to come and see him. She smiled at Annie apologetically before walking away. Annie moved into the chair that Lynsey had vacated and tentatively took hold of Robbie's hand. "I thought I'd lost you," she whispered.

"Well you haven't," Robbie reassured her. "You don't get rid o' me that easily. I'll mend, don't worry mum, I always mend."

Clive came to join them, affectionately kissing the top of his wife's head before sitting beside her. "I can't tell ya how glad I am t' see ya son." He said to Robbie. "They told us yer having trouble remembering some things lad. Well at least y' know who we all are an' the rest'll come back t' ya, ya'll see."

"I know." Robbie pondered. "I didn't even know who I was t' start with though. I mean, I know I'm Robbie McAndrew now but I was so convinced that I was called Michael t' start with. God knows where that came from but I was really convinced. I thought that copper was a nutter when he told me that I wasn't." He looked at his mum. "An' when he first mentioned your name t' me; I'd thought ya were me Auntie or summat. It wasn't 'til he said both yer names together that it hit me, Clive an' Annie, mum an' Clive, o' course it is."

Annie felt that sudden fleeting wave of nausea hit her again for the briefest of moments; she closed her eyes in a prolonged blink. Robbie hadn't noticed, but Clive had, though he didn't say anything. He probably felt that he didn't want to draw Robbie's attention to it. After all, the poor lad had enough to contend with at the moment.

"I'm goin'tae let our Richard come an' see ya Robbie. He's been very good, letting everyone else in first. I'll go an' get a cup o' tea while he comes in okay love?" Annie suggested.

Robbie smiled and nodded as Annie squeezed his hand. Not wanting to make eye contact with her husband for fear he'd be able to read her soul, she walked away. Clive knew something wasn't right, but he didn't feel it was the time or the place to be asking her about it. Though he would be asking her. She looked like she'd aged ten years over the past twenty-four hours, which he understood, but he'd thought that she'd be different now that Robbie had been found and she wasn't. Though he wasn't sure what exactly the problem was, he was sure that there was one.

When Annie had come back through, Rich was in the process of explaining the big search to Robbie. "...An' Mark an' me went into the flat together; we didn't know what we might find in there. My heart was pounding like ya wouldn't believe bro, I can tell ya."

"Who's Mark?" Robbie had asked. Bringing it home to Rich that though his brother had survived his ordeal, he still had a way to go.

"Mark Pallister? Y' know? Your mate from work. You were working' on this Mortimer thingy together. You were gonna be doing a presentation on it for yer bosses I think."

Robbie shook his head before digressing. Studying his brother's tattooed arms he said; "Didn't I let you tattoo me once Rich? I've got a tattoo haven't I?"

Rich smiled. "Ya've got three bro. All me own work." He said proudly.

"Don't you believe it," Annie interrupted, feeling a little better now. "You were his guinea pig when he was practicing his art. The first one he did was rubbish."

"Yeah, but I did a decent job of the cover up," Rich protested.

"Pally!" Robbie suddenly exclaimed.

"Ya what?" Rich asked.

"From work. I've remembered. It's Pally isn't it? Mark Pallister, tall, dark hair? I remember him now." Robbie appeared really pleased with himself for finally remembering. "It's like a delayed reaction. I didn't have a clue who he was a minute ago, but then it just seemed t' jump into me head when you were talking about tattoos. I don't know why."

"Well at least ya've remembered, doesn't matter how or when. Just proves that it's all still in there buddy."

Lynsey came back through. "The Sister's asked if we can leave within the next fifteen minutes. I just wanted a bit more time if that's okay?"

"Of course it is love," Annie replied. "Come on Richard; let's give them a wee bit o' time together. We'll come back in the morning Robbie, I promise."

"Okay mum. I am getting a bit past it now if I'm honest. I'll see ya tomorrow then."

"You absolutely will sweetheart," Annie replied. "I love you Robbie, never forget that."

"Love ya mum."

# Chapter Eleven

Clive and Annie had decided to stop off at a coffee shop on their way home. Clive was concerned that Annie hadn't eaten; he thought that if they stopped off somewhere she might have something, even if she just had a scone or a bowl of soup, anything really.

She looked quite drained and gaunt somehow. Normally, she didn't look anything like her sixty-eight years, but at that moment she did, that and then some. She'd always looked after herself, always groomed herself, she had fabulous skin, beautiful grey-blue eyes with a definite twinkle in them. She was elegant both in her dress and in her manner. She was still dressed as she would normally but something wasn't right and though he'd expected some degree of turmoil given the current circumstances, it was more than that. Clive was finding it hard to put his finger on just what it was, but he knew that something wasn't right. He decided to go with the flow for a while; see if there was anything in what she might say that would enlighten him without him having to goad it out of her. He was finding the whole situation quite difficult. She was his best friend as well as his wife; he'd helped bring up her boys from when Robbie was eleven and Rich just five years old. He had a great relationship with them, always had done. He put that down to how

Annie was: relaxed, kind, always amiable and approachable, traits that had certainly rubbed off on the boys.

So if anything, it was becoming glaringly obvious that something wasn't right. He understood the emotions of the past twenty-four hours. He knew that she would've been going through hell, but they'd always turned to each other when times had got tough in the past. This time Annie had turned inwards and Clive didn't understand or like it, nor was he too sure how to deal with it.

"A toasted teacake and a pot o' tea would be nice love, thanks." Annie had begun to notice that she hadn't eaten too. It was probably the rumble in her tummy that she'd felt in the car on the way there that had given it away.

Clive smiled at the waitress. "Same for me please lovey," he said. He looked at his wife sitting opposite him; she smiled back, one of those forced, tired smiles that people do out of politeness. "Would y'rather just go home?" he asked her.

She shook her head. "No. I'm sorry. I know it must be difficult for yae too. It's just taken it all out o' me, all this worry, that's all."

Clive wasn't convinced and he wasn't going to let it lie. "Are y'forgetting who it is yer talking to Annie?"

She looked puzzled. "What d' ya mean love?"

"Annie Wilkinson; I know ya better than I know meself. I know when yer unhappy, I know when yer worried, scared, when yer being nosey as opposed t' curious. I know what makes y' laugh an' what makes y' cry." She didn't say anything, just listened. "The point I'm making, is that *I know you;* an' I know that ya've got summat more running through yer mind than what yer trying t' make out."

The waitress brought their order, not to mention a welcome interlude for Annie, who began pouring two cups of tea. She went on to butter her teacake while Clive picked up his cup and took a sip. He'd decided not to mention anything else until she'd eaten something. He didn't want her losing her appetite again, though he was really struggling walking on a sea of egg-shells around her. She'd never made him feel uncomfortable before; this just wasn't like her.

***

Driving home, Clive had decided to go the long way round. Rather than go on the bypass, he'd thought to go over the tops, across the moors. They used to go for drives over the moors a lot when the boys were younger. They'd stop off for ice-creams and watch the boys play and climb up the rugged boulders on the Glenside.

It was the tail end of winter now though and there would be no business for a fool hardy ice-cream vendor at this time of year.

Clive pulled the car into the same lay-by used by the ice-cream man in the summer months and parked up close to where the land fell away and the views were magnificent on a clear, sunny day. Not that today was one of those, but you could still see for miles across the valley, beyond Baildon and Shipley and on towards Bradford in one direction and Leeds in the other.

They'd met in Baildon about thirty-two years previously. Annie had worked in the old Bay Horse Tavern at the time and Clive was working as a drayman. He'd fancied her right from the start and manipulated the deliveries so that the Bay Horse Tavern was always on his list which had meant he could see Annie once a week at least. He'd always thought that she was out of his league, but she was so easy to talk to and to get along with, that he'd decided to finally chance his arm and ask her out. On that day when she'd accepted, he'd felt his life begin again and he'd never looked back since. Clive had already had one failed marriage which had ended some years previous to that and Annie had been a widow with two young boys to fend for. But now, now she was his wonderful wife and he loved her with all of his heart. He loved her sons like they were his own flesh and blood too.

*** 

"Why are we stopping here?" Annie asked. "Isn't this where we used tae bring the boys a lifetime ago?"

"It is love, yeh," Clive confirmed. "I thought it might do us good if we had a bit of a trip down memory lane. I kinda got the impression that y' might want t' clear yer head a little."

Annie looked worried. "But what about Robbie? What if something happens an' they need t' get a hold of me?"

"If anything happens, they've got my mobile number Annie, don't worry. If anyone needs us, we're only a phone call away," Clive reassured her. "Besides, nowt's gonna happen. Robbie's gonna be fine love. You heard what that doctor said same as I did."

Annie's shoulders dropped as she sighed. Feeling a little more relaxed, she sank back in her seat and gazed out across the heather strewn moorland.

"We've always been honest wi' each other Annie haven't we?" Clive said the words with a certain amount of trepidation, unable to gauge the response he might be met with. "It's just that...well I know...I know there's summat yer not telling me love. I'm not stupid, I know ya, an' I know when summat's not right Annie. An' it's doing my head in you not telling me. Ya've never shut me out like this before, not in all the time I've known ya." He paused for a moment, trying desperately to reach her, to read her. "Please tell me love, whatever it is just spit it out. I know it's got t' be summat t' do wi' what's happened wi' our Robbie; just tell me, I can help. I want to help."

Annie maintained her gaze out across the moors, remaining silent for a few moments. Clive could almost hear the cogs turning as a single isolated tear spilled down her pale cheek. "Guilt," she finally said. "I feel such a sense of deep, catastrophic guilt. Something I've spent my life trying tae bury, but I've clearly not."

Whatever her response might have been, Clive hadn't quite expected it to be that. "I don't understand love," he queried. "What have you got t' be feeling guilty about? Surely y' don't mean yer guilty in some way wi' what's happened to Robbie? That wa' nowt t' do wi' you Annie. You couldn't o' done owt about that."

"I know," she said softly. "It's a lot o' things Clive. There's so many things I should o'...so many years...I've lied...secrets." She began to weep. "I feel so bloody guilty."

Clive was beginning to worry. However this conversation was going to go, it wasn't anything he felt he could second guess at. "Guilty why?" He pushed her for an explanation. "Surely y' not beating yerself up ov'r Robbie being in hospital love? He wa' just in the wrong place at the wrong time. There's nowt y' could o' done about that, there's nowt anyone could o' done. It's life, an' sometimes really bad thing happen t' really good people y' know?"

"Oh I know alright." Annie cried. "Believe me I know. But yae don't understand Clive. Yer a good man an' I love yae dearly, but yae don't understand the promise I made."

"For God's sake Annie! What promise?"

"I promised I'd always be there for him. Always take care o' him an' I've failed, just like I failed before an' I so hate myself for it Clive. I made a promise that I couldn't keep an' I feel useless, helpless."

Clive took her shaking hand in his. "Robbie?" he asked again. "I don't get it. You've been a wonderful mother t' both o' them boys Annie; they'd be the first t' tell y' that. What promise are y' talking about? Their dad? Did y' promise their dad?"

"No," Annie whispered through her tears. "His mother; I promised Robbie's mother."

# Chapter Twelve

Stunned beyond words at what his wife had just disclosed, Clive drove them home. He'd remained silent the whole way and Annie just wept with the occasional "Oh God", the only indicator of the depth of her despair.

She was a wreck; she looked haggard and crushed as Clive led her into the house. He poured her a large vodka and orange and himself a whiskey and ginger before almost collapsing on the sofa beside her. "Right love," he said in as reassuring manner as he could muster. "I think y' need t' tell me now. I need t' know just what's going on. No more smoothing over, no more swerving the subject. You've basically just told me that our Robbie's not our Robbie, an' that's one hell of a bombshell t' be dropping. Come on now Annie, I'm yer husband and *I need to know.* You need t' tell me."

Annie took a long slurp of her drink and wiped her eyes with a tissue from the box beside her. "Oh Clive I'm so sorry," she managed. "Of course yer right, I know that. I just don't know where tae start. It's so complicated and..." She hesitated.

"And what love?" Clive coaxed her.

"And, well...probably very illegal."

Clive was struggling to make sense of everything; *illegal,* what the bloody hell did she mean by that? *Oh Christ this is going from bad to worse* he thought to himself. "What do y' mean; illegal? Y' make it sound like ya've kidnapped him..." A fleeting glance in his direction gave away more than it should. "Oh shit, oh no, Annie, please tell me y' didn't steal him from his mother! It wasn't one o' them illegal adoptions was it? He wasn't snatched from his mother an' sold?" He jumped to his feet in panicked disbelief and began pacing the room, repeatedly running his fingers though his hair. He could feel each breath he released shaking as it left his lungs. He perched on the armchair at the other side of the living room. "Right. From the beginning Annie. Everything, an' I mean everything! If you're really not his mother, then who is, an' where is she now?"

Annie put her cupped hands to her face for a while, took a couple of deep breaths and then rested back into the sofa. "She's dead," she said finally. "She died when he was just five years old."

"So you haven't had him since he was a baby? If that's the case an' y' promised t' look after a friend's little lad, then why all the fuss? Why's that illegal? An' why have y' never said owt?"

"Like I said Clive, it's complicated, very, very complicated. I did kidnap him ya see, after she'd died. I stole him from his father. That man was a monster, a nasty, vindictive, cruel alcoholic. He'd killed her, I know he did it. No-one could ever prove it an' the powers that be woulda never believed it. But he killed my little sister alright an' I couldn't *not* act. I couldn't just leave her wee boy in his hands."

"Oh my God!" Clive began to fit one or two pieces together. "Oh Annie, he's your nephew! Robbie's your sister's child? Why couldn't he stay with his dad? What was so bad about him?"

Annie contorted her mouth in disgust. "He was vile Clive; a horrible man. He used tae beat my sister black an' blue. Oh she'd be the dutiful wife an' tell folks that she'd fallen, walked into a door, the usual. But the whole village knew it was him. After the boy was born, my sister fell pregnant a couple more times. Each time he accused her o' carrying another man's bastard an' beat the poor mite out o' her.

"She was found one morning by some local fishermen, caught up on the rocks at the foot o' the cliffs. The coroner said she must've been there all night, died of a massive head injury and multiple other injuries the likely result of a fall from the cliff. There was no water inside o' her, so she hadn't drowned. He left the verdict open, said he couldn't decide if it was accidental or suicide. But I knew; we all did.

"Mona would o' never left her own child like that, especially knowing what his fate'd be, the same as hers eventually no doubt. He used tae hit the boy too, she'd do her best tae protect him, but it just meant she took his beatings as well as her own.

"It'd been throwing it down the night before she was found, an' she certainly wasn't dressed for the weather. She'd a flimsy summer frock on an' sandals with a low heel. She wouldn't have been out walking at the cliff top dressed like that; she wasn't stupid. He killed her; I know he did. He either pushed her from the cliff himself, or else she was already dead when he threw her over." Annie struggled to maintain her composure as she recalled the event.

Clive's heart bled for his wife's pain. "Wasn't he ever questioned? If the whole village knew what he wa' like, didn't anyone get involved?"

Annie shook her head. "They tried God love 'em. We all did. I was living in England by then with my husband and Eban had banned Mona from seeing me at all. She was reduced tae phoning me in secret. Some o' the villagers, good people, went tae the Church elders."

"Why the Church?" Clive seemed puzzled. Why not the police?

"Because Eban was the Minister, the Vicar. The man o' God that no law or Church elder would ever question, not in them days anyway. They were scoffed at for even suggesting that their Minister would behave in such a way. They thought they were getting somewhere once, when the Bishop from the Free Church came tae visit. Eban was his usual, gracious self tae the Bishop. An' that stupid man swallowed everything Eban fed him. He only went an' told him what the nature o' the complaints against him were an' as usual, Eban charmed his way out of it. Said that he'd had a run in with a couple o' local men over their drinking habits an' general demeanour, that he'd had tae pull them up on their family responsibilities. The Bishop believed him when he'd said that it was their apparent revenge on him, an' not tae worry, that he would pray for them and help them find their way."

Clive didn't quite get it. "Still, I don't get why more wasn't done? It seems archaic, even for thirty or forty years ago"

"That's because it was," Annie explained. "You have tae understand Clive; this was coastal, rural Scotland in the nineteen-seventies an' the village was very isolated. Everyone went tae the Free Kirk on Sundays. No shops were opened, the pubs only opened for a couple o' hours at lunch an' for three an' a half hours in the evenings, no food was sold. No exceptions, no-one broke the rules an' that's just the way it was. The whole community was led by the Church an' the Minister *was* the Church in a small wee place like that. An' the Minister was Eban Whithorn, Mona's husband, my brother-in-law. The monster in the dog-collar."

"How can y' be so certain that it was him? I mean, I don't doubt he was a bastard to her, but it doesn't mean that he definitely killed her either," Clive asked.

Annie was beginning to look exhausted, but now that she'd opened the flood gates, she couldn't shut them again. "Mona had been planning on leaving him, running away because she couldn't ever have done it properly, told him I mean, she was gonna take her boy an' just leave. No warning, no goodbye. It wa' the only way. They wa' gonna come tae England an' live wi' me. Peter had died in a car accident three months before an' I was alone an' pregnant with Richard. When I'd buried my husband, my own sister hadn't been allowed tae stand by my side at his funeral. He wouldn't let her come. Told her I'd lost my husband 'cause I was such a bitch an' it wa' God's punishment. That bastard, that evil bastard!"

Clive went back over to his weeping wife and held her in his arms to comfort her.

"I think he must've found out," Annie continued. "I was due tae meet them up in Ku'koo'bree the day after she was found. I'd driven up. Mona was meant tae take the bus from the Isle to Wigtown, an' then another on tae Ku'koo'bree. I was tae collect them an' we'd away back tae England, the three of us. I'd taken a room the night before in a B&B. When she didn't show, I phoned our friend Izzy McStay, the village school teacher. I remember I collapsed tae the floor when she told me about Mona. It'd only been three months since I'd lost Peter, an' now my sister too. Our parents had died some years previously, mum when I was twenty an' dad just after I lost my Robbie..."

Clive stopped her. "Your Robbie?" This was news; his head spun.

Annie shook her head at the whole sorry situation, realising she had opened a can of worms and had a huge mess ahead of her. "Yes, my Robbie." She smiled in gentle remembrance. "Ya see Clive, that's how I knew that the man in the hospital was Robbie, our Robbie. The minute that policeman, Bash, said that there was a confusion 'cause the man thought his name wa' Michael, I knew it *was* him. He really is Michael ya' see, Michael Whithorn, son of the Reverend Eban Whithorn an' my sweet, lovely sister Ramona Cummings as was. She called him her angel. Oh how she loved that wee boy, my Ramona's angel. He'd been born thirteen weeks after I'd had my baby, Robert, my own angel an' the apple o' his dad's eye. He wa' just shy of eight months old when he went tae sleep one night an' nev'r woke up. A cot death they said, no whys or wherefores, just *'it's a tragedy Mrs McAndrew, but it's just one o' those things with no rhyme or reason to it.'* But it was so much more than a tragedy, it broke my heart an' it broke Peter, he was nev'r the same after that. Mona cried all the time, she felt so guilty that she had her baby while I'd lost mine, but she comforted me, she was there for me.

"It took us a year or so t' get our heads around what had happened. Eban was very nice tae us at the time, prayed for us, said all the right things. Anyway, Peter an' I decided we needed tae get away, a fresh start somewhere. He took a job in England, Chesterfield tae be exact. But if I'd have known then, I'd have nev'r left her there. I felt so ill, so guilty when I found out what was going on, but by then it was too late, he wouldn't let her visit, he wouldn't let her speak tae us at all. Peter had offered tae go an' get her an' the bairn, but back then she wa' still in denial, she believed him when he said he wa' sorry, she believed him when he promised tae ne'er do it again. An' she trusted that he *would* change. He didn't, he just got worse an' poor wee Michael saw it all.

"After she died I couldn't leave him there. Izzy an' some o' the other villagers would tell me how withdrawn and terrified the boy was, how he would cower when his father walked into the room. How could I leave my sweet sister's angel with that man?

"I went back up tae Ku'koo'bree an' met up with Izzy, her husband an' three others from the Isle. That's when we planned it; we all knew it was the right thing tae do. The Church an' the police weren't interested in our concerns for the child; we'd tried them. Eban was a Minister, a man o' God, the least likely person to hurt a child.

"At first it felt like an abomination tae even think of using my own dead baby's identity. But it was for the greater good, an' I couldn't think o' any other feasible way tae conceal Michael. He'd have been found in no time under his own name. We decided tae get him out by sea, that way we could avoid the roads, in case Eban discovered what we were doing an' called the police, plus it gave us a believable excuse tae leave behind.

"Ya see the plan was that the men would say that they'd taken the boy out fishing with them. They often did anyway, so no-one would question that, not even Eban. They were gonna say that there was an accident an' he'd fallen overboard. They'd raise the alarm, look for him, the works; but they were gonna return full o' grief at another poor soul lost tae the sea."

"An' did they?" Clive asked. "How did y' get a little lad like that to go along wi' it? Even if he wanted to, surely he wa' too young t' be able t' pull it off wi' out raising suspicion?"

"Aye, that worried me too if I'm honest. It was a big ask of a small boy. I'd moved from Chesterfield to Doncaster a week earlier. It was all part o' the plan, a new place where no-one'd know he wasn't mine. I'd planned on moving us around a few times while I got Michael tae become Robbie. I was already seven months pregnant by the time we rescued him anyway. I wa' just gonna tell my new neighbours that he'd been staying wi' family 'cause I'd been having a difficult time of it.

"But, as it turned out, Michael took no convincing at all. He really did fall overboard ya see. There was a storm an' the sea wa' rough. We were in a small fisher being thrown all over by the waves. Just as the boat wa' heading into Wigtown bay, Michael wa' thrown out when it listed. I saw him go under, an' I screamed for all I wa' worth. I prayed tae a God I no longer believed in, I begged for him, for my sister's child tae be spared. He was all I had left, an' I thought he wa' being taken too.

"In what seemed like a heartbeat, Jamie, one o' the men that was helping me, hit the water just near where Michael had gone in. I couldn't see either o' them; I couldn't see much o' anything wi' all the wind an' rain an' my own tears blinding me. Then I heard Jock shout at me; '*Take the wheel Annie; do it now!*' I did as I was told an' scurried into the pilot's hut. I felt the boat pull tae one side as Jock dragged them back on board. The two o' them threw Michael onto his belly an' pushed down on his back. It looked like they were punching him, but then all this water an' vomit came up from his stomach an' the poor child started tae gasp for breath. He wa' freezing cold, it was October, it was dark an' he'd been in the icy sea. He *was* breathing, that wa' the important thing. A few cuts an' bruises as he'd been dragged aboard but it wa' the hypothermia made him confused an' disorientated an' made the next bit easier.

"As soon as we got ashore, we got him in my car, wrapped up with the heater on full. I drove him straight tae the hospital in Dumfries. I'd wanted one o' the men tae come with me, but if the story was tae be believed back in the Isle, they'd both have tae go back in the boat. I was distraught at the time, but Jock shouted me down. He was right o' course, I was just so scared that's all.

"I told 'em at the hospital that Michael, or Robert, which is what I booked him in as, had fallen off the jetty in Ku'koo'bree, that he'd been playing an' hadn't heeded me. I said that a gust of wind had knocked him off balance an' he'd gone in. I was terrified that I'd be found out, but I wasn't. They checked him over. Once he'd warmed up he was talking again an' every time a nurse called him Robert, I'd distract him, worried that he might correct them, but he didn't. I think it'd been the last in a long line of traumas for him and after that his memories became distorted an' confused. He might remember something an' ask me who the lady was that used tae pick him up from his old school; I'd tell him that was me. Sometimes he'd look a bit puzzled, but he'd just accept it. Over time, he replaced the memories of his life in the Isle village with memories of me an' Peter. I used photos of Peter that he just incorporated into his memories as if they'd always been there and...basically, that's how Michael Whithorn became Robbie McAndrew."

Clive felt like he was in a dream, like this whole conversation, this explanation hadn't really happened. It was so farfetched that if he'd have been watching a television drama with this storyline, he would've turned over, thinking it too unbelievable. "He doesn't know does he? He genuinely believes he's Robbie?"

Annie sighed. "Yes he genuinely believes he's Robbie, but somewhere deep inside, he clearly knows he's Michael too. He mentioned Auntie Annie before he put us together as mum an' Clive. I *was* his Auntie Annie; that's how he would've known me, how Mona would've referred tae me."

"No love," Clive said. "You *are* his Auntie Annie, an' y' need t' decide where we go from here."

"I don't know Clive. I've been living in the hope that if I close my eyes, when I open them again it'll have all gone away, like a bad dream."

Clive leant in towards her, resting his hands on her knees. "Annie I love the bones of ya, but this isn't going away. An' we're gonna have t' deal wi' it one way or another, but what we can't do, is ignore it. He needs t' know love, he really does. He deserves that doesn't he? None o' this has been his doing."

Resigned to what must be, Annie held onto her husband's hands. He was right and she knew it. She'd always wanted to tell Robbie the truth, but hadn't known how to. She wanted him to know about his mother and how much she'd loved him, but she was afraid, afraid of how he would cope with knowing and, if she were to be honest with herself, afraid of what would become of her. She'd broken the law when all said and done and so had the villagers who'd helped them. There was Richard to consider too. He didn't know any different, as they'd grown up as brothers. Would either of them ever forgive her or understand?

## Chapter Thirteen

"Okay, thank you very much. What time can I come in tomorrow? Right, thanks." Lynsey finished her call to the hospital and replaced the receiver. Natalie was in the kitchen making them both something to eat. She called through to her sister to check that everything was alright with Robbie then returned to check on dinner.

"Yeah, he's okay Nat," Lynsey called. "I'm just gonna ring his mum an' see how she is. Robbie was a bit worried earlier that all this has put her through the wringer a bit. I promised him I'd check on her."

She was busy on the phone when the entrance buzzer went off. Natalie rushed from the kitchen to see who it was. "Okay, I'll buzz you in Mark," She said. She bobbed down to the end of the hallway to unlock the door in readiness before rushing back to the kitchen to rescue dinner.

Mark knocked lightly before popping his head around the door and calling through. "Hiya, it's only me, am I okay t' come in?" Natalie confirmed his request from the kitchen and so he entered, closing the door behind himself. He stopped at the door to the kitchen to speak to Natalie. "Hello, we meet at last," he said with a smile. He'd spoken to Natalie on the phone previously; she'd been the one to fill him in on the news regarding Robbie's discovery and the state he was in.

Lynsey came to join them once she'd finished on the phone. Mark greeted her with a kiss to the cheek. "Well you look so much better than the last time I saw you Lynsey. It'll be the relief no doubt."

Lynsey laughed. "Yeah, I imagine it is. I can't tell ya how exhausted I feel though; it's kinda hit me like a truck. Now that the worst of the worrying is over an' I know he's safe an' where he is an' all that...I think I was functioning purely on adrenalin t' be honest Mark...oh, can I just ask? Do ya prefer Mark or Pally?"

Mark looked back at her with an odd expression on his face. Lynsey giggled. "It's just that when Rich was talking to Robbie earlier, he mentioned you an' Robbie didn't have a clue who ya were, then he just piped up with it a few minutes later. *'Oh Pally'* he said, *'I know who that is now'*."

Mark saw the funny side immediately. "It doesn't really matter," he said. "I answer to either; but you're right, Robbie usually calls me Pally."

"After I'd had chance t' think about it, it'd made sense to me. Robbie talks about Pally from work, but when y' phoned me an' introduced yerself as Mark Pallister, I didn't make the connection," Lynsey explained. "Think I wa' just too distracted at the time."

Mark shrugged it off. "T' be fair; ya did have a lot more on yer plate."

Natalie interrupted them. "Speaking of plates; teas ready," she announced. "D'ya want some Mark? There's plenty." She began dishing up while Lynsey searched the drawer for clean cutlery.

"How was his mum?" she asked Lynsey.

"I'm not sure, I didn't actually get t' speak to her. Clive answered the phone. He said she was alright, but when I asked if I could have a word, he suddenly announced that she'd gone for a lie down, which is fair enough. It's bound to have taken its toll on her. It wa' just the way he said it; a bit cagey, not how he normally is. Made me wonder if she wa' sat in the background shaking her head an' not wanting to talk t' me. I hope I haven't offended her. I know it's been difficult today 'cause we all wanted t' be in there with him an' it was so restrictive, only two at a time an' not tiring him out etcetera. I hope I didn't come across like I was trying t' push her out an' wanted him all to myself. I mean I did, but I'm not stupid, I know that his family needed t' be with him too."

Natalie wasn't convinced. "Now you're just being daft," she said. "Letting your imagination run wild. Maybe she really was knackered, an' let's face it, who could blame her. She's been through the mill too y' know, an' she's no spring chicken. Or maybe they'd had words, her an' Clive; you might've called in the middle of a barney."

"I wouldn't have thought they'd be arguing today, not with everything else that's gone on." Lynsey reasoned. "Besides, they're just not like that; they always seem t' get on so well, but thinking about it, she was very quiet at the hospital. We were in that waiting room for hours before they let us in t' see Robbie. She barely spoke to Clive in all that time, she didn't say much to any of us t' be honest."

"Well there ya go then." Natalie said. "She'll be dead on her feet, that's all. Don't worry about it an' for God's sake, don't tell Robbie about it when ya see him tomorrow."

Lynsey agreed that her sister was most probably right, though she couldn't quite shake the feeling that all might not be well in the Wilkinson household. She did feel just a tiny bit guilty for the fact that she had slightly resented giving up time with Robbie for Annie and Rich. It was completely irrational and totally selfish, she knew that, but it was hard and for all she knew, that could be how the others felt too. All wrapped up in their own desperation, not knowing whether they were headed for grief or joy at the time. She tried not to think too much about it and sat down to eat. "What have they said at work Mark?"

"Well naturally they were all really concerned. They're more bothered about how he is than anything. Asked me t' keep 'em updated, let 'em know if there was owt you or Robbie needed. One o' the directors came down himself an' had a word. Asked me how ya were. They were gonna send a car an' driver to take ya to an' from the hospital y' know, they've been really good. Oh sorry Lyns, it never occurred to me...I just told him you had yer sister here to help wi' stuff like that...I can get it sorted if ya like?"

Natalie laughed. "Aw, that's really nice of them, but I think we've got it covered."

"Yeah that is kind," Lynsey added.

"Well they think a lot o' Robbie at work y' know; he's one o' their top software developers. After yours truly that is," Mark joked. "Have the police said anything more? Do they know what exactly happened yet?"

"Not yet," she answered. "They think it's more likely that he was just targeted randomly but, 'cause he can't remember anything about it, they don't want t' rule anything out." She hovered over her food for a minute before continuing. "There isn't anything that you can think of is there Mark? I mean, I don't know, something t' do with this Mortimer project perhaps?"

Mark grinned, trying to stifle a laugh. "Nah," he scoffed, "It's not that sort o' thing. Certainly not worth jack-shit to anyone else outside Fletcher Dean's. It's just a new programme for storing an' sorting internal data. We dubbed it Mortimer after my old head o' year at school, 'cause he was weirdly OCD, y' know, *everything in its place an' a place for everything* which is pretty much how the software works. It's just a more refined programme, less complicated for the user an' more efficient all round. Means we can update that aspect for our clients, but they're contracted to us anyway, so it wouldn't be worth anyone else's while. Besides, not the usual way industrial espionage'd take place I imagine."

The two girls laughed it off, mostly to cover slight embarrassment on Lynsey's part. It did seem farfetched. Natalie asked if there was anyone at work that Mark didn't get on with, anyone he'd pissed off, but Mark couldn't think of anyone. It seemed more likely that Robbie and Mark were the office clowns than anything else. Lynsey couldn't recall Robbie ever saying anything detrimental about anyone he worked with. It did seem to be the least plausible reason for the attack he'd suffered, though it was one hell of a beating for the sake of a Smartphone too, no matter how much it may or may not be worth.

Exhaustion was beginning to overtake Lynsey shortly after dinner. "I'm sorry guys," she apologised to Mark and Natalie, "I'm really knackered an' now I've stuffed my face, I'm struggling to keep my eyes open. D'ya mind if I call it a night?"

"Not at all," Mark said. "I wa' ready for the off anyway."

Lynsey quickly rested her hand on his forearm in protest. "Oh no, no I didn't mean for you t' go. It's early yet. It's just me

122

that's done in. Please stay an' keep Nat company. Honestly, I'd be happier if y' did." Despite all she'd been through and how sleep deprived she was feeling, she hadn't failed to notice how well her sister and Mark had been getting on, that little spark between them that had been evident all evening. She threw a sly wink in her sister's direction as she got up from the table leaving them both there.

# Chapter Fourteen

Once Robbie had embarked on the road to recovery, there was no stopping him. He'd been moved to a different ward, reflecting the fact that he was on the mend. He'd even been deemed fit enough to undergo further surgery. The Orthopaedic surgeon had used metal pins to fix the lower Tibia and Fibula bones in his broken left ankle; she'd explained that there was also a hairline fracture of the Talus and some tendon damage, all of which would take a long time to heal. He already had a cast on his right arm to fix the simple fracture there and was wearing a neoprene shoulder brace which helped to reduce the demand on the injured side. When he'd first woken up, his right arm had also been in a sling type device, but that had been removed and Robbie was encouraged to gently move the joint a little each day. Despite all of that, in what seemed like no time at all he was able to sit up in bed, he was eating normally, his voice had recovered and he still displayed the same sense of humour that was so familiar to those around him. His memory, though improving, was still quite sketchy though and he sometimes took time to recall events, work colleagues, what sort of car he had, that kind of thing.

Lynsey had taken the rest of the month off work so that she could spend most of her day at the hospital with him. Annie visited each and every day, mostly with Clive but sometimes alone.

Richard had bought his brother a new mobile phone and on the days he didn't visit, he'd call him instead. Mark had been to visit a few times too. He'd brought one of work's old laptops as soon as he'd found out that the hospital had Wi-Fi; he didn't want his pal getting bored. Plus, seeing the company logo on the desktop had jogged Robbie's memory a time or two. It had helped him remember the names of other colleagues and his boss as well as the project he'd been working on. All in all, progress was good.

***

Lynsey had gone to the supermarket with her sister while Annie was with Robbie. Liam Drake had just left; he'd continued to check on Robbie every day or so since his arrival. If he were to be honest, Robbie fascinated him. He'd been the first real serious trauma case that Liam had dealt with in A&E and he found it intriguing to follow his progress, to think back to when he'd first arrived looking like shit, not knowing if he'd even survive the night or not; and then to see him now, so positive despite his ordeal. The younger man liked Robbie, he'd got to know him more as a person which is something A&E staff rarely got the chance to do. They're not with their patients for any extended time really, they just patched them up and shipped them out to wherever.

Annie was listening to Robbie telling her all about the things he could remember from work; like the time some person called Craig had leant too far back in his chair, the leg had snapped off and the chair went over covering Craig in the heavily vinegarred chips he was eating at the time. Someone else had been filming him on their phone as he'd balanced the chair on two legs; she'd caught the whole thing including the hysterical laughter that broke out around the office as it happened. The footage had made its way onto YouTube and gone viral. Though Annie didn't really know what that meant, she smiled and listened patiently while he told her about it. "I'm gonna try an' find it later now that I've got my laptop," Robbie said.

She was so glad to see him in such good spirits, but it didn't do anything to ease her heavy heart. Every time she looked at him now she thought of Mona and of the Isle, of the life she and her younger sister had grown up with as children, of Buyyoch farm where their parents had raised cattle. The Cummings' had been one of the few families in the area that didn't earn their living from the sea…and she thought of Eban. She'd no idea if the man was dead or alive, but she knew that she'd have to find out, eventually.

It broke her heart to think of the life her poor sister had endured, her death under somewhat dubious circumstances, and of Michael whom she'd saved. She'd done it for Mona. Yet Michael was now a man and he was here in front of her in his hospital bed, healing and being jovial, with no apparent memory of Mona, of the mother who'd loved him more than life itself. Annie felt guilty for so many things. Oh she'd loved her sister's child like he was her own, but then she'd given him the name of her own boy. Had she distorted the boundaries in doing so? Once she'd got him back to

England and a new life, he'd been happy and loved, he'd gone to school, made friends, he had a new baby brother, but he didn't have Mona. Annie had never meant for him to never know of Mona. She'd truly wanted him to know what he'd meant to his mother and she'd always wanted to be able to share her memories with him, but she was afraid to.

At the time her intentions had been good, and though she didn't regret getting the boy out of that awful situation, she did however regret that she hadn't really planned things better. She hadn't given any thought at all as to how she was going to pull it off in the long term and after the first couple of years when she began to feel that they were going to be alright and safe from discovery, it had dawned on her that she *couldn't* tell him. He'd become Robbie by then, he'd lost his Scottish accent but for the odd word like 'wee' instead of small which most people put down to the fact that his "mother" was Scottish. He believed that *she* was his mum. How would he have taken it, having his world shattered yet again? And what if he'd said something? To a teacher, a friend's mum? He could've ended up being returned to his father. Eban would have certainly been able to convince the authorities of his plausibility; he'd had plenty of practice at it. Annie herself could well have ended up in gaol and she had baby Richard to consider by then too.

\*\*\*

The recent events had reopened a door that she knew could never be closed again. She was glad that Clive knew now as at least she could lessen the guilt of keeping such a thing from him for all of this time, but each day after spending time with Robbie, she'd go home to her loyal and loving husband and cry.

The crying was releasing years of pent up stress, of the self resentment she felt at the way things had happened and the years of grief. Clive had been trying to reassure her that if it came to it, if, once it had all come out, someone informed the police, that it would be her grief that saved her. Clive thought that as she'd lost her parents within a few years of each other, her baby a few months later, then her husband and her only sister; that she would be looked on more mercifully. He'd told her that they would take those things into consideration and perhaps even consider that she wasn't in her right mind at the time.

"But I *was* in my right mind," Annie had protested. "I knew exactly what I wa' doing and what the potential consequences were...are."

She'd told Clive that she no longer cared if she was to be prosecuted, or convicted for her crime. She just cared about Robbie and what he would think of her for doing what she'd done. And Richard, what about Richard who'd never known any different? How would he feel about his mother's lies?

"What if something had happened tae me Clive? Before I'd told you even," Annie cried. "I could've gone tae my grave an' that poor boy would o' never o' known any different. He would o' gone tae his own grave still believing he's Robert McAndrew."

"He wouldn't be the first," Clive had argued. "What about all them adopted people? I know nowadays most seem t' know they're adopted, but it hasn't always been the case has it?"

"What if my sister could speak? What would she think of me for erasing her from her son's life, his memories? An' ya know today while I was with him, he was trying tae pump me for information about his childhood. He asked me if he'd ever had a wee friend called Michael 'cause he's still hung up on why he'd thought it tae be his own name."

"Then those memories that y' seem t' have convinced yerself that ya've destroyed are obviously still there somewhere, buried." Clive was nothing if not blunt. "Y' said it yerself; the poor kid had a terrible time. Is it any wonder that he took no convincing t' put it behind him?

"An' as for yer sister. Well...come on, really? You put yerself in Mona's shoes for a minute love. 'Cause I tell y' this for nowt; if y' really had o' been in her shoes, an' ya'd suffered what she did at the hands of a man like Eban, would y' have resented her for taking *your* child? Especially if ya'd already made her promise t' look after him if owt happened t' ya. I'm sure she'd be happier knowing him t' be safe an' happy wi' nowt by way o' memory of her, than she would t' think of him remembering her, but having to endure what she did at the hands o' that man, spending his childhood wondering why she'd left him, feeling lonely, miserable an' abandoned. He might never o' known that she loved him anyway. Who's t' know what Eban would o' told him about her? What he'd o' done t' the lad.

"Oh Annie y' need t' stop going over the 'what ifs'. One thing y' can't do is change history. It's happened an' there's an end to it. The question now is: where do we go from here? How are we gonna handle this, and when? What we need is a plan of action."

Annie got up and went to stand by the window. Looking out into her garden and the late afternoon sun, she sighed. "I know you're right, but I don't know where tae start Clive, I really don't. Other than waiting 'til Robbie's fit again...home from the hospital I mean. I couldn't drop this on him in there. It wouldn't be right...I wouldn't know where tae start. Where d' ya start wi' something as big as this?"

"Y' start by task breaking love." Clive answered. "D'ya mind me making a suggestion?"

"All advice welcome," Annie replied. "What did ya have in mind?"

Clive got a pen and a pad of paper. "Well, t' start wi'...I reckon we ought t' do the bulk o' the donkeywork as soon as we can. While our Robbie's still laid up, if we can find out what we can before we have t' tell him, then we'll be armed wi' all the facts so as t' be able to answer all his questions, 'cause there's bound t' be plenty of 'em."

"I've no idea how tae Clive. I decided after the first year or so not tae stay in touch wi' Izzy McStay; we thought it safer for both of us. Said we'd only get in contact if it was a dire emergency. But o' course since then, I've moved house several times, so she'll not have known where tae find me."

Clive wasn't for giving up. "Right," he said. "Sit down lovey. You need t' think back t' what you *can* remember. D'ya still have Izzy's address? Even if she's not there anymore, they might know where she went or where she is now. She'll be retired by now, like us."

"She might even be dead Clive. She was a good ten years older than me I think, an' I'm sixty-nine this year," Annie said. "But I'll have a look. I'm sure I've still got my old address book somewhere."

"And what about the others? The folk that helped you all them years back. Can y' remember all their names Annie?"

"Oh yes. I'll never forget them." Annie took a seat and began to recall what she'd considered at the time to be Michael's rescue, while Clive put pen to paper. "Isabel an' Joe McStay. Catriona McGuffie, but she was an oldish woman back then. She can't possibly still be alive, but her son should be, Jamie McGuffie: the fisherman. He was the one I told you jumped in the sea that night when Robbie...I mean Michael'd fallen overboard. Him an' Jock saved the boy twice that night. Jock Maguire, the Isle harbour Master, again, I'm not sure if he'll still be with us. I think he was around the same age as the McStays. Then there were the Alexander's, Morag an' Ross. They had the pub on the harbour, the Solway Harvester. We didn't see them the night we left, but the plan was that they'd refuse tae serve Eban that evening. Start up some argument or something. He'd be forced tae the only other pub in the Isle then, which was in the other direction. Ya' see they'd no way of avoiding going past the Harvester that night; if he'd o' been in there he might o' seen 'em. I'd deliberately not gone tae the house myself for that reason. If he'd o' seen me in the village, or someone else had an' told him...well he'd o' known for sure that something was afoot. Even if it was after the fact an' he'd found out I'd been there, he'd o' never o' believed that Michael was lost tae the sea like the story we'd agreed on. He'd o' known I was involved."

Clive had written a list of all the names. "Okay. Right, y' need t' take a deep breath now love. When wa' the last time you wa' there?"

"Not since that night. I've never been back. Why?" Annie answered nervously.

"Well yer gonna have t' bite the bullet, 'cause we need t' go there. Y' need t' go back Annie; it's the only way we'll find out what's what. We don't even know if his father's still alive do we? We'll find that out if we go there. The only other alternative is to approach the Scottish Church, the Free Church you called 'em. They'd know what happened to him if he was a vicar, or if he still is."

"Oh Clive!" Annie exclaimed. "I don't know if I can. I've not seen the Isle since that night. And what if talking tae the Church raises more questions than we're comfortable with"

"Then we've no choice love. We have t go there. You'll have t' go back." He saw the blood drain from his wife's face as the reality hit and a painful fear took its place. "This time I'll be there with ya." He put a reassuring arm around her. "This time ya'll not be facing things alone. We'll do it together Annie, me an' you, 'cause I'm going nowhere love. I don't care what y' might o' done or the rights an' wrongs of it. I'll never leave ya t' face owt alone. I've never done so yet have I?"

Clive kissed his wife's forehead and held her close to him. She'd stopped shaking, as if she'd begun to resign herself to what lay ahead. *I'll do this* she was thinking to herself, *for Mona and for Michael.* And so that she could openly cherish the memory of her own lost baby, the real Robert McAndrew who was lying in the ground in his tiny coffin just three mile from where he'd been born, a piece of her heart in there with him and another piece in the plot beside him, where Peter lay at peace. The only solace that she'd had during these long secret years was in knowing that they were together. That her baby wasn't alone and that Peter had been reunited with his heart.

# Chapter Fifteen

Annie was reluctant to go anywhere while Robbie was still in the hospital. She didn't want to leave him, nor did she relish the thought of creating yet another lie in the form of her and Clive's reason for going. They would have to tell the boys something, but what? She didn't really want to have to think about it.

She'd partially regretted telling Clive everything, though on the other hand Robbie was still puzzling over why he'd thought himself to be Michael. He was convinced that he must know a Michael and because he couldn't yet remember everything himself, he quizzed his visitors from time to time. It had become a kind of mini obsession for him, driven by a mixture of boredom and nightmares. He'd asked Mark if there was a Michael at work, but the closest Mark had come up with was a Mick who worked in accounts, someone that Robbie would have been aware of but wouldn't have worked with directly. Even Rich had been recruited to go into the coffee shops that Robbie used to see if there was a Michael working there. He'd also quizzed Liam to try and find out if any of the staff who had looked after him in A&E or thereafter were named Michael, but nothing. He wasn't going on and on about it, but he clearly hadn't forgotten about it either. He'd told his mum that when Bash had visited and told him who he was, that he'd known immediately that it was indeed the case, that being Robbie felt right and normal straight away. Yet before that, before he'd found out who he really was, when he'd thought of himself as Michael, that had felt equally as right. Annie knew that her time would be limited. She'd sensed that as his memory returned a little at a time, there was a strong possibility that some of those buried memories would find their way back too and he wasn't five any more. She had neither the energy nor inclination to try and manipulate things the way she once had.

It was that familiar feeling in itself that puzzled Robbie and that he couldn't quite let go of. If someone had told him at the time that his name was Tim or Ben, would he have been equally convinced? It was just that strange feeling that if he wasn't Michael after all, then he must know a Michael quite well and when he spent any time thinking about it, that unanswered question was really bugging him.

***

"So, I don't mind driving us love, but how do we get there?" Clive asked. "I mean, I've never even heard of the place. Dumfries an' Galloway area y' say? South-West Scotland then."

"That's right, down at the very bottom of the Machars, it's not that hard tae find. Ya just head north up the M6 an' turn left when ya get tae Gretna. It's out o' the way, but the roads there are fairly straight forward," Annie explained. "It shouldn't be much more than a couple o' hundred miles from here."

Clive took his AA roadmap out from the sideboard drawer. It was a few years old, but he couldn't imagine that the major routes had changed much in that time.

Having found the Isle, he proceeded to trace the route with his finger. "Yer right love. Does look a bit out on a limb doesn't it? Looks t' be about three or four miles t' the next nearest place. Not much round it."

"Just fishing and agriculture, always has been," Annie said. "I don't want tae stay there Clive, I don't think I could..."

Clive looked back down at his map. "Stennoch, that's the next place, or somewhere called Sorbie?" he suggested.

"No." Annie was adamant. "Still too close. There's Wigtown, that's not too far away, but far enough so as I won't feel trapped. I just need tae know we can get out o' there if it gets a bit much for me, a bolt-hole." Annie couldn't help but display the nervousness that she'd given up trying to hide. "There's a distillery just outside the town too Clive. You like yer whiskey, yae'll like it there." Not that he needed any convincing. Annie was simply conscious of the fact that she might be making things a little more awkward than Clive maybe thought they should be.

"Okay." He agreed. "I'll try an' find us a list o' B&Bs then. An' don't worry, if it gets too much for ya, I'll be the first t' drag you out o' there."

*** 

Robbie was looking better by the day, even sitting in the chair beside his bed a lot of the time, just for the change. When Richard visited, he'd help him into a wheelchair and wheel him off down the corridors and sometimes to the hospital canteen, though he'd soon learnt to make sure he told a nurse when he was going to leave the ward, as they'd both had an almighty bollocking the first time they'd gone and neglected to mention it.

Lynsey wasn't quite so brave. She was nervous of taking Robbie off the ward, frightened that something might happen or that she'd bump the wheelchair into something or someone and hurt him, but he was working on her.

Mark had taken him out a couple of times too, but he mostly visited in the evenings after work and the canteen was shut by then. Though Mark had been the one who'd wheeled him down to A&E as Dr Liam had let him know when the same team would be on duty and Robbie wanted to go down to see them, he remembered Liam saying that A&E staff never got to see what happens to their patients once they left the department.

They were very busy, but each made time to speak to him, commenting on how well he looked compared to the last time they'd seen him.

"My God!" Sister Miller exclaimed, turning to Liam. "Is this really the same person we received three or four weeks ago?" She was grinning from ear to ear. Then to Robbie. "Wow, I can't believe how different you look...now that you're conscious for one thing," she joked. "I really wouldn't 'o known it was you though. Liam's been keeping us up ta date, but bloody hell...You look really, really well Robbie."

"Thanks," Robbie beamed. "I just wanted t' pop my head round an' thank all o' ya for what y' did." He suddenly felt quite choked-up as the reality of his state that morning hit home. "You erm...y' saved my life."

Sister Miller smiled back at him sympathetically. "It's what we do Robbie, it's our job. An' trust me, seeing you here looking so well is reward enough. We never see anyone at times of joy in their lives, so it's lovely that y' came down from the ward to show us how well you're doing an' we get to see the positive outcome of our work. Oh wait..." She stopped abruptly to grab a hold of the arm of a passing paramedic who'd just transferred a patient to a cubicle.

"Ya'll never guess who this is Bridget," she challenged the woman who stopped to take a good look at Robbie. Bridget examined his face before conceding defeat to Lisa Miller.

"Robbie, this is Bridget. She was one o' the paramedics who brought you in." She turned to Bridget. "This is the guy who'd been attacked on the tow path Brij: the jogger."

"Oh my God!" Bridget gasped. "Oh wow, is it really? We didn't know if you'd survive, an' look at ya. Y' look great. Oh I'm so pleased yer doing so well. Just wait 'til I tell Bobby, he wa' my crewmate on that day. He'll be chuffed t' bits."

Robbie suddenly felt quite overwhelmed and a few tears spilled down his cheeks. He was embarrassed that he couldn't control himself, but the enormity of what had happened to him and of the people who'd come together as a team and saved him. People he'd never met before, strangers, it all seemed to hit home in one almighty blow.

Mark felt his friend's embarrassment for him and placed a reassuring hand on his shoulder. "It's alright mate," he said.

The paramedic looked so sorry for him. "It must be really weird for ya," she said. "But you'll get there pet, an' one day you'll put this all behind ya."

Robbie sniffed up and wiped his eyes with the back of his hand. "I'm sorry, I feel a bit pathetic really. I didn't expect t' come over all emotional like this," he laughed. "I just...I can't put it into words how grateful I feel."

"You don't need to," Lisa said.

"Yeah, I do." Robbie insisted. "Y' see, my mum would've had t' bury me. My other half, Lynsey, well I don't even know where t' start wi' how she would o' been affected. I'm a brother, an uncle, then there's all my mates, d'ya see? If you all hadn't o' done what y' did, then I probably wouldn't be here now. How can a mere *'thank you'* ever be enough for that?"

"Right. That's it," Mark intervened, making an attempt to lighten the mood. "Get a grip now soft lad or I'm not buying ya that pint I promised ya for when y' get out of 'ere."

It worked. They all cracked up laughing before saying their goodbyes, Robbie promising that the next time he came to see them, he'd be walking in, with no crutches, straps, casts or bandages.

***

"Robbie," Clive said tentatively and in such a way that Robbie knew a question was going to follow.

*"Yehhs Clive?"* Robbie said expectantly.

"I was just wondering how ya'd feel about me taking y' mother away for a few days? Past few weeks have really taken a toll on her. I wa' thinking she might benefit from a bit of a break. Not too far mind, she wouldn't wanna go too far away from ya, just a break that's all."

"Oh is that all?" Robbie laughed. "I thought there wa' gonna be some major revelation then. How disappointing. Yeah why not.

It'd do her good. You taking my mother for a dirty weekend, you old duffer?" he joked.

"Behave yerself y' cheeky beggar," Clive chastised half-heartedly. "She might not go yet anyway; when I mentioned it before she didn't wanna leave you."

"Why? I'm not going anywhere am I? Nah tell her t' make the most of it. Best to have a break now, tell her, 'cause when I get home I'm gonna have her run ragged. She can be my nurse while Lyns is at work," Robbie grinned.

"She'll like that y' know," Clive said. "She'll be in her element looking after ya."

"Yeah I know. She'll spoil me rotten an' I'll lap it up. Never bothered *me* keeping one o' them apron strings attached. I'm not proud!" Robbie knew that letting his mum come and help him once he was well enough to go home would be as much a tonic for her as it would for him. "Where ya gonna take her then? One o' them spa places?"

Clive shrugged. "Haven't decided yet. Thought about just visiting family or summat."

"Pfft...d'ya know, ya've just got no sense of adventure Clive," Robbie teased.

Clive wanted to relish these moments, the days before anything changed. Robbie was a good lad, always had been, but even Clive daren't try and predict how he was going to react once he knew everything. He could only pray that he'd understand.

# Chapter Sixteen

Bile rose up suddenly in the back of the old man's throat, accompanied by that strange unease he'd been feeling recently. He tried to stem it but he couldn't and it spilled out down his chin and the front of his shirt. It tasted disgusting and was making him gasp for breath a little. He couldn't understand where it had come from; he'd not felt sick, it'd just come on all of a sudden.

He did his best to wipe himself, but it was no good; he knew he'd have to press his call button for help and tolerate a moron cleaning him up. He looked down at the button around his neck, with gloopy yellow vomit covering it. He pressed it anyway and just waited.

***

"Can we stop off at that florist and get some flowers please Clive?" Annie indicated towards the flower boutique across the road from their B&B as they pulled up outside. "Can we just drop the bags off for now? I can't settle 'til I've visited Mona. She's buried at the Kirk in Stennoch, by the Priory. I'll show ya when we get there. Ya don't mind, do ya Clive? I just want tae be there with her a wee while. My baby, Peter, Mum an' dad are there too an' I haven't set foot on Scottish soil in all these years an'..."

Clive put his hand on her knee to stop her. He didn't need any explanations from her; he already knew how hard this was and how much harder it was going to get, especially for Annie. "I'll drop the bags off an' get us signed in love. You go an' choose some flowers. Meet y' back at the car."

Annie got out of the car and crossed the quiet street to where the florist's shop was situated between what looked like two book shops. There'd always been a lot of book shops in Wigtown as she recalled, but there seemed to be even more now. She didn't recall the florist shop though, that's not to say it wasn't there, just that she couldn't remember it.

She and Mona had spent a lot of time in Wigtown as children, at the markets mostly. Dad would bring them to the cattle auction with him and there was an annual fayre for farmers too, where the best of the herds were shown against each other. Dad's prized Beltie bulls had won quite a few times over the years. Things like that were important to the farming community. It wasn't just about pride; life was very tough and the family income could be boosted if you happened to have a prize beast. Other cattle farmers would pay handsomely for the offspring, or for the stud services of a prize beast, and Annie's father and grandfathers before him had built up an excellent reputation for their Belted Galloways.

She paused outside the florist's and gazed along the main street to where the stalls for the market used to be. "Hello there.

145

Can I help yae wi' some'ing hen?" A middle aged woman wearing a navy blue, tartan print pinny tied round her ample waist had come out of the shop, the proprietor no doubt.

"Oh, hello," Annie replied. "I was just wanting some flowers...for my sister."

"Oh, does she live in Wigtown?" The woman asked.

Annie smiled, but couldn't be bothered with a complicated conversation. "No, Stennoch. But we used tae come here as girls, wi' our da', tae the farmers market," she explained. Aware at how quickly her Scottish accent broadened when speaking to a fellow Scot. "Does it still happen? The farmers Market I mean?"

"Och no hen. There has nae been a farmers market in years. It all happens away in Dumfries now," the lady said. "There's still the weekly market though, every Friday. Yae can still buy yer fruit an' veg then, an' handbags, an' haberdashery, yae know the sort'ae thing," she chuckled. "D'ya know the sort'ae blooms yer sister likes hen?"

"Lilies," Annie said. "She always liked lilies. D'ya have some?"

"Aye. Come inside hen, I'm sure there's some'ing yae'd like."

"How long's yer shop been here?" Annie asked her once the two women were inside.

"I'm the fourth generation tae run a business here. But it's only been flowers for twenty-five years. I'm from a family o' leatherworkers, saddlers an' the like."

"Oh, oh yes I remember now," Annie recalled. "It must've been here we'd come for our bridles an' head collars fixing. We'd come in wi'ae broken one. If it wa' only a wee job, we'd leave it wi' the man in the morning an' pick it up again at home time. If not we'd pick it up next market day. Wasn't there a farrier worked out back?"

"Aye that's right." The woman seemed pleased to recall the old days. "I imagine yer da' dealt wi' my grand'da. He'd'ae been running the show back then. His brother wa' the blacksmith. Made a load'ae the gates an' railings yae'll see about town so he did."

"Not much call for saddlers nowadays I don't suppose," Annie noted.

"No there's not unfortunately. Working animals became few an' far between, people started mainly riding horses for the fun o' it. All the equipment can be made cheaper in China or Korea now. Och half o' it's synthetic these days anyways; an' what wi' the internet..." She pointed at a sticker she had on the top of a glass counter. "Interflora; even I've had tae embrace the business I get from the phone an' th'internet. Yae have tae move wi' the times, or else yae just plain ole don't move at all'."

Annie selected a lovely bunch of white scented lilies with a splash of greenery throughout. "These are lovely," she said.

"Well I hope yer sister likes them hen." The woman smiled. "I'll maybe see yae again afore yae leave town."

It felt so strange walking across the almost deserted street back to the car. It was almost like slipping back in time in some ways. Apart from the fact that there were modern cars parked here and there, and the odd satellite dish visible, nothing had changed. The place looked just the way it had all those years ago, right down as far as the cenotaph and the Church where the grave of the Wigtown Martyrs lay.

Clive was already sitting in the car. "Beautiful flowers," he said as Annie got in.

"D'ya know Clive; there was always a hustle an' bustle about this place in the old days. Now look at it; it's mid-afternoon an' it's all but deserted. I suppose they all work outa town somewhere now, now that everyone's got cars. When we were kids, my parents woulda known everyone who traded on this street. The farming families all met here, helped each other. It's so, so sad tae think all that's gone now."

Once they reached Stennoch, Clive parked the car in a parking space that looked like it was in the middle of the street, which was split into one way traffic, heading south along the left of the parked cars and north to the right. The town was almost as quiet as Wigtown had been. Just across from them was an old white building which comprised an archway with two windows above it and what appeared to be a royal crest of some kind in between them, a throwback to days gone by when some long dead King had graced the town with his presence.

"Through there." Annie pointed towards the archway. "Through the Pend House, that's the way tae the Kirkyard. The old priory's beyond it, but the graves are through there on the right. That's where Mona an' my..." There was a renewed reluctance in her tone again now as she sat transfixed by the archway, as if lost somewhere deep in memory and grief.

"C'mon lovey," Clive encouraged her. "Ya've come a long way t' do this."

Annie turned to him. "D'ya mind me going on my own Clive? I just feel...I dunno...I buried my sister last time I was here an..."

"It's okay," Clive said. "You do what y' have to Annie. I'll be here when y' need me."

149

Annie stepped out of the car and walked towards the archway where two women and a child were stood chatting. It sounded really strange to her, to hear familiar Lowland accents around her. It reminded her that she'd come home; it was comforting. It gave her the strength to walk through the arch of the Pend house and into the graveyard.

Standing silently for a moment by the gate, Annie slowly glanced around her to get her bearings. She could see immediately the graves of her parents lying side by side. She went over to them and crouched down as she ran her fingers through part of the worn inscription on her mother's headstone *'Beloved Mother of Ann Rose and Ramona Mary'* it read.

*Oh mum,* she thought to herself, *I wish ya'd o' been here, yae'd a' known what tae do, what was right.* Taking one of the lilies from the bunch, she carefully placed it between their graves. They were tidy at least. She was pleased that the graveyard was kept well. Standing up again she gazed diagonally beyond her father's stone, knowing that Peter and her beloved baby weren't far away, though she wasn't yet ready to stand at their graves, she couldn't yet bring herself to look upon the headstone that bore both of their names. She felt a pang of nerves. It was silly really but she couldn't help it. She could feel her heart pounding as if she'd been called to the hangman's noose.

Making her way slowly towards her sister's grave, she noticed that there were flowers lying on it. Not quite fresh, but no more than two or three days old. Annie squatted down to pick them up, searching for a card or some clue as to who'd placed them there, but there wasn't one. She placed her own offering beside them before raising her eyes to read her sister's inscription, though she knew what it said; it was branded hard in her heart. *'Ramona Mary Whithorn, much loved wife of Rev Eban Whithorn and mother of Michael Whithorn, chosen by God'*. The dates of her birth and death below it. It was emblazoned in Annie's memory from the last time she'd laid eyes on it shortly after the funeral.

She raised her gaze to read it again, but was quite taken aback by what she saw. Before the original inscription, at the very top of the stone in much smaller script, it read; *'In loving memory of Michael Whithorn, aged 5, lost to the sea but found by God'*. She hadn't expected that, that was shock enough to cause her to take in a deep breath. Of course most people would've thought Michael to be dead, especially Eban. She knew that to be the case because Izzy had told her that Jock and Jamie's version of events had been accepted, and those that knew different had kept their silence to protect the boy. Yet seeing it cast in stone like this had still given cause to stir her somewhat. She took a few minutes to be alone with her sister and her thoughts, her heart bleeding with grief for the way things should have been.

Returning to the car, she told Clive about the other flowers she'd found on Mona's grave.

"They could be from her friend, Izzy," Clive reasoned. "It'd make sense if she *is* still local that is. Ya've no other family round abouts that might o' left 'em?"

"None that I'm aware of," Annie said. "Mum had been an only child an' her own mum died giving birth to her. She'd spent a lot o' her childhood wi' her grandmother, Ramona. That's who my sister was named after; she was Portuguese. My grandfather was a naval man once upon a time, just brought her home wi' him one day apparently. I was named after my dad's mother. He had two brothers but I never met the eldest; he died in France in the war. I remember Uncle George, but he died o' the pneumonia when I wa' twelve or so. I think my auntie Margo, his wife took their children back tae be wi' her own family after that as far as I recall. She was a Highlander; I don't know from where exactly. I remember she spoke Gaelic to my cousins though. I suppose we just all lost touch. Times were really hard back then Clive. It was a hard life whether yer living came from the land or the sea.

"It must be Izzy that left them, or Joe. I can't think anyone else would do it, not after thirty-five years. She an' Izzy were good friends though…must be her."

"How far is it t' the Isle from 'ere love?" Clive asked.

"Not far, ten minutes, fifteen maybe.  Why?"

"Did ya want t' go there now?"  He noticed Annie visibly withdraw.  "Just for the drive?  We don't have t' stop an' get out or owt love, just have a bit of a reccy."

Annie continued shaking her head.  "No, not yet Clive.  It's been a hell of a long day an' I'm tired.  I'm no' ready.  Tomorrow, we'll go there tomorrow."

There was a small part of her that longed to go to the Isle.  After all, she'd grown up there, gone to the schoolhouse there, played in the fields, fished.  But then there was this big dark cloud which hung over her too, a sense of pain and loss that was there in the Isle and until she actually went there again and faced it, she was unsure of which feelings would prevail.

# Chapter Seventeen

It was the middle of the night and the ward was in darkness and quiet, well not as quiet as it could have been. Someone could be heard snoring and every now and then the phone would ring and a nurse could be heard answering it, but in the bay that Robbie inhabited it was fairly quiet. There were four beds to a bay and only three of them occupied. The two opposite had patients in them, but the one next to Robbie was empty for now at least, though it wouldn't have been unusual for it to be filled, even in the middle of the night, by some random patient, newly admitted, on a sleep-out because the ward they should be on had no beds available.

Robbie was sleeping; though he didn't look to be too peaceful in his slumber. His face kept twitching and he screwed his eyes up from time to time, there was the odd grunt or an incomprehensible word muttered. He was dreaming again. He took in the occasional sharp breath and his arms would jerk a little, then he'd moan as his brain acknowledged discomfort in some of his movements, though he dreamt on.

\*\*\*

*Trapped in a cave somewhere, he could hear the sea all around. It was a small cave with only one way in and out. He could see out of it to the pebbled beach below. No sand, just huge football* sized smooth rocks and pebbles with sea birds resting on them. The sea was lapping over them as the tide crept in, but he knew he'd be safe from the water because it wouldn't rise as far as the cave, would it? He could see right out of the mouth of the cave. It was twilight and it was getting colder. Then it dawned on him that he wasn't trapped at all; he could walk outside if he wanted to, yet he was afraid to. Frightened of leaving the cave, he was trapped by his fear and nothing else. He knew that if he tried to leave the cave that something really terrible would happen.

Then, he was startled by a sudden feeling that he couldn't breathe. He was drowning, looking up at the surface of the water but unable to get there, paralysed by cold and fear. It was very dark up there but he could make out a boat. He drifted off into nothingness before finding himself back in that cave.

Just as suddenly he found himself by an open fire, warm and safe. He could smell roast beef cooking, but he had that same sense of fear; he couldn't bring himself to look round. He could hear voices but couldn't make out what was being said. He felt like a child, as if he wanted to cry, but he was too afraid to make any noise at all.

He was back in the cave for a moment before he heard a woman's voice asking him what he'd drawn. He turned towards her and found himself in a classroom full of children. The woman bent down and picked up a piece of paper from in front of him. 'That's

*nice', she said. 'Is that you an' yer mammy?' He felt a small burst
of pride as the lady smiled down at him. She'd got curly, dark-
auburn hair and hazel eyes. She turned to the children. 'Look
everyone; Michael's drawn this lovely picture of himself with his
mother. Has anyone else finished their picture?' No; he'd drawn it,
not Michael. What was she talking about? That little burst of pride
he'd felt vanished as his heart sank.*

*Next minute; he was under some blankets, in bed. There was
a lot of banging and shouting and it was getting closer. He was
bursting for a pee but he daren't move, he just lay as still as he could
beneath the covers, terrified and trying not to shake so much. Then
all of a sudden the covers were dragged off him and the shadowy
figure of an enraged man loomed above him, arm raised in
readiness. A woman began to scream. He covered his face and
began to scream too. He could feel someone shaking him. Gasping
in fear, his eyes sprung open.*

***

"Hey buddy, it's me, Andy. It's alright. It's just a
nightmare." The Charge Nurse stood over him, speaking in a
lowered tone. There was the first threat of daylight beginning to
make its way through the gaps in the window blinds. "Bloody hell,
yer wringing wet. Must o' been a bad 'un mate. You okay?"

Robbie was momentarily disorientated on waking up so
suddenly. "Erm...yeah, yeah I'm okay. I need a pee," he said.

"No problem Robster. I'll get you a clean pair o' peejays too, them ones look like they're stuck t' ya wi' sweat."

Robbie lay there, knackered but relieved. He'd been having nightmares most nights since been in the hospital and it wasn't the first time he'd woken up lathered in sweat, but this was the first one he'd been woken from, which is probably why he could still remember it in fine detail.

"Was I making' a racket Andy? Did I wake anyone up?" he asked the Charge Nurse while he helped him to change.

"I don't think so," he replied whilst looking round at the other two sleeping patients. "Ya were having the odd grunt most o' the night. But then y' just started yelling out. Luckily I wa' just coming in here anyway. So I think it were all over wi' in a flash. Doesn't look like it bothered these two sleeping beauties." He nodded his head towards the patients opposite.

"An' did I say owt? When I wa' yelling I mean. Was I just yelling or was I actually yelling summat understandable?" Robbie was curious.

Andy shrugged. "Mostly just yelling, but y' did shout at someone t'stop it, then ya yelled summat that sounded sort o' like 'dahhhh, I think it was. Maybe it's t' do wi' when y' were attacked."

"Maybe...I dunno," Robbie said. "It wa' mostly about the sea. I wa' drowning at one point." Though he was okay now, it had left him feeling a little disturbed in all fairness.

"Well y' were attacked on the canal towpath. I know it's not the same, but it's a body o' water isn't it? Might be relevant, y' never know," Andy suggested. "Why don't I fetch y' some paper, write it down while y' can remember it. Might make more sense t' ya when ya've fully recovered."

He wasn't completely convinced, but Robbie agreed that writing it down might help him remember something relevant. 'Dahhh'? What did that mean? Dad? It could be dad. Robbie couldn't remember much about his dad. Peter had died when Robbie was about five, so his memories were sketchy but he'd grown up with good stories of him. His mum had never given him the impression that his dad was anything but a warm and loving man. Whoever that man was in his dream, he definitely wasn't giving off any warm and friendly vibes. He began to scribble down what he could. At least he could compare this latest nightmare with any subsequent ones to see if there were any similarities.

He hated this feeling of not being able to recall details. He'd improved so much over the past few weeks but he still couldn't remember anything at all about the actual attack he'd suffered. Was there one attacker or more than one? Did he know him? Had he seen him before?  Had they argued?  He simply couldn't answer any of those questions and it was frustrating to say the least.

He finished jotting down what he could about his nightmare, then closed his eyes in the hope of getting a little more sleep before the whole place burst into life again for the day.

Rich and Jodie were coming to see him later.  He was looking forward to that because he knew they'd take him off the ward for a while.  He was going to have to whip Lynsey into shape with that one though.  The consultant had told him that if his physio was going well enough, he'd think about releasing Robbie for day visits to home providing he had someone there to look after him.  So he needed to build Lynsey's confidence and recruiting Rich and Jodie to help with the task of Lynsey-boosting, would hopefully serve to speed things up.

# Chapter Eighteen

Robbie was still a little shaken by the content of his latest nightmare by the time Rich and Jodie arrived, and he was still pretty tired too.

"What's up?" was Jodie's initial greeting to him as she plonked herself in the comfier of the two chairs beside his bed. "I mean; y' look done in. Didn't y' sleep much last night?"

Robbie smiled but shook his head. "Another nightmare bro?" Rich asked him.

"Yeah. Night staff had t' wake me up, I wa' yelling out apparently." He went on to tell them what his nightmare had been about and how it had left him feeling. Rich just seemed to shrug it off as one of those things; an after effect of the head injury maybe. In truth, Rich didn't really know what to say. Jodie on the other hand was far more intrigued.

"I think ya've done the right thing, writing it down, t' be honest," she said. "Might be summat an' nowt, like Rich says. Could be what they call crypto-amnesia."

"What amnesia?" Rich questioned her with distain.

"Crypto-amnesia," she repeated. "Buried memories. Means that y' might be remembering details from summat ya've seen years ago an' don't remember. Like a film, or a book ya've read when y' were a kid. Ya've forgotten about it, but somehow the memory of the story has got mixed up with your real memories an' this is how it manifests. You taking such a blow to yer bonce being the catalyst in some way. I've read about it."

"Have ya now?" Rich maintained his nonchalant attitude to the subject.

Robbie however, had pricked his ears up. "D'ya know Jodie; you might just have summat there. I'd been racking my brains thinking I must know who this Michael is, but y' could be right. Happen I saw a film or summat as a kid an' this Michael's a character from that. It'd make sense me feeling like he were a kid in my dream."

"For fuck's sake Robbie! Don't encourage her," Rich said sarcastically. "She'll be convincing ya you're a reincarnated dead dude called Michael next."

Jodie flashed her husband a scolding glance. "Well that's a possibility too. Y' never know," she scoffed.

Robbie cocked his head to one side as he looked at her in puzzlement, his expression somewhat similar to that of a curious

Labrador. "What's a possibility? That I'm the reincarnation of someone else an' it's his memories an' not my own?"

"Yeah pretty much," she responded. "It's not as uncommon as people think." She scowled as the two men looked at each other and burst out laughing.

Though Robbie didn't mind indulging Jodie's lateral train of thought, he had to admit that he was of the same mind as his brother on this occasion. Jodie's reasoning and explanations made perfect sense, but he just couldn't bring himself to accept that such a thing were possible, though he was slightly more tactful than his brother when voicing such an opinion. Jodie didn't push it; she knew she was outnumbered.

Robbie swore them both to secrecy about his latest nightmare. He didn't want Lynsey finding out. "Ya know what she's like; she'll just get all flappy about it. An' listen, we need t' get her a bit more confident wi' me off the ward. Don't get me wrong, they're brilliant here, but I'm so stir crazy it's beyond a joke. I need t' get home an' the sooner Lyns can hack it the better. It's just confidence with her, so keep it light when she gets here eh? No mentioning any nightmares or owt okay? Just happy thoughts today people." He grinned at them like a Cheshire cat as he reached out for his brother to help him into the wheelchair.

***

"Did y'ever see that seventies film...'The Wickerman'?" Annie reminisced as they sat in their parked car on the near side of the harbour looking out towards the Cairn. "Well the whole village was star struck many moons ago Clive. Down there, the pier. All the women an' girls got all giggly an' silly once, an' one or two o' the men had their chins on the floor too. Edward Woodward, Brit Ekland an' a few other cast members went out for a day's fishing from there. Must o' been seventy-one or seventy-two I think. They had some time off, so some o' them wanted tae go out sea fishing, it was a lovely day for it. They did a lot o' the filming up in Creetown, but they used Burrow Head an' St Ninian's Cave for some o' the outdoor scenes, just up the coast there." Annie indicated along the coast road leading west, out of the village.

Clive raised his eyebrows in surprise. "Really? Yeah I've seen it. Christopher Lee were in it too as I recall."

"Aye that's right. But he wasn't with them when they came tae the village. That night, the Solway Harvester, over there look." Annie pointed across the harbour to the pub on the row. "Well I don't think it'd ever been s'busy. I think the majority of the villagers squeezed into there that evening when they'd come back in from their fishing. I wouldn't be surprised if most o' the households here in the Isle weren't in possession of several autographs from back then an' the odd hastily snapped photo maybe. I know when they were filming on the beach by the cave, the kids used tae run up tae the cliff tops tae watch them. Izzy once told me that she'd had

163

tae go up there an' round 'em all up. They shoulda been in school ya see, an' her classroom was nigh on empty."

Clive rested his hand on top of hers, drawing her gaze back round to him as he did so. He smiled at her softly. "Speaking of Izzy..." he said.

Annie smiled back, acknowledging that his meaning hadn't gone unnoticed. "I know," she sighed nervously. "It's that one over there on the Main Street, near the end wi' the dark wood door...that's new," she added, referring to the door. "She might not be there anymore ya know Clive, she might o' moved."

"She might," Clive conceded. "But we'll not find out by just sitting 'ere will we?"

***

"Right Lyns, this is how it is," Rich began. "Y' need t' get used t' being on yer own a bit wi' our Robbie. So me an' Jodie's gonna leave y' both 'ere t' finish yer coffees okay?"

Lynsey initially laughed before she'd realised that they weren't joking. "What? No. I don't think I'll be able t' manoeuvre this thing on my own." She tapped the wheelchair that Robbie was in. "An' he's got t' go t' physio after this. I don't even know where that is."

Rich tried desperately to keep a straight face, but Robbie was just killing himself laughing at her panic. "It's not sodding funny," she insisted. "I might have an accident wi' this thing." That was it, Rich couldn't contain himself anymore and the two brothers doubled up, unable to speak through their combined laughter.

Jodie, though quite amused herself, attempted to be more sympathetic. "It's just that Robbie said ya'd not be happy about it. An' ya kinda reacted how he said y' would, that's why they're laughing. We're in a hospital Lyns. Nowt bad's gonna happen. An' even if it did, the place is full o' doctors an' nurses."

Lynsey finally saw the funny side and smiled while shaking her head in mock disgust at being the butt of their joke. "Okay, okay," she said. "I know what yer all up to. An' I know you've put 'em up to it Robbie McAndrew." She wagged her finger at him. "Right, okay. I'll take ya to physio, on my own." She stressed the last part. The brothers let out a combined cheer. "Yeah!" Rich then held his hand up for Robbie to 'high-five'.

"But ya'll not be on yer own love," Robbie stated. "I'm going too." That was enough to set Rich off laughing again, as Jodie yanked his jacket from the back of his chair and thrust it at him.

"Come on trouble," she insisted. "Time we went an' picked the kids up before Lynsey wallops ya an' yer in need o' physio yerself." Then turning to Lynsey. "Ya'll be fine Lyns, honest. You'll see. I'll give you a ring tonight, okay?"

Lynsey smiled and nodded her agreement and the two women hugged, though she jokingly scowled at Rich before hugging him too. Turning her attention to Robbie she sighed. "Right then ya cheeky beggar. I hope *you* know yer way ta physio matey, 'cause I sure as hell don't."

She made him hold her handbag on his knee by way of punishment, while she cautiously began to steer the chair out and away from the canteen table. Robbie directed her, telling her it would be easier to go through the door backwards, then along the corridor to the lifts.

It wasn't actually as scary as Lynsey had imagined. She'd bumped the chair a couple of times, but nothing much and it certainly didn't appear to have bothered Robbie. She hated to admit it but they'd been right, she just needed to build her confidence up. Robbie was well and truly on the road to a good recovery, but she still had that nightmarish image of him stuck in her mind, all battered and broken in the intensive care unit. But that was weeks ago now and he was better, much better and stronger. She made a conscious effort to take his lead in his recovery, instead of being over cautious all the time the way she had been doing. She wanted him home desperately, and she knew that she'd have to re-adjust her thinking in order to help him make that possible.

"We're here," Robbie said as they approached the double doors with the words 'Physiotherapy Dept.' above them. "It's usually locked. You have t' press that buzzer at the side," he instructed her.

"*Can I help you?*" the disembodied voice asked.

"Robert McAndrew t' see the physio," Robbie responded. A short tone indicated that the doors were now unlocked and Lynsey pushed her backside against them until they opened, pulling Robbie in after her, backwards of course.

She asked Robbie and Claire, one of the physiotherapists, if she could stay and watch. "As long as there's no sound effects," Robbie insisted. "I know you, ya'll sit there sucking in air, pulling faces, moaning; all 'cause ya'll be thinking I'm gonna fall or summat," he quipped.

"I won't. I promise," Lynsey complained. "I'll be quiet as a mouse; ya won't even know I'm here. I can take ya back t' the ward then can't I?"

Lynsey couldn't help but get a little teary-eyed as she marvelled at how far Robbie had come. She'd not realised that they had him up and walking. He used a crutch to support his weight on his left side, but because he still had a cast on his right arm, they couldn't let him use one on that side too. Instead, they gave him a metal walking stick with three small legs on it. He'd been told not to take his weight on that side, but to just use it to steady himself while taking his weight with his left arm.

He looked a bit awkward, but he was doing it; he was on his feet and walking. Lynsey felt so emotional watching him, so proud that he'd been through so much but had fought back with such strength of character. She daren't speak for fear of putting him off, but she secretly took a few pictures of him on her mobile. She sent the best one to Clive's phone there and then, knowing how pleased and proud his mum would be to see how well her boy was doing. She spent the remainder of the physio session in silence, just staring at him, beaming and wiping away the odd happy tear. Having seen him in action, she no longer doubted his ability to cope, nor did she want her own *inability* to cope to be the reason he was held back.

# Chapter Nineteen

The inside of Robbie and Lynsey's flat was looking all spic and span. The kitchen and bathroom were spotless; the two bedrooms were bright and freshly made up. The living room had everything in its place, though a small side table had been placed on the other side of the sofa from where it would normally be and a footrest was close by it. It was the footrest that came with the lounge suite anyway, but it normally lived in the spare bedroom out of the way as they didn't usually have any particular need or use for it, until now that is.

There was a kafuffle around the entrance as the door opened and Rich walked in carrying a holdall, which he quickly placed to one side of the hallway before turning round to help his brother in through the open door.

"It's alright, I can do it," Robbie insisted as he hobbled inside using his crutch and walking stick. He was followed in through the door by Lynsey, Clive and finally his mum. "Bloody hell," he exclaimed, "I wa' beginning ta think I'd never see this place again." He'd been out for a couple of day trips with Lynsey and his family previously, but this was the first time he'd been home and he couldn't believe how good it felt. "Oh this is great. Are there any beers in the fridge Lyns? Rich fire up the Xbox my good man. I can feel a Need for Speed coming on."

"Erm, first things first." Lynsey stepped in. "We've just walked through the door for God sake. Why don't we swap the beers for coffees and leave the Xbox 'til next time ya get shore leave Captain eh?"

Robbie scoffed at her suggestion. "Pfft...there's no next time about it Mrs! I'm here now, I'm not going back."

"What?" Rich laughed. "What d'ya mean? This is only a day visit, y' do know that don't ya?"

Robbie was grinning with a victorious gleam in his eye. "Nah, I'm stopping here now. I'm not going back." He continued making his way into the living room where he took up residence on the sofa, bringing his left leg to rest on the pouf that he'd managed to drag towards himself. The others all looked around at each other in stunned, momentary silence.

"Robbie!" Lynsey was the first to break the quiet. "Ya can't, yer not ready."

"Ready as I'll ever be." He was unwavering in his resolve. "I'm not going back into hospital Lyns; I'm staying here, at home. They've been fantastic in there, don't get me wrong, but I'm sick of it now. I need t' be home where I can toss it off on the Xbox all day if I want, make myself a cuppa in my own kitchen whenever I want an' piss in my own frigging toilet whenever I want without someone knocking on the door asking if I'm okay, or shoving a plastic fucking container at me an' asking for *yet another* sample of my piss *'just to test for kidney function Mr McAndrew'*. My fucking kidneys are fine. I'm not an idiot; I'd be the first t' say if summat didn't feel right." He looked round them all one by one. "So, I'm staying here, okay?" Though the question was quite clearly rhetorical. "Mum, *you* know I'll be fine don't ya?"

Annie was just as concerned as the rest of them, but she knew him well enough to know that under such circumstances, when his mind was made up, there'd be no budging him. She relented without a fight. "Well, they did say that when ya finally came home, there'd be an intermediate care team, district nurses or something. I suppose they'll just have tae start calling in sooner."

"Annie?" Lynsey seemed appalled.

"I know what yer thinking love," Annie said to her. "But ya know Robbie well enough tae know that he means it. So we either help him, or watch him struggle. Either way I doubt he'll go back under his own steam, do you?"

Lynsey was furious, and scared, but she knew that Annie was right. Once he'd made his mind up about something, there wasn't going to be hell, high water, or any number of wild horses that would shift Robbie. In this frame of mind he'd happily stand his ground against an army of JCBs attempting the task.

"Look," Annie reasoned with her. "We'll manage. We'll make sure someone's here all the time. Me an' Clive can sort out the days while you're at work. An' I'm sure our Richard'll pitch in, won't ya love?" She turned to him.

"Yeah, no probs," he said. "We'll be right Lyns, honest. I'll even stay overnight for a bit if ya want?"

"Now that's a good idea," Clive reinforced. "Then if our Robbie needs the loo or owt, y' know."

Robbie laughed out loud. "If Robbie needs the loo in the middle o' the bloody night, Robbie knows where it is thank ya very much. But yer more than welcome t' stay over Rich. Might put Lynsey's colly-wobbles t' sleep if nowt else."

Lynsey wasn't happy about it, but she agreed. And if she were honest with herself, if she were in his shoes she'd probably feel exactly the same. "Should I sleep on the sofa?" she asked. "Only, what if I roll into you or kick you in my sleep or something."

"I were hoping ya would roll into me." Robbie grinned while Lynsey flushed with embarrassment. "Seriously though, if ya sleep on my left; there's a bloody great cast on that leg. If ya do kick it, it won't be me it hurts." He lifted his right arm. "An' this thing, well the arm doesn't hurt, cast's coming off day after tomorrow, shoulder's just a bit tender still, that's all. We'll be fine Lyns, honest. If I didn't feel up to it, I wouldn't be doing it would I? Like I said, I'm not an idiot."

"And the nurse'll be coming in regularly," Clive added.

"Have ya got the number for the ward Robbie?" Rich asked. "Someone's gonna need t' tell 'em they've been dumped."

Annie went into the kitchen to put the kettle on and make something to eat for everyone. Clive followed her in. "Well, seems he's coming home sooner than anticipated love," he voiced in a lowered tone. "We really are gonna have t' sort out telling him."

"I know," Annie answered without looking up.

"I mean, it's not like we haven't held off long enough already Annie."

"Yes I know."

"Only, if we don't say summat soon it'll never get said love an' it'd be wrong t' say nowt."

"For Christ sake Clive! I know," Annie snapped. It was nearly three weeks since they returned from Scotland and Annie had been through the mill during that time. They'd managed to find out quite a lot whilst there, but it'd taken its toll on her. She'd been quite ill on her return with some kind of chest infection. Weak and depressed by it, she'd taken to her bed until it'd passed, knowing that it wouldn't be wise to visit Robbie in the hospital while she was so ill.  She spoke to him each day by phone instead for about ten days or so, until she was better.  Though she was still harbouring a residual cough, she wasn't feeling anything like as poorly as she had done.

"Let's just give him chance tae get settled eh?  Besides, I've changed my mind about telling him an' Rich together.  I don't think we should say anything in front o' Lynsey either," Annie whispered.

"What?  Why?  I thought we'd agreed that he'd need a bit o' moral support."  Clive was surprised.

"An' he likely will," she replied.  "But that's not a decision either of us should be making for him.  He's a forty-one year old grown man Clive, an' he's had s'many decisions made for him without even his knowledge, let alone his consent.  Enough.  If we drop something like this on him in front of another person, then whether he likes it or not, his hand'll be forced, he'll have tae do something about it.  An' what if he doesn't want to?  What if he decides he wants tae carry on regardless?  He won't be able tae if anyone else knows.

"An' as for our Richard…don't ya see Clive?  This is gonna devastate him too.  Robbie's his brother; he's never known him as anything other than that.  Plus, how d'ya think he'll feel towards me?  When he finds out what I've done?  When he finds out that his real brother is lying in a grave somewhere?  Part of his whole life has been a lie too. Christ, neither of 'em even know about Peter's grave, I was so terrified they'd want tae visit. That they'd go there an' see baby Robert's stone too. The dates on it woulda given them more than food for thought. I told 'em that their father was cremated an' that I scattered his ashes." Annie took a breath and held it for a moment, by way of control.

"My God, y' certainly thought of everything Annie didn't ya?" Clive realised that she couldn't have risked the boys wanting to visit their father's grave. Part of him felt dreadfully sorry for this desperate woman, his wife. Yet another part of him couldn't help but be cautious about just what she'd been capable of. He could see all the mistakes she'd made, but he could also appreciate that in the heat of the moment, she'd done her best, done what she'd believed to be the right thing.

"Okay then," Clive said. "Let's give him some settling in time. But this needs doing Annie, an' soon."

\*\*\*

That evening, Mark, Rich and Robbie challenged each other to games on the Xbox, while Mark fended off comments the other two kept making about him and Natalie.

"Must admit mate," Robbie said. "I'd o' never o' put the two of ya together. I mean she's ace an' everything, but would o' thought she'd be a bit...I dunno...high maintenance maybe?"

175

"Well she's not," Mark defended her. "We get on well enough. Besides, it's early days yet, we're just having a bit of a laugh that's all. We'll see how things go."

Rich cracked up laughing. "Roughly translated Robbie that means they're shagging a lot an' they haven't really had a conversation."

Mark threw one of the cushions at Rich. "Wanker," he joked.

Lynsey walked in from the kitchen with a plate full of sandwiches. "What you lot laughing at?" she quizzed.

"Nowt love," Robbie lied. "Just getting competitive over our Xbox skills. They can't handle that even wi' one broken arm I'm still better than 'em."

"Dream on hop-along," Mark said.

"Yeah, that were obviously one hell of a blow t' the head y' got bro, 'cause yer clearly still in cloud-cuckoo land."

Lynsey blindly accepted what they'd said and left the sandwiches on the coffee table for them while she poured herself a glass of wine. "I've told yer mum not t' bother tomorrow Robbie, I'm gonna take the day off, so she's gonna come in Friday morning, okay?"

"Cool, yeah that's fine love," he replied. He sensed that she wanted to be with him and wasn't too keen on the extra company, but he also wanted to prove to her that he could manage at home, that she didn't need to worry, and so for now at least, that meant getting used to having a houseful.

# Chapter Twenty

By the following week, Robbie was doing so well that the Intermediate Care team were happy to just call in when needed. He no longer had the cast on his right arm; that had been taken off the previous Friday and he was keeping up with the physio exercises he'd been set to strengthen it. He'd just finished on the phone to the hospital when his mum arrived. "Hiya mum, no Clive today?" he called through to the hallway when he noticed she was alone.

"No love, not today," Annie replied. Clive had come with her each day that she'd been round to help look after Robbie, but today she'd asked him not to, because today she wanted to be alone with Robbie.

"That was the hospital on the phone; they want me back in on Monday t' take this off." Robbie pointed down to the florescent green cast on the lower half of his left leg. "Will you be able t' take me again mum?"

Annie put down the small bag she was carrying and took off her coat. "Aye, of course. Isn't it a bit soon though? Surely ya'll not be able tae walk properly on it yet?"

"Oh it's not done wi' yet," he reassured her. "They're gonna gi' me one o' them pneumatic walking boots instead. That way when I'm not on my feet, it can come off. I'll be able t' crack on wi' physio on that ankle then. Ya know, start rotating it, that sort o' thing. An' when I wanna be up an' about. I can put my weight on it an' walk, while the boot takes the strain an' cushions the joint. It's gonna be ace compared t' this bloody thing." He lifted his foot off the floor to emphasise his point.

"Sounds good," Annie smiled. "Must be very frustrating for ya being more or less confined tae quarters? I'm sure ya'll be out an' about much more with that. Just don't overdo it son eh? I notice yer not bothering with that crutch around the flat now either."

"Yeah, short bursts between rooms is fine," he said. Then glancing towards the sofa, "So what's in the bag? You taken up knitting or summat?" he joked.

Annie's heart skipped a beat and she coughed a little. "I'll go an' make us both a brew love, then I'll show ya."

***

Placing Robbie's mug of coffee down next to him and with her heart in her mouth Annie took a large brown envelope out of the bag she'd brought with her. Handing it to Robbie, she gestured for him to look inside, which he did. Pulling out a pile of different sized photographs he began to study them closely.

Hovering over one of a young woman holding a baby and sitting on a garden wall, he smiled. "This is us isn't it? I don't remember seeing this one before."

"Not quite," Annie replied. She rooted round the other pictures until she'd found what she was looking for. Passing it to Robbie, he noticed that it was another picture of a woman and baby, this time standing just outside the doorway of a house. Robbie looked from one to the other.

"Aren't they both us?" he queried, a look of puzzlement pulling at his brow. "I can't tell if that's you in both of 'em mum, is it?"

Annie began to chew on the inside of her lip; she could hear the blood pulsing through the arteries as it rushed past her ears. "No love, one of them is my sister, Mona. We were always very alike though, even though there was two years between us."

Robbie looked satisfied. "Ah yeah, I remember y' telling' us you had a sister. Died a long time ago didn't she? Is this her cuddling me? Aunty Mona?" He held up the photo of the woman and baby by the doorway. Annie nodded and smiled affectionately as she took hold of the picture again from Robbie. "Then this must be us," he said as he looked back at the woman sitting on a garden wall holding a baby. Annie's eyes prickled with tears and she couldn't stop a couple as they escaped down her cheeks. She was hoping desperately that Robbie wouldn't have noticed, but of course he had. "Mum." He put his hand on top of hers. "Oh I'm sorry, y' must miss her. Y' were really close weren't ya?"

"Aye we were," Annie sniffled. "So close that we made each other promises should anything happen tae the other of us."

Robbie was beginning to become suspicious. This was more than just sentimentality that Annie was displaying. "Come on mum, y getting me worried now. What is it? What's up?"

Holding both photos, one in each hand, Annie took a deep breath as she gazed at them both through blurry tears. Then looking up at him she passed him the first. "This is me, with my baby Robert." Then passing him the second. "And this is Mona with her wee Michael. This is *you* Robbie, with Mona, with yer mother. Oh I'm so, so sorry Robbie."

Shock took away Robbie's words for a few moments. He sat back in his seat raising both arms up and running the fingers of both hands through his hair. He half smiled in disbelief as he looked at her for confirmation that this was some kind of joke, but there was none.

Annie's tears were running freely now. "Oh Robbie I'm so very sorry. I nev'r intended that you'd be kept in the dark, it was just so...complicated an' I didn't know how..."

"Wait a minute!" Robbie stopped her. "All this time; all the time I were in the hospital; all the fucking confusion over thinking I wa' called Michael. I thought I wa' going mad y' know. An' now yer telling' me I wa' right? I am Michael? Oh this is too much." He got up and made his way towards the balcony doors. He hobbled outside and leant against the top rail as he drew in a few deep gasps of the cold, fresh air. Annie followed him out.

"Please let me explain Robbie?" she pleaded. "There's so much more tae it. An' whether ya end up hating me or not is irrelevant, but ya do need tae know the whole story. Ya need tae understand why."

Robbie was far too distracted trying to absorb what had just happened to be able to try and rationalise it. He ambled back into the living room and grabbed the photo of Annie. "And this!" he demanded to know. "Your baby you said? Robert?"

"Cot death," Annie sniffed. "My wee Robert died when he was only a few months old. At the time it seemed logical that you'd just become him, but it was an awful time Robbie, an' decisions were made in haste."

"I don't get it. Are you sayin' that every time I've produced my ID, every time I've renewed my passport, or when I got my driver's licence…are you saying that I used someone else's birth certificate t' do it? But that's mine! That's my birth certificate. I keep it in 'ere wi' all my papers." Robbie banged his hand down onto the top of a chest of drawers. Annie sat on the very edge of an armchair, feeling ill and weak but knowing she had to go on.

"When's my birthday?" Robbie snarled. "Twenty-second o' March. That's my birthday isn't it?"

Shaking her head Annie looked down at her intertwined fingers. "Fourth of June. It's the fourth of June, nineteen seventy-one. There was only about nine or ten weeks between ya, but Robert was born on the twenty-second o' March an' you were born on the fourth o' June. Oh Robbie, there's so much ya need tae know," Annie pleaded.

Robbie couldn't bring himself to look her in the eye, and each time she moved towards him, he moved away. Nothing else that she was saying was going in. He came to a stop again back out on the balcony. Closing his eyes he could sense her behind him. "Get out!" he spat. "I know ya've got loads more t' say, but not now, just not now. I can't listen to it now, you need t' go."

Annie was beside herself. "Robbie I can't leave ya on yer own all day, please? We don't have tae talk about it if ya don't want, but ya can't be on yer own."

"Yes I can mum...Annie...whatever the hell I'm meant t' fucking call ya. Just go! I want you out...now!" This was too much for Robbie. He felt like his head could explode at any minute. He couldn't cope with conversation on top of everything else, he just wanted to be left alone, to not have to talk to anyone, least of all to Annie.

When Annie left, Robbie was still outside clinging onto the balcony rail. It was a clear sunny day and he could see right across the city, but it was cold. He got the afternoon sun on his side of the building and it was only nine-thirty, so it was still in shade and chilly. He turned his back to the city and stared back inside through the open balcony door towards the sofa. She'd left the bag and the photos and Robbie couldn't shift his gaze from them. His leg was aching a little and he wanted to go and sit down, but he couldn't bring himself to move from his self-imposed, fixed location, his isolation.

Eventually he went back inside, closing out the cold as he did so. He picked up his coffee that Annie had made him previously; the cup was cold so he continued on into the kitchen to make a fresh one.

He spent what seemed to be an age sitting in the armchair cradling his coffee and staring blankly at the bag on the sofa. In fact it was only a matter of minutes, but time had become distorted to Robbie and he had to glance at the clock, surprised to see that it wasn't quite ten yet. He put his cup down and reached over, scooping the photos back into some semblance of a pile as he sat back down with them on his lap. The phone started to ring, but he didn't want to speak to anyone so he ignored it.

Holding the two photos next to each other he could see that Annie had been right, the two women were very similar. Repeatedly looking from one to the other, he tried to get his head around the fact that it wasn't the same baby in both pictures being held by two different women. Only one of them was him, the other a dead cousin whose name he'd taken. Closing his eyes he felt dizzy almost, he felt like a grave robber. He suddenly recalled seeing an old movie where a fat, greedy man had just polished off a steak pie and really enjoyed it, only to find out that the person who'd made it and served it to him had actually killed his beloved dogs and it was them he'd just eaten and not steak. Not quite the same thing, but with the emotion he was feeling he didn't know how to rationalise it any other way. He'd enjoyed his life, his childhood and his family only to find out that it was someone else's after all. He wasn't who he'd thought himself to be and more to the point, he wasn't who they'd thought him to be.

Did anyone else know? Clive? Richard? Did they all know? Was it just him who hadn't realised? What was all this going to mean for him? What was he going to tell Lynsey? He'd been adopted and no-one had thought he needed to know...for forty-one years? What about Rich? Was he adopted too? They did have a similarity, they must be family, but was he Mona's child too or not? There were so many questions, things he knew he'd have to bite the bullet and get Annie to answer for him, but just not yet.

He began to look through the other photos in the pile. There was one of Annie and Peter holding hands and Peter was holding a baby in his other arm, Robert. They were smiling at the camera and Annie's head was tilted slightly in towards Peter's shoulder. They looked happy, and young, a lot younger than he was himself. There were various photos in the pile; one was of Mona on her wedding day. Black and white like most of the other ones, she didn't look very old, but she looked happy. Her husband had a dog-collar on, a vicar? Was that his father? He looked to be a fair bit older than Mona, at least ten years if not more. There was something written on the back; *'Reverend Whithorn and his new bride Ramona Cummings, 12th Sept. 1969'.* He knew 'Cummings' to be Annie's maiden name too. So Mona was short for Ramona was it? There was no first name for the vicar, just a last name; Whithorn. Was that his own real surname too? Is that who he really was? Michael Whithorn? He'd kicked Annie out before he'd had chance to even think of such questions, let alone get answers to them.

He wasn't sure where to go from here and he wasn't sure what to think. He was Robbie McAndrew, that's who he'd grown up as. That's who he'd been known as and that's what felt right. Looking through the rest of the pile, he came across a school photo. It looked to have been taken in the playground outside what appeared to be a small schoolhouse. There were about twenty-five kids in the picture, all of varying ages and size. He recognised himself to the left of the front row. He knew that it was himself he was looking at and some of the faces looked familiar too but he wasn't sure. Until that is, he saw the face of the teacher; *McStay,* he thought to himself; *that's Mrs McStay.* The only photos he had, or rather Clive and Annie had, had been taken at Marley Primary School and this looked nothing like Marley Primary. Nor were these the classmates he would have remembered, but he remembered that teacher as soon as he saw her in the photo. He turned it over to see if any clue was written on the back. There was a photographer's stamp, then the year written in by hand '1976'.

Robbie had a sudden overwhelming sensation of detachment, as though this were happening to somebody else. Almost as if he were an intruder in someone else's life, peeping in through a window, watching events unfold while not actually being a part of them. The anguished feeling of loneliness was like a knife to his heart. He picked up the phone and dialled. "Rich it's me; can y' come over? No, I'm okay, I just need ya t' come over…soon as, please. Oh an' don't say owt, don't worry anyone. If ya've got someone there t' cover, then just come over...please?"

## Chapter Twenty-One

He could feel his heart pounding as the German bloke arranged his food dishes on the table in front of him; it was racing and the hairs on the back of his neck were prickling, causing him to breathe faster than normal. He felt sick again but he didn't know why. Was he having a heart attack or something? He didn't know, there was no pain, just a tight feeling in his chest and he felt a bit light headed.

The German Nurse had noticed something wasn't right, he looked concerned. *'What is it? Are you ill?'* He'd asked a couple of times, but the old man couldn't concentrate on what he was saying as the feelings of anxiety gripped him.

*** 

Richard arrived to find Robbie back out on the balcony. He'd only noticed the photos spread out on the sofa and coffee table in his peripheral vision as he'd passed them, but even before Robbie had turned to face him, he knew something was wrong. "What is it Rob? What's happened? Have you hurt yerself? Where's mum? I thought she wa' meant t' be here today."

"I sent her home," Robbie said, an almost blank expression on his face. He looked a bit pale and puffy around his eyes as though he'd been crying.

"Robbie?" Rich's concern was growing. "Summat's happened hasn't it? What's happened Robbie? Is it mum?"

"Mum's fine. I'm fine. It's nowt like that, it's just..." He moved towards the sofa. "She brought these with her today." He picked up the two separate photos of the sisters and handed them both to Rich, pointing to the one with Annie in it. "This is Robert with *your* mum. The other one's me with my mum, Annie's sister, my real mum."

"Ah," Rich responded in what could only be described as a 'not too surprised' tone of voice.

Robbie was exasperated. "What the fuck's that supposed t' mean? Did you know? How come you knew an' I didn't?"

Rich put the photos down on the coffee table. "Robbie calm down! No, I didn't know, not really," he tried to explain.

"Either y' knew or y' didn't Rich; just fucking tell me."

Rich sat down. "D'ya remember when we were kids. You must o' been about fifteen an' me about nine. Mum an' Clive had left us at home when they went out t' Clive's work Christmas do. I told y' I wa' gonna go crimbo present hunting while they were out.

You were pratting around the living room, dancing t' summat on Top o' the Pops I think."

Robbie screwed his eyes up, half embarrassed at the many times he must've done such a thing.

"Well I wa' looking for pressies in the bottom o' that huge wardrobe they used to have. There were some shoe boxes an' I thought knowing mum, she might 'o hidden some stuff in there. Anyway they mostly just had shoes in 'em; apart from one that had old photos an' papers in. I found my birth certificate in there, an' then I found yours." Rich stalled for a moment. "Then I found yer death certificate too."

"You what?" Robbie was dumbfounded. "Why the hell didn't y' say summat?"

"Say what?" Rich argued. "I wa' nine years old for fuck sake Robbie. I'd just found a piece o' paper wi' my brother's name an' date o' birth on it that said he'd died not long after he were born. An' yet I knew he were downstairs prancing round the living room like a fucking great jessie. What were I meant t' say?"

"Well what were y' thinking? What wa' going through yer mind when y' saw it?" Robbie quizzed.

"I dunno." Rich seemed irritated by the question. "I were a kid. It might o' crossed my mind that ya'd been adopted, but I didn't understand the death certificate bit, so I just ignored it I suppose. Thought it were a mistake 'cause I knew y' weren't dead. Haven't thought about it in years. To be honest wi' ya Robbie, if you hadn't o' just told me what you have, I probably wouldn't o' thought about it at all. It'd gone; buried."

"Crypto-amnesia," Robbie stated. Rich looked at him, remembering back to them both teasing Jodie about it a few short weeks back when Robbie was in the hospital still. "D'ya remember what yer wife said to me that day Rich?" Rich nodded his acknowledgment. "Well betchya can't guess what my real name is?" Though Robbie knew that Rich wouldn't need to think about it too hard.

"Michael?" Richard said. "Oh fuck me; you were called Michael weren't ya?" He got up from his seat to stand in front of this man he'd thought of as his brother for the whole of his life. Fighting hard to stem the tears building in his eyes, he threw his arms around him. "Oh Jesus, oh fuck. I'm sorry bro. If I'd o' known, if I'd remembered or been old enough t' make more sense of it…" The two men stood hugging each other as if they'd just found each other after years of searching. "Right," Rich finally broke their pain. "What d'ya' know? What's mum told ya? If y' remember being called Michael, y' can't o' been a baby."

Robbie handed him the school photo he'd found. "I wasn't. That's me there." He pointed to the little boy on the front row. "I don't remember them, the other kids. I mean, not really. But I remember her, the teacher. An' there's this." He passed Rich the wedding picture. "These are my parents. Well she's definitely my mother, and I'm assuming he's my father, the vicar. Me, the son of a preacher man eh?" The irony would have been amusing under different circumstances.

"Did you find yer birth certificate? That'll say if he is. Is it in the bag?" Rich asked him.

"I dunno, I haven't got round t' looking in there yet." He picked it up and took out the contents. There were a few more photos, some child's drawings, and a certificate. A death certificate, Robert's, but there was no other birth certificate. "She must've destroyed it."

Rich wasn't convinced. "Why would she? If she adopted y' from her own sister or anyone else for that matter, why would she need t' destroy yer original birth certificate? What purpose would it serve?"

"All I know is she made me into Robert McAndrew. Into her dead son an' that's sick. I'm sorry but it is. She probably wanted t' destroy all evidence of who I wa' before."

"Then why keep all these pictures?" Rich asked. "I know y' must be really pissed off at her Rob, but y' can't think she's done this out o' some kind o' wicked intent. Come on…Mum? She's just not like that."

"She's just not my mum either Rich."

"Yeh…she is. She might not o' given birth t' ya, but she's been a good mum. D'ya think she's treat us differently? Have you ever gone without?"

Robbie shook his head conceding to the fact that if nothing else, Annie had always been a good mum to them both. He'd never felt less loved or cared for than Richard was, she'd always treated them equally. "There's so many things I don't know," he said.

"Then we'll go to mum's. I'll drive us. There's no point festering here. If anyone's got the answers y' need, it's her," Rich suggested.

"I threw her out. She might not want to."

"She'll understand. An' she obviously does want t', otherwise why bring all this?"

Robbie's mobile began to ring with Lynsey's name flashing up on the display. "I can't. She'll know summat's wrong if I talk to her."

Taking the phone from him, Rich answered it. "Hiya Lyns. It's Rich. He's just on the loo…yeah he's fine…oh I've taken the day off, so I sent mum home. Listen, I'm gonna take him out for a bit, get him out o' the house, okay? Yeah...I'll make sure he doesn't overdo it love. I dunno what time we'll be back though, so don't panic if we're still out when y' get home...yeah, will do. Bye then, bye."

***

A blue Vauxhall Vectra turned out of their parents' cul-de-sac as the boys turned in. Rich knocked on the door then immediately opened it and walked in. "Just us, the gruesome twosome," he called out. Clive rushed out of the kitchen, a little startled at seeing them. He and Robbie looked at each other for a moment, both of them knowing why they were there.

"Yer mum's in bed. Doctor's just gone, she's not well." Clive said, reading the look on Robbie's face.

"What's happened?" Rich asked, concerned.

"Doctor thinks she's not quite over this chest infection she's had, still fighting it a bit. She erm...she had a bit of a faint earlier when she got home," Clive explained nervously.

"You know Clive don't ya?" Robbie said calmly. "How long have y' known? Since I were a kid?"

Clive gestured for them to go through to the dining room and out of the hallway by the foot of the stairs where Annie might have heard them.

"Yeh, yes she did tell me son, but only after you were in the hospital. I swear I never knew a thing about it 'til then. Even if I had, I'm not sure what I'd o' done about it," Clive stuttered quietly. "She wa' going out of her mind wi' it Robbie. You waking up thinking' y' were called Michael, it wa' tearing her apart, making her ill. I knew there wa' summat going on so I badgered her 'til she told me. Trust me lad, I didn't know before that; but now that I do, I want to help, both o' ya; you an' yer mum I mean, 'cause she is still yer mum. She said y' were angry, that's t' be expected, but this tale is so vast an' complicated. All I ask Robbie is that y' listen t' the whole thing. There must be a mountain o' questions y' want answers to, an' ya'll get 'em. No-one's looking' t' keep owt from y' now lad. The ball's in your court now Robbie. I just want y' t' remember t' have a care for y' mum, she's my wife, an' she's not the villain o' the piece." Clive was visibly shaken at the anticipation of Robbie's reaction, which was silent and stony faced if anything.

Rich answered on his behalf. "This is affecting all of us, Clive. We're all a bit shocked. It's hard, especially for our Robbie."

They all sat down around the dining table. "Am I Michael Whithorn?" Robbie asked after an initial awkward silence.

"Yes son, you are," Clive answered him. "I can tell y' everything that I've found out, that's not a problem, but even I don't know the full picture yet Robbie. Each question just seems t' lead t' more at the moment."

"That's what I don't get Clive," Rich pondered. "Surely an adoption's not that complicated. An' why'd mum go to all that trouble t' keep it quiet? I know she had a sister that died before I wa' born; but if she took on that sister's kid, our Robbie here, then why'd it need t' be kept a secret? He is *legally* adopted after all isn't he?"

The look on Clive's face gave them the answer to that question straight away. Robbie rested his elbows on the table with his head in his hands. "Oh Christ. What's going on Clive? I don't understand any o' this."

"Is that why mum changed his identity? To hide him from the law?" Rich continued.

Clive felt caught between a rock and a hard place. He knew how it must look to the boys, but he also knew that they didn't have all the facts. "It's not as simple as that," he tried to explain. "Yes, I suppose by doing what she did, it hid y' from the authorities Robbie, but that was secondary t' who she wa' really hiding y' from...y' father, Eban."

Stunned, Robbie sat bolt upright in his chair. "Hang about! Are *you* saying that I wasn't even a fucking orphan? My dad wa' still alive? I just assumed they must o' both been dead?"

Clive didn't feel qualified to be going through all of this with the boys, it was complicated and he was concerned that he might not put Annie's case across fairly enough. "It was yer dad that wa' the problem Robbie. Y'know he were a vicar, right?"

Robbie nodded. "Yeah, I saw the photo of their wedding day."

Clive stared into space for a moment before continuing, trying to get things in order in his own mind. "The thing is son, when yer mother died, Mona I mean, yer real mum, well when she died it were in somewhat dubious circumstances. He were abusive ya see, Eban. He weren't a nice man at all. It seems Mona wa' planning on taking you, an' getting' y' both away from him. She wa' gonna go an' live wi' Annie. Peter had died a short time before an' Annie were pregnant wi' our Richard an on her own, so they'd planned on a way of helping Mona an' you get free of Eban."

"Why didn't she just leave like anyone else?" Robbie wasn't convinced.

"Because of who he was an' where they were, I suppose is the simple answer," Clive said. "He wa' the head o' the Church in that village. People tried complaining about him, about how he behaved an' how he treat Mona, and Michael." He looked tentatively at Robbie as he used the name Michael. "But he wa' the local holy man, an' the Free Church stood by him. The local constabulary ignored what they deemed as gossip. He were adept at talking the talk when he had to an' he were believed by them that should o' known better.

"Seems the whole bloody village knew that Mona were a battered wife. Little Michael were terrified o' the man, an' so when Mona died, the verdict wa' left open. The coroner couldn't decide if it were accidental or suicide. But yer mum an' Mona's friends were adamant it were neither. Annie thinks he found out that she wa' gonna run away the very next day, taking Michael with her. Annie had even driven up there that night, so she could collect 'em early next morning in a nearby town, but when they never showed up...well let's just say, when she found out what'd happened to her sister..."

"How d'ya know?" Robbie asked. "How d'ya know it wa' definitely like that? I mean, what if they just didn't get on?"

Clive was less than happy at the implication Robbie was making about Annie perhaps embellishing what had happened for her own gain. "Now you listen 'ere!" he insisted. "I understand yer not happy about this, an' I don't blame ya, but that woman rescued you. Yes she had t' do it in a less than conventional manner, an' yes she should o' maybe thought things through better at the time. But

198

she wa' grieving. She'd not long lost her husband an' now she'd just lost a sister, a sister she wa' trying to help, a sister who made her promise t' take care o' you should owt happen to her, an' it did didn't it? How could she leave you alone wi' a man like that? It wa' bad enough when Mona were alive, but at least she could protect y' t' some extent. Annie felt she couldn't let her sister down, dead or alive."

"But why call me Robert McAndrew? That's just sick. It's not right," Robbie complained.

"An' that's summat she's had t' deal wi' every day of her life Robbie. But at the time she didn't know what else t' do. You an' Robert were the same age near enough. She had t' change who y' were for fear o' ya being found. Like I said, no-one who mattered believed what Eban were like; you'd o' been returned to him if ya'd o' been found an' she couldn't risk that. She hated having t' use her own child's identity like that; she knew it were wrong on every level, but she couldn't think how else t' protect ya. It meant she could produce a birth certificate for ya, get y' into schools, doctors' surgeries etcetera. It wa' for the greater good, so she just had t' come t' terms wi' it."

"But how d'ya know he wa' that bad Clive? You didn't know him, ya've only got what she says t' go on." Robbie was struggling.

"We went up t' Scotland," Clive admitted. "The other week when I said y' mum needed a break, we went up there. I've met people that were around at the time, I've spoken to 'em. Annie wasn't exaggerating the cruelty o' yer father, Robbie. It seems it were very much true. I'm sorry son, I don't know how else t' convince ya. I don't know what else I can say. You've been wronged, no-one's denying that, but Annie tried her best at the time. She couldn't o' left y' there but she didn't know how else t' go about getting you out safely, so that he couldn't get y' back."

"Didn't he look for me?"

"He were told y' fell ov'rboard while out fishin' wi' some o' the local men. Y' used t' go wi' em sometimes anyway. It were quite rough on the night Annie took ya an' y' really did fall overboard, but y' were rescued an' you an' Annie were put down in a harbour some way away. The fellas went back an' said ya'd fallen ov'rboard an' couldn't be found. Sea wa' searched for a couple o' days, but when y' weren't found it were just accepted ya'd died at sea. Like a lot o' folk had from there abouts."

Robbie screwed up his eyes as he laboured to remember things from that time. He couldn't, but he could remember some of the nightmares he'd been having since his attack. Rich looked across the table at him. "Crypto-amnesia bro," he said. He remembered Robbie's nightmares too. "She wa' right after all, my Jodie."

"Annie took ya t' the hospital, ya'd nearly drowned y' see. But they said y' were okay. She said y' memory were a bit sketchy after that so she played along, manipulated the thing's y' did remember a little, that sort o' thing," Clive said.

Robbie laughed, though not with amusement. "Isn't that called brain-washing?" he said sarcastically.

"I suppose it is," came a voice from the doorway; it was Annie. She was wearing her dressing gown, looking pale and tired. Robbie couldn't bring himself to look at her. He loved her; she was the only mum he knew, but he felt so betrayed by her too, so angry.

Clive got to his feet, concerned. "Annie love, should y' be up? Doctor wanted ya t' stay in bed, rest a while."

"I'm alright Clive, please don't fuss," she insisted. "A cup o' tea'd be nice if yer making one?" She smiled at Richard before sitting in the chair that Clive had vacated opposite Robbie. "It was the best of two evils Robbie. I know it's difficult for ya' tae understand, especially in this day and age...but in them days, back then things were so very different. We were in a very isolated community, in the days when the people in authority could pretty much do what they wanted an' get away with it. It's different now love, all these historical abuse cases we hear about on the news an' the like. It doesn't matter who you are nowadays, ya just wouldn't be able to do those things without being found out, but back then...once Mona had died, all the options I had where you were concerned were bad. I chose the one that I believed tae be the least bad. I couldn't just leave ya there son. I desperately wanted ya tae know all about yer mam. She was such a sweet, lovely girl; she called *you* her angel ya know. But the longer time went on, the harder it got. It wasn't planned that way Robbie, it's just the way things went."

Finally Robbie looked up, making eye contact with Annie. "Okay," he said. "Tell me."

# Chapter Twenty-Two

Robbie sat in silence while Annie recounted events. She told how things had been back then, about the happy, if not hard, childhood she and Mona had. How they'd grown up on a farm midway between the villages of the Isle of Stennoch and Cutreach. She explained how in nineteen sixty-six the old Minister of the Free Church had retired and that after a few months of having several different Ministers standing in, the village finally got its own Minister again: a much younger man of twenty-nine at the time, Eban Whithorn. He was the younger son of missionaries and had seen quite a bit of the world. He was handsome and single, something that had appealed to one or two of the local girls at the time, but he wasn't interested in them.

Mona was only fifteen at the time, but she'd caught his eye. He'd behaved like the perfect gentleman towards her, never put a foot out of place, never said a wrong word. He was always friendly and charming whenever he saw her or any of the family, which had endeared him to their parents. It wasn't until about three years later that he began courting her properly. She'd just turned eighteen and was Annie's Maid of Honour when she'd married Peter, one of the few men from the Isle who didn't fish or farm, but trained as an engineer. Eban had officiated at the wedding; he couldn't take his eyes off Mona the whole time. Annie and Peter had their wedding breakfast in the village hall. She smiled as she recalled the moment when the harbour master had interrupted the party looking for some of the men to help because the pier was collapsing. It hadn't been watertight for years, but it had chosen Annie's wedding day to finally give up the ghost. Eban had gone with the men and Annie had seen how Mona's gaze had followed him to the door. That's when she'd known for certain that her sister had fallen in love. Eban had been her rock when their mother died of ovarian cancer four months after the wedding.

The Minister from Stennoch town came over a year later to officiate over Mona's marriage to Eban. She was nineteen and him thirty-three but no-one had batted an eye about the age difference. The fact that he was a man of God had been good enough for their dad. Eban's brother who was also a Minister in Ireland somewhere, had been the only member of his family to attend the wedding as the Best Man. That had been the first and only time anyone had ever met Jacob; he never visited again. Eban's parents were apparently in India, doing whatever it is that missionaries do. They'd sent him a letter wishing him well, but they never visited at all. Mona had never met anyone from Eban's family apart from Jacob, and that was only the once.

The following year the sisters had both found themselves pregnant. With hindsight, Annie could see that something wasn't right, but at the time it hadn't been as apparent and Mona had never made any suggestion to the contrary. Annie had gone on to have a son, Robert, born on March twenty-second nineteen seventy-one. Then tragedy struck again on April twenty-ninth, when they'd lost their beloved father to pneumonia. He'd been taken ill less than a week before he died, it was very fast. The family had only been tenant farmers and with no-one to take over, the tenancy had been awarded to Freddy McGuffie who'd been a farmhand for their dad since leaving school. He had a wife and children of his own and the sisters were glad to see that if it had to go to anyone, it had gone to them. It left the girls with no other relatives locally though; they only had each other and their husbands.

Mona's boy Michael was born on the fourth of June the same year and she'd been immediately besotted by him. Peter travelled with his work, often around England, taking his young wife and baby with him most of the time. Annie hated leaving Mona behind, but she'd got her own family, her husband Eban who adored her, or so it had seemed, and her beautiful baby boy. She had a lot of good friends in the village too, people who'd known her all of her life. Mona had been the first to encourage Annie to take that leap of faith.

Then Annie's whole world imploded, on the morning of November the sixth. She'd found her baby Robert in his cot. He was cold to the touch, his skin was almost white and he was blue around his lips, hands and feet. There'd been no reason for it; the coroner had documented it as a cot-death with no known cause and no suspicious circumstances. This was the worst kind of grief that Annie had ever experienced. She'd felt agonising pain when her parents had died, but nothing, (not even that) compared to the inconceivable grief of losing her baby.

Mona was heartbroken for her sister. She did everything for her; she even helped to dress her on the morning of Robert's funeral, combing her hair for her and tying it back in a neat bun. Annie felt comatose. She couldn't function, and even breathing was an effort. And she just wasn't capable of dealing with Peter's grief. He was distraught but the two of them were like strangers, each locked in a solitary world of despair. Mona had insisted that they both return to the Isle with her and Eban, just to give them some time to heal a little.

Mona was wonderful; she'd taken care of them both so well. Eban had counselled them, especially Peter. They'd prayed together most days. But Mona cried as much as Annie did. She felt so guilty that she had her baby when her sister's had been taken so cruelly. At first she'd tried to avoid letting Annie see too much of Michael in case it upset her. But it had the opposite effect, it helped her. Each time she held Michael, fed him, changed his nappy, each time he smiled up at his aunt, it helped her to accept that the world couldn't stand still, no matter what had happened and nor should it. She knew that she would never get over the loss of her child, but that she was doing the memory of him no favours by stagnating either. Peter was offered a permanent post in Chesterfield soon after. So eventually, he and Annie moved to their fresh start in England.

Again with hindsight, she should have picked up then that things between her sister and Eban weren't right, but she was too caught up in her own grief to take a proper note of all the times her sister would shut up the minute he walked into the room. The time he'd reached above her head to get something from on top of a kitchen cupboard and Mona had cowed like a bomb had just gone off. Annie had witnessed so many tell-tale signs, but she just hadn't processed them properly, and Mona wouldn't have said anything, not at a time like that.

Halfway into the following year, after her move to England, Annie and Mona were talking on the telephone one afternoon; Mona's was one of only three telephones in the Isle back then. There was one at the post office, one at the Solway Harvester Inn and one at the Manse (vicarage), Mona's. Anyway, Eban had overheard Mona's side of the conversation; she was telling Annie that she wasn't happy, that things weren't as they seemed. He'd been furious, banning his young wife from ever using the telephone again without his permission. He wouldn't let her visit Annie and Peter, nor would he allow them to visit her again after that. It turned out that he'd been beating her all along; he terrorised her. He'd told her what he would do to her and the baby if she ever told or tried to leave him. At first he'd been full of apologies after the fact, but that didn't last long. Mona had tried to keep the peace between them, but he'd become so unpredictable that it was impossible to tell what was going to set him off. She'd become almost housebound. If he saw her outside talking to someone, especially a man, he'd go mad when she got home. He'd accuse her of being a whore and a liar.

Annie's only contact had been writing her sister letters and posting them to Izzy McStay's house, then waiting anxiously for the reply. She'd offered to go and collect her sister and baby Michael on several occasions but Mona had refused, misguidedly believing that Eban would calm down again one day, but he never did. Within two years of Michael's birth, Mona was pregnant again. She'd lost the baby before she'd even begun to show having suffered Eban's violence yet again. He'd called her a whore, accused her of carrying another man's bastard and he'd beaten her so badly that she lost the baby that night. Isle folk were all sympathetic when she returned from hospital, but they believed that she'd fallen down the stairs because that's what Eban had told them, and who would question a Minister?

But Izzy knew and fairly soon it became more and more apparent to others too. Eban had given up trying not to mark her face and she was often seen with black eyes, strangle marks and the like, but she was too ashamed to do anything but defend him when people asked. And if anyone dared to challenge Eban on the matter, it just made it worse for her; she'd suffer his wrath when he'd get home. That was why Annie daren't be seen anywhere near the Isle either, if she'd have been anywhere near and Eban had found out, God knows what he would have done to Mona.

He used Michael as a way of controlling her; he'd threaten the boy. The poor child would often wet himself as soon as his father raised his voice.

Mona was over five months pregnant when she lost her next baby to that monster. He'd fallen over one of Michael's toys when he'd come home drunk and launched at him, so Mona had stood between him and the boy. Michael ran out of the back door screaming as Eban laid into Mona. He'd got her to the floor and repeatedly kicked her in her back and belly. Michael had run to the McGuffie house, and by the time Catriona had arrived, Eban was gone to his bed and Mona was in agony on her hands and knees on the kitchen floor. Desperate and knowing the futility of it, Mona refused to go to hospital. The district nurse was the only available medic and within a few hours, Mona had delivered another son, but this one was dead, way too tiny to have ever stood a chance on this earth. *'It's the will o' the Lord',* had been Eban's only comment on the matter. But that had been Mona's tipping point, that was the day that she'd decided she had to get herself and her son out. She had to bide her time though.

There was no internet access back then, no emails, mobile phones or the like. When someone from the village had tried to help previously by going to the police and the Church elders, they'd been dismissed as busy-bodies, and when the Bishop had visited and asked Mona if all was well, of course she'd said yes. She was terrified of her husband. What else could she say? Eban would make her pay dearly for any other comment out of turn. The local Bobby knew the score, but he couldn't get anything done either, though Eban was always wary around him for some reason, always a little more cautious.

But the older Michael was getting, the more he'd be on the wrong end of Eban's temper too, and Mona couldn't tolerate that. He could do what he wanted to her, and he did, but she couldn't allow such a small boy to suffer that too, not her sweet angel. Which is when she'd enlisted Izzy's help to try and hatch a plan of action.

The only contact she had with her sister at the time was through Izzy. She'd found out through Izzy that Peter, Annie's husband had been killed in a terrible accident. Annie had rung the Manse and spoken to Eban, but he'd kept it from her. When her sister really needed her, Eban had kept it from her. It was three weeks after the event when Mona eventually found out. Annie had written to her at Izzy's, grief stricken yet understanding of Mona's predicament, writing for her to not blame herself for not being able to come to the funeral, that Peter had been buried and that his work colleagues had paid for the funeral and headstone, that she was being looked after and not to worry. Poor Annie, she'd had so much grief. She'd told her in a previous letter that she was expecting another baby, the first since Robert and she'd sounded so happy. But then this, her lovely husband snatched from her too, how terrible. Mona so wanted to be with her sister. She wanted more than anything to get her boy out of the village and away from Eban's cruelty, but she knew it wouldn't be easy.

"She was going tae come tae England wi' ya Robbie," Annie said. "Ya were both meant tae come an' live wi' me until Mona had got herself a job an' a place for ya both. I'd even done all the research into which solicitors would be the best, tae help her. She wanted tae divorce Eban, but she needed tae be sure that he couldn't get you. Women's rights weren't brilliant in the seventies, even in England, but they were a hundred times better than they were in rural Scotland. In those days when a woman married, she was still promising to 'love, honour and *obey*' her man. Domestic violence was swept under the carpet, so we needed a sympathetic solicitor who'd be willing tae take on Mona's case, knowing he'd be asking the court tae take her word above that of a Minister. It was going tae be difficult however we went about it, but we'd prepared, we'd done all the groundwork we could think of...an' then..."

"She died," Robbie finished for her. "An' you think my father killed her."

"No Robbie...I *know* yer father killed her," Annie insisted. "I can't prove it of course. Don't ya think if I could that I would o' done so a long time ago? He did it alright an' nothing'll ever convince me otherwise.

"I'm not ashamed that I took you away from him son. I just wish things had been done differently. I wish I could've brought ya

211

up knowing that I was only yer auntie an' being able tae tell ya all about yer mum. She'd be so, so proud o' you." Annie's eyes began to well up. "But I didn't know how. We'd o' had a hard enough time convincing the court tae let ya stay wi' yer mam if Eban contested it; but they'd o' never o' let me keep ya over him. I was naive I know, but I didn't know what else tae do. I'm sorry!"

Robbie ran his hand up one side of his face and sighed. "Is he still alive?" he asked. "Eban, my father. Is he still alive?"

Annie looked to Clive and him to her. "Aye Robbie, he is," she informed him.

# Chapter Twenty-Three

Robbie had been very quiet all evening. At first Lynsey had thought him to be in a bad mood, but he'd not been snappy or irritable, just quiet. She'd decided he must just be getting really fed up of not having the sense of independence that he was used to. He was up and about, mostly without the need for crutches. Thanks to the pneumatic walking boot he'd literally come on in leaps and bounds. He couldn't drive yet though. Partly because of his ankle but legally because of his head injury.

Apparently the DVLA are informed of any serious head injuries and place an immediate temporary driving ban on the victim. Seemed quite harsh at first but it made sense. It was to do with the fact that some head injury victims go on to develop epilepsy or other problems which may affect their safety behind the wheel. Robbie had been told that he wouldn't be allowed to drive for six months, after which he'd be re-assessed. If he had any problems within that time then the ban would be extended and possibly become permanent. Luckily he hadn't had anything go wrong with his recovery at all and so it had become just a matter of biding his time really.

Snuggling up beside him in bed, Lynsey allowed him his pensive moment. He smelled of the Lynx shower gel that she'd bought him at Christmas; he smelled good. He turned his face into

213

her hair and she could feel his breath as he began to kiss the top of her head, his fingers stroking gently up from her elbow to her shoulder. He wanted her and she him. He began to caress her neck with his lips, pushing her hair back behind her before moving slowly down to her breasts. She'd been so cautious of having sex with him since what had happened, and had even tried to avoid his advances on previous occasions for fear of him doing himself an injury. But now she had no such inclination; he needed her. Before it had felt like he just needed sex, but now he needed her.

Pushing his hand between her legs he began to gently rub back and forth as Lynsey writhed beneath his touch. He hadn't said a word and neither had she, just kissed and caressed each other in silent ardour. She put her hand to his chest as he tried to climb on top of her, causing him to stop what he was doing. "Lay down," she whispered, and as he did so she straddled him, kissing and licking at his body before she finally allowed him inside her. He moaned as his manhood found its target and he pulled her body close to his, her hair falling into his face a little more with each thrust.

Sensing that he was close to climax, Lynsey sat upright and groaned a little more as she felt him reaching his crescendo. Holding his hands to her breasts she threw her head back, squeezing at his forearms as she came. Moments later and with one final, violent thrust of his pelvis, Robbie had joined her in their private moment of paradise.

Sweaty and panting, though completely sated, Lynsey rested herself back down onto Robbie's chest. He held her, gently stroking up and down her spine with his fingers. He kissed her forehead. "I love you, ya do know that don't ya?" he said.

"I know ya do Robbie, an' I love you too. More than ya could ever imagine."

He really hoped that she meant it. He hadn't told her about his recent revelation; he hadn't known how to. How do you tell the woman that you love, that the man that she loves isn't who she thinks he is? He'd had this conversation with Rich, who'd been quick to point out that he hadn't lied to Lynsey; he hadn't been living a double life or keeping things from her. None of what had happened had been of his doing and he couldn't be held responsible for any part of it. He wanted to tell her; he just wasn't sure when, or how. He'd just needed some space in his head first, time to process the whole and understand the sum of its parts. He'd been having an increasingly strong urge to go to Scotland, to the place of his birth, the Isle of Stennoch. The more he ran over things in his mind, the more urgent it felt that he go there. All the dreams he'd had, all the nightmares. The photographs of the community he'd been both born into and lost to. All of those familiar feelings he'd had, which had made no sense at all at the time, were now fast becoming an unstoppable cascade of jigsaw pieces waiting to fall into their rightful place, but that needed to be there, where it mattered, and not here in Leeds, where it felt more like a drama unfolding on some cleverly devised television programme.

He couldn't *not* tell Lynsey; she'd never forgive him. He'd want to know if the tables were turned. Plus; how could he possibly live with her and keep it from her at the same time? Would she be implicated if he told her? Even though she'd done nothing wrong, if he told her and then she said nothing to no-one, but it came out anyway and the police became involved, would she then be in the wrong? Oh Christ this was all getting too much for Robbie; he couldn't sleep. Looking to his left, Lynsey's eyes were tight shut and her breathing had fallen into that soft, steady rhythm of slumber. Would she stay if she knew? Or would it all be too much for her too?

Turning back to stare up at the ceiling, Robbie knew what he had to do. He got himself up out of bed and went through the living room and out onto the balcony for some cool night air to help him think. The city looked good at night, all lit up like a Christmas tree. He could see some kind of emergency vehicle about a quarter of a mile away, its blue lights distracting his vision from everything else. There was no sound of sirens, just the blue lights. *Silent running,* he'd thought to himself, some emergency night crew having to work and yet trying to be considerate to those who didn't, those who were sleeping in their beds, like he should be, but wasn't.

He went back inside, barely noticing how cold it had been outside until the warmth of the flat enveloped him on his return. Lynsey was sleeping. He sat beside her on the bed, just staring at her, wondering, thinking to himself that these were the last moments of normality for her and drinking in the sight of her so that he'd remember, just in case it all went tits-up.

"Lyns," Robbie said softly as he stroked her hair. Her eyes flickered for a moment. "Lyns. Wake up love. I need y' t' wake up. There's summat I need t' tell ya."

## Chapter Twenty-Four

Lynsey was in the kitchen already when Robbie awoke; he could hear her clattering around in there. He'd decided on showering before facing her as he wasn't sure how she'd be feeling; this was the morning after the night before and she would've had time to let things sink in by now. He looked at the clock beside the bed: five past eight. She'd normally set off for work by quarter past. Maybe she'd be gone by the time he'd showered. That could possibly be a good thing. He felt ashamed though logic told him that he'd done nothing wrong, but what he felt in his heart was that he'd deceived her in some way. That he'd somehow been responsible for the lie that he'd been living, the one that she'd inadvertently been caught up in too. If she couldn't cope with knowing, then she might leave him and he wasn't ready to face that prospect yet. No, better to jump in the shower, let her go to work and then face up to the consequences of her conscience this evening, when they'd both had more time to prepare.

He made sure that he took long enough in the shower so that she'd have left before he'd done. He kept listening out to see if he could still hear her moving around. He couldn't, but he'd not heard the flat door go either. It was spring loaded and normally closed itself really slowly until the last few inches when it would bang shut all of a sudden. It was possible that she'd controlled its closing, wanting to leave silently and without a fuss.

He hoped she was okay, that she hadn't lain awake all night worrying. She'd been very quiet when he'd told her, looking up at him, examining his face for any clues as to how he was feeling, for any signs that this man that she'd loved wasn't her Robbie after all. She'd said very little about it, just wept a little and held him closely all night. He felt so sorry for her. She hadn't asked for any of this; this wasn't what she'd signed up for. It was as though he'd trampled into her life, set off a Molotov cocktail, and retreated to the safety of the barracks without her. He tried to rehearse in his mind what he might say to her when she got home later. How would he convince her that he too had only just found out? What if she didn't believe him? Shit! What if she didn't come home? She would though, wouldn't she?

Leaving the bathroom with only his towel wrapped around his waist, he went back into the bedroom to get dressed. It wasn't until he'd already got his boxers and tee-shirt on and was sitting on the edge of the bed pulling on his socks, that he became aware of Lynsey's presence in the bedroom doorway. She was leaning against the door frame just watching him. They stared at each other in silence for a few seconds before he broke it. "Morning love," he said. "Won't you be late for work?"

"I'm not going." Lynsey answered. "I...I don't know what t' say t' you, or how to help. But I love you Robbie McAndrew...Michael Whithorn, or whoever the fuck you are. I love you so much...an' I just need t' be with you today." Her eyes were welling up and tears were beginning to spill down her cheeks, but she continued to try and reassure him through her sniffles. "I'm going nowhere. For as long as *you* want me here, then I'll be shoulder t' shoulder with y' Robbie. Shit. I don't even know if it's okay for me t' still call y' that."

Scooping her into his arms, Robbie held her close as she sobbed. Hearing her say that was what made him realise that no matter who he'd been in the past, no matter what had happened to him, rightly or wrongly, he was now Robbie McAndrew. He'd spent less than six short years as Michael Whithorn and thirty-five as Robbie. There were parts of Michael still inside him; he had no doubt about that. But he'd lived as Robbie for as long as he could remember.

Those initial emotions he'd had when Annie had told him his story, those feelings of wanting her to stop, to not talk about it and to try and pretend it hadn't happened, those emotions had transitioned from feelings of detachment and disbelief, through to a marginal curiosity and finally an outright need in him to find out the truth: to speak to the people who remembered him and his mother, Mona. He wanted to see the places he'd been, the school he had vague, jumbled memories of, but most of all, he wanted to meet his father. If Eban was indeed, still alive, then Robbie needed to see him.

***

"Have y' spoken to our Richard?" Clive asked.

"Yeah," Robbie replied. "I've told him t' tell Jodie everything, just make sure she'll keep it to herself."

"Y' didn't have t' do that y' know Robbie. Might be better t' not let too many people know," Clive reasoned.

"I know, but she's his wife. She's family an' it's not fair our Rich having summat like this in his head an' no-one t' talk to about it. She's a good lass is Jodie, she'll not say owt," Robbie explained.

Lynsey came into the dining room and sat at the table with Clive and Robbie. "Right, I've booked two double rooms at the Solway Harvester Inn Robbie. Are y' certain y' want t' stay in the village? We can always cancel an' stay somewhere else?"

"No," Robbie insisted. "I want t' be in the village as much as I can. I want t' be there for when the sun rises, an' in the dark too. Anything, don't y' see? I just want t' give it chance t' make me remember. I know I were only little, but maybe the sights, the smells, even the way the bloody light falls on the rooftops or the water might help. I don't know really, just feels right that's all."

"But what about yer mum? Clive said she couldn't face being in the village before. That's right isn't it Clive?"

Clive nodded. "Yep, but that were before. It wa' the first time she'd been there in thirty-five years. I'm sure she just wants t' do her bit now. Don't you worry about yer mum Robbie. If it does get a bit much for her we don't have t' stay, I can always take her somewhere else."

"How is Annie now Clive?" Lynsey asked. "Is she feeling better? D'ya think she's well enough t' go back again?"

"Oh aye," Clive reassured. "She wants t' go. She's got t' go for some tests in a couple o' weeks, up at the hospital. Just t' make sure this infection's buggered off. Needs a chest X-ray doctor says. But she's brighter than she has been; think this last lot of anti-biotics has done the trick, finally."

They finished putting the last of their bags into the back of Robbie's car. Lynsey was going to drive them all up to Scotland and Clive would take over if she got tired, at his insistence that is. He was only trying to be chivalrous in his own, old fashioned kind of way, but Lynsey had been quietly a little offended that he didn't think she could cope with four or five hours driving on her own.

"Lynsey'll be fine Clive, honest," Robbie had defended her. "She's done journeys like this before. Besides, we'll be stopping' off for a coffee I dare say. An' y' know what you're like wi' yer toilet stops. You and 'Mr Frusemide'." Robbie joked, making reference to the water tablets that Clive took. It was quite right though; he couldn't go for too long without emptying his bladder.

Annie appeared in the doorway with her jacket in one hand and her handbag in the other. "Right, I think that's everything," she said. She looked a little anxious and still found it difficult to maintain eye contact with Robbie for too long. They were pleasant to each other and had got over that frostiness which was a blessing, but they both still felt a little awkward in the other's company. Annie still felt terribly guilty for the way things had panned out, but couldn't see how she could have done things any differently. And for his part, it seemed that Robbie understood that, because he'd racked his brain to think how, if what he'd been told about his father were true, things could have realistically been done any other way.

He didn't think that Annie was lying about Eban's character, but he still needed that confirmation himself. He needed to hear firsthand what the people that knew Eban had thought of him. If they remembered him or Mona. He desperately wanted to know about Mona, to put flowers on her grave, to see the farm where she'd grown up and the fields she'd played in as a child. Even though he didn't hold any animosity towards Annie any more, he couldn't help but blame her a little for all the Mothers days and birthdays where Mona's grave had lain barren of a bouquet from her only child.

Robbie knew that Annie had loved Mona with all of her heart and that she'd done everything she could to help, especially given the torment Annie had suffered herself at the time. He'd initially assumed that Annie had jumped at the opportunity to replace her own dead son with her dead sister's child. But the more they'd talked and the more chance he'd had to get things into perspective, the more he'd realised that what Clive had told him from the beginning was actually true. Annie really had struggled with the prospect of giving him her baby's identity. It had been a massive and traumatic thing that she'd done, but she'd done it for Mona and the promise she'd made to her, the promise she'd kept for thirty-five years. It was an act of unselfish love that had caused the decisions she'd made back then and not the selfish obsession of a bereft woman, which is what he'd originally accused her of, to his shame.

Annie took her place in the car sitting behind the passenger seat. She'd lost a little weight through her illness and still looked pale, but the stress of recent events must have added to her condition too. Still, she was smiling as Clive finished locking up the house before getting into the back seat beside her. She reached for his hand. "Are we all ready then?" she asked. "I think our Robbie's sanity is depending on this trip. Isn't that right son?"

## Chapter Twenty-Five

Leaving Todhill rest stop on the M6 motorway they soon see the big blue sign informing them that they are now entering Scotland. Robbie hadn't really wanted to stop off at all, for him he couldn't get to the Isle fast enough, but he'd had to concede defeat as it was three against one for some respite. He knew that they'd only covered just over a hundred miles and had nearly a hundred still to go.

Annie leant forward touching his shoulder. "The second half o' the journey won't take as long Robbie; the roads are pretty straight and fairly quiet once we get past Gretna." Then addressing Lynsey, "Just stay on the A75 an' follow the Stranraer signs; it's a straight line 'til the Wigtown turn off love."

"No problem," Lynsey replied. "D'ya mind if I put the music back on anyone? I promise not t' blast yer eardrums."

No-one objected and so she nudged Robbie to do the honours. He tapped the 'on' switch and within a couple of seconds they were driving along to the sound of Snow Patrol singing Shut Your Eyes. Somehow Robbie found this track somewhat more haunting than he had before, he'd never really listened to it that closely. Now though, as he gazed out of his window at the not so distant hills the lyrics seemed to mean more to him than just a good tune.  He sang along silently in his mind.

He must have drifted into a semi trance like state, still aware of everything around him, though time seemed to pass without him having noticed at all.  He was roused from this borderline dream state by Annie's voice, reminding Lynsey that at the next roundabout she'd need to take the first exit and follow the signs for Wigtown.

"A few miles down this road Lynsey, ya'll start tae see signs for Stennoch.  Keep an eye out for a right turn towards Stennoch love; it should turn us off before we reach Wigtown, okay?" Annie instructed.  She paused for a moment, sitting back in her seat.  She looked at Clive for reassurance before continuing.  Clive smiled at her and gave her hand a little squeeze in acknowledgement and understanding.  Annie took a breath.  "Oh...erm, Robbie love, we have tae drive through Stennoch tae get tae the Isle.  I don't know if you'd like tae stop off there?  It's where Mona's buried, an' yer grandparents.  You were so little at her funeral, an' ya just...We don't have to if you're not up tae it yet love," she faltered a little.  "Robert's there too love, only...well, that might feel a bit...ya know?"

Robbie hesitated for a moment before answering.  "No, I'd like to.  It'd seem wrong t' just drive past without paying' my respects."

Annie smiled to herself; she somehow felt that she was bringing Michael back to his mother after all of these years. She tried to picture her sister in her mind's eye, smiling. Mona had smiled her way through childhood, always so happy, so kind. How could Eban have taken something so precious and destroyed it, leaving bones in the ground, the only testament to a life lost too soon? Why would anyone deliberately do that to another human being? She'd lost sleep night after tortured night over the years trying to find answers to those questions, but she never did find any. It had made no sense to her at all back then, and it made even less sense as time had gone on. One thing Annie had come to terms with long ago, was that no matter what anyone said, time *did not* heal those wounds at all. The only thing that time did, was to teach a person new ways of masking their pain.

Stepping out of the car, they all turned to face Robbie. "D'ya want us t' come with y Robbie?" Lynsey asked. "It's okay if ya'd rather go on yer own."

"We'll all go I think if that's okay wi' you lot?" Robbie replied.

Standing with his hands in his pockets and Lynsey linking arms with him, Robbie read the words on his mother's headstone quietly to himself. He gently shook his head as he noted the dedication to Michael at the top of the stone. *In Memory of Michael Whithorn...*it felt like a dream looking at that inscription, quite

227

literally carved in stone and dedicated to some poor dead child, but knowing that Michael wasn't dead after all, that Michael was standing right there, reading his own memorial. 'Weird' didn't even come close to describing the sensation; it was way more than weird.

It didn't quite feel real to think of his mother's remains lying in the ground beneath his feet. It was hard to imagine that whatever was left of her down there had once been a living, breathing person, full of vitality and hopes for the future. A loving and dutiful daughter, sister, wife and mother. He'd still been out partying and living it large when he'd been the age that Mona was when she'd died. A sudden rush of emotion washed over him and he had to draw in a long, deep breath to keep from blubbing right there and then. This was his mother, the woman who'd brought him into the world. She'd loved and cherished him and done her utmost to protect him as best she knew how. The sudden, immense love he felt for her was overwhelming.

Fighting back tears he turned to Annie. "I remember her," he whispered. "I remember her holding my hands an' spinning me round. I can remember the sight of her at the gate, waving me in t' school." The tears won the battle. "She was my mum, an' I loved her."

Annie's face was also wet with tears as she nodded in recognition of his grief. She and Clive had both noticed the nearly fresh flowers on the grave again, but neither chose to mention it.

She couldn't speak; she could only stand there clinging onto her husband's arm, quivering with emotion as the memories of Mona and Michael were finally reunited. Ramona's Angel had at last come home.

***

Three miles later the Isle of Stennoch village came into sight. There were countdown markers for the reduced speed limit. A row of old cottages lined the left hand side of the road with some newer builds set back on the right. Robbie leant forward in his seat. "Slowly," he said to Lynsey.

"I'm only doing twenty," she replied.

"Go slower," he said. She slowed right down to a speed that any curb-crawler would have been arrested for.

Up ahead on the left, Robbie caught sight of the Queens Arms. It was all shuttered up, looked like it hadn't been in use for a long time. Diagonally opposite was the small, stone built building that he knew was the post office, even before he saw the sign. It was closed up for the day, but he insisted on getting out of the car there.

"The Harvester's only across the harbour there son," Clive said, a little confused as to why Robbie didn't just want to drive round. "We can come back here in a bit."

Shaking his head, Robbie stood outside the post office, staring at the small, whitewashed Church building a little further ahead. "Why's it built out into the water?" he asked. The Church had been built on a platform of bedrock to raise it above the level of the sea, but he was right, there were no other buildings jutting out into the harbour like that.

Annie leant her head towards the open door from the inside of the car. "It wa' built that way 'cause the Laird at the time wouldn't allow any land for the villagers tae build their own Free Church. He thought everyone should go tae his. So the villagers built it into the sea. The Laird didn't own that."

Robbie had a look of puzzlement about him, if not a little apprehension too. Clive got out of the car and leaning back in he told the women that they should carry on round to the Inn, that he would stay with Robbie. "It's a lovely, sunny day girls," he said, "an' there's no rush is there? Let's do this bit at his pace eh?" Reluctantly the two women agreed to leave Clive and Robbie to it, Annie insisting that he let her know immediately if anything happened.

"What d'ya thinks' gonna happen mum?" Robbie asked. Annie didn't know the answer. "I'm not five anymore, I'll be fine." More satisfied, though still a little worried, they left them to it.

"It's a beautiful place isn't it?" Clive said as he looked out onto the twinkling water in the harbour.

"Yeah," Robbie said. Though Clive wasn't too sure if he'd actually heard the question, he appeared very distracted by his surroundings. "This way," he suddenly said as he set off towards the direction of the Church before crossing the road. "Here, look...there's a gap between the houses; that's where the school is Clive, I'm sure it is."

Sure enough, there was a gap just where Robbie had said it would be. They walked between the houses into what looked like a small car park. "This wa' the playground," Robbie stated as he panned round to his left. "There! That's my old school."

"It looks like it's a private house now lad," Clive said. There was a dry stone wall down the centre of what was once the playground, a car park to the right of the wall and the garden of the school house to the left. Beyond it were what looked like retirement bungalows on what had once been the school playing field and over the boundary to the right the sea, lapping in to within a few yards of them.

There were rocks protruding from the water with seagulls resting on them. "We used t' scramble about on them rocks when the tide were out Clive, I remember it, me an' my mates." He screwed his eyes up in concentration. "I can see 'em so clearly but I can't remember their damn names." He turned back to face the schoolhouse. "There were only two classes; Mrs Johnson an' my teacher, Mrs McStay, the one mum said helped t' get me out. She wa' friendly wi' mum, Mona I mean, my real mum."

He noticed a woman working in the garden of the schoolhouse. "Excuse me," Robbie interrupted her. "How long has the school been closed down?"

The lady stopped what she was doing and walked over to the gate to speak with them. Surprisingly she had an English accent. "Oh quite a few years now. Nineteen seventy-eight or nine, I think. Why?"

"I used t' come here when I wa' really little," Robbie told her. "Did you grow up here?"

"No," she replied with a smile. "I came on holiday with my husband a few times; we loved the place and so decided to live here."

"Who lived in the house before you if y' don't mind me asking?"

"Not at all, but no-one lived here before us. A local joiner used the building when the school closed and we bought it from him in ninety-one." She explained. "My name's Jean by the way. Stop and chat again if yer passing."

"Thank you," Clive finished. "I'm Clive an' this is my lad, Robbie. Thank y' for yer time Jean."

Walking back through the gap onto Main Street, Robbie paused as he looked across at the Church again. "It's funny Clive, but it seems smaller than I thought it'd be." Its whitewashed walls and black window frames looked just the same as they did in the wedding photo and apart from the fact that the picture was in black and white, nothing else had changed. "I'm sure there used t' be a shop there Clive." Robbie indicated to the far side of the Church. "Like a big garden shed, a shack really, with a bench round the back that we'd sit an' eat lollies on." The ground was void of any kind of structure now. It looked as though the only thing it was used for now was as a dry dock for various small fishers, dinghies and sail boats.

Turning his back to the Church and the dry dock, Robbie looked across Main Street to the row of cottages opposite. He looked them up and down. "I can't remember which one it was. In my dream it's got white walls an' pale blue window frames Clive, but none o' these have an' I don't know which one it was that I lived in."

"Annie told me it were that one ov'r there son." Clive pointed towards the whitewashed cottage with mustard coloured window frames. "It were the Manse back then; don't think it is now though."

Robbie examined it for clues as to his place of birth. It did look familiar, but then they all did. He wasn't getting any sense of home there though, not like he had when he'd rounded the corner and seen the school.

"Come on," Clive said. "It's coming' in colder now, it's getting towards tea-time an' we'll be wanting to eat soon. We can look round some more tomorrow. It'll be getting' dark by the time we've had our tea anyway Rob."

Robbie still had a slightly anxious look on his face as though he were struggling to remember details and it was causing him some kind of inner turmoil, but he agreed that they should go to the Solway Harvester and get settled in before tea. He was feeling a bit on the hungry side if he were honest anyway.

The landlord, so Annie had informed him, was the son of Jock Maguire, the Harbour Master whose boat had been used the night Annie had taken Michael from the Isle. A man in his mid fifties, he didn't recognise Annie, a fact that she was glad of as it would've raised too many questions. She tried to covertly find out about Jock without arousing his suspicions by saying that she used to visit the Isle in her younger years and remembered a Harbour Master by the name of Maguire, and that having noticed that same name on the licensee's plate above the door, she wondered if there was a connection. *Hmm, subtle,* Robbie had thought to himself.

"Aye that's right," the man said. "I'm Angus Maguire, It'd be my da' yer talking about, Jock. He were the Harbour Master for a lot o' years he wa'. He died about twenty year ago now, hen. Wa' one o' the life boat crew went out tae rescue a fisher in rough water wi' engine failure. They got the wee boat back in, but me da' had took ill out at sea: chest pains. He never made it as far as the hospital; died in the ambulance 'afore Newton Stewart."

"Oh I'm sorry," Annie said, feeling genuinely choked. She knew it'd be a miracle if he was still alive, but he'd gone before his time and he was someone she owed so much to. "I remember him as a big man with a heart o' gold, a very kind man."

"Aye he was," Angus reflected. "A fact borne out by the size o' the turnout at his send off. Came from way beyond Ku-koo-bree tae see him off so they did. He wae a very well respected man my da' wa'. A good man. It's an Englishman by the name o' Phillips is Harbour Master now hen, He's alright, but he's no Jock Maguire, yae know what I mean?" With that he tipped a wink in Annie's direction as he cleared their empty glasses and moved on to the next table.

A few minutes later a waitress served them their food. "I hope yae enjoy yer meal," she smiled. Robbie turned and thanked her, noticing that beyond where she stood, was an old man sitting by the window in the corner looking towards him. He didn't look away either when he'd noticed Robbie had caught him staring. He just smiled and raised his glass in their direction. He looked to be eighty if he were a day, wearing a bottle green fleece with a black body warmer jacket over it and a battered looking trilby hat. Robbie put it down to possible senility, or just the 'old man rights' that some old folk seem to think they've got, as if they can't be bothered with what they deem to be the triviality of etiquette and just get to the point instead.

He thought no more of it until he went to the gents and the old boy came in as he was washing his hands. "Now then laddie. Yer looking well."

He was bonkers, he must be, either that or some kind of old perv who liked to follow men into the gents to get his jollies. "Erm...thanks," Robbie said before beating a hasty retreat.

Taking his place back at the table, he looked a little flustered. "Mum, have a look at the old fella just coming out o' the toilets; d'ya know him?"

Annie continued eating her food but scanned the old man's face as he walked past them. He smiled at Annie and she suddenly looked a little uncomfortable but felt obliged to smile back. "No, I don't think so love," she said to Robbie. "Why?"

"Oh nothing," Robbie lied, not wanting to distract anyone too much. "Just with him been old that's all, I wondered if he were around when y' lived here."

"Oh, right," Annie puzzled. "Well I wouldn't like to swear tae it, but I can't say I recognise him." Though she never raised her gaze to look at him again.

Annie said she was tired and wanted to go up to their room as soon as she'd finished her meal, though she'd only eaten about a third of it. She told Clive that she still hadn't got her appetite back, that those last anti-biotics had made her feel full more quickly. Seemed a bit lame, but no-one argued. Robbie and Lynsey stayed in the bar area and had a couple more drinks, before Robbie decided he wanted to go for a walk outside.

"It's dark now," Lynsey complained. "An' it's cold out. Can't we go tomorrow?"

"Okay, you go up then love," Robbie agreed. "I won't be long. I just want t' go outside while it's dark, just as far as the pier that's all. I just want t' see the harbour in darkness. Y' don't mind do ya?"

Lynsey sighed. "Okay, just don't be long will ya?" She kissed him, collected her jacket from the back of the chair and went through the door marked 'accommodation'. Robbie drained his glass, pulled on his coat and went outside. He stood for a moment looking across to the other side of the harbour, before turning to his left and heading down towards the pier.

He was leaning on the wall looking out in the direction of the open sea when he became aware of someone behind him.  He looked back over his shoulder to see the old man from the pub standing there.  Robbie didn't want to be rude, but he was sorely tempted to tell the freaky old duffer to fuck off, but what the old chap said next stopped him dead in his tracks.

"That's a fair old limp yae've got there Michael; sporting injury is it laddie?"

# Chapter Twenty-Six

Holding out his hand to shake, the old fella could see how dumbfounded he'd made the younger man feel, especially as Robbie just stood there and didn't reciprocate the greeting. "I'm sorry tae have caught yae off guard laddie, but I knew it wa' you. Och don't get me wrong, I was'nae one o' the people involved, no' directly at any rate, but I never believed yae tae be dead either."

Robbie didn't know how to react. His initial instinct had been to deny any knowledge, to make out like the old guy had lost his marbles. After all, it could cause a whole host of trouble if anyone knew who he really was. Michael was legally dead and Annie, along with anyone else still living who was involved that night could go to prison for what they'd done. But he knew. The look on the old man's face told Robbie that he could deny it all he liked, but this old man knew.

"My name's Robbie McAndrew," he attempted a deflection.

The old man chuckled to himself a moment. "Well that explains why yae wa' never found. I always wondered. I thought maybe yae'd been taken abroad. I remember yer aunt yae know an' Peter McAndrew; they'd a baby, Robert. Died didn't he?" He sounded genuinely sad, but the intonation in his voice left no doubt in Robbie's mind that this man was no fool, but he was afraid to answer, in case he gave too much away when he wasn't supposed to. This man knew what he was talking about alright.

"I'm sorry, but who are ya?" he finally asked.

Again the old man held out his hand to shake and Robbie responded this time. "I'm Gregor Scoular. I was the village Constable when you were a bairn. An' I remember yer mammy an' Annie when they were girls too. I attended both their weddings, an' I was at yer christening too, and Robert's, God rest his soul. Yae probably don't want tae hear this laddie, but yae've a look o' him, it's no' too strong, but I can see Eban in yer face too. Yer mammy's in yer eyes though, an' yer spirit I hope laddie."

Robbie could feel himself shaking inside. A policeman, a fucking policeman. This was the last person he'd want to know. "Mum...I mean Annie didn't recognise y' back there in the pub."

"Really?" he didn't sound convinced. "Still, it's been over thirty years, I'm a wee bit rounder an' greyer than I used tae be. But if I were wearing my police uniform, what's the betting she'd know me then eh?" He smiled and sensing the growing panic in Robbie he went on to explain more. "Let me tell yae some'ing boy. Back then, when Eban first arrived here, I knew he was'nae right, there was always some'ing about the man. I mentioned it tae yer mammy's da' afore they married but Eban were a Minister an' he'd a way about him." He stopped for a moment and drew in a long breath, then looked straight back at Robbie. "I know I wa' only a lowly bobby Michael but I was a bloody good copper, yae know what I mean?" He tapped the side of his nose with his finger. What he meant of course was that he'd known more about the Isle's state of affairs than he'd maybe let on, or that folk had given him credit for.

The two of them weighed each other up for a while as they engaged in small talk before continuing with the real crux of the matter.

"Pardon my plain speaking but I knew what that bastard wa' doing tae yer mammy, an' tae you laddie, there's no denying it. I even walled him up one night outside this very same pub, threatened tae rip his guts up through his throat so I did if he ever laid another finger tae either o' yae." He pursed his mouth and clenched his fists just thinking about it. "But all it did were tae anger him more, an' he went away an' took it out on yaer mother."

Robbie was caught between the proverbial rock and a hard place. Partly afraid to converse with the old chap further, for fear of giving confirmation of whom he was, yet also intrigued and thirsty for more knowledge about Eban and Mona. Something told him he could trust this man's character. After all, if he really had known for all of this time and not said anything, then he would be unlikely to do so now, it could only hurt the wrong people now. "Why didn't y' report him?" Robbie questioned. "There must've been summat y' could o' done?"

Gregor walked to a nearby bench, his old frame growing weary, he sat down. "Och Michael I tried laddie, I really did, but I were just the bobby an' he were a Minister. My superiors accused me of exaggerating, of trying tae make a name for myself so as I could get on in the job yae know. I remember my sergeant telling me that a wife sometimes needed tae be pulled intae line by her man. Imagine that? Yae'd ne'er get away wi' a comment like that nowadays that's for sure. But times were different then. Many o' menfolk'd gi' their missus a clip round the ear an' get away wi' it. But what Eban did tae Mona went way, way beyond that."

Robbie sat down beside Gregor trying to pull at the strands of his memory, some long, but most very short. "Y' said y' weren't directly involved; what d'ya mean exactly?" he queried.

Gregor looked at him, shaking his head a little. "Just that I s'pose. I was nae directly involved. Don't get me wrong, if I'dae known about their plan tae spring yae, I'dae been sorely tempted tae help 'em anyways, but I'm guessing they didnae wanna put me in an awkward position in case they couldnae pull it off, so no-one ever told me at the time. But I'd seen Jamie sneaking Jock's fisher, the Charlie Peake, round tae the old lifeboat launch just as the sun was going down. I knew they were up tae some'ing, just didnae make the connection 'til after they'd come back claiming yae'd gone overboard an' were lost tae the Solway.

"I pulled Jock tae one side an' asked him tae his face what had happened to yae. Oh his mouth repeated the agreed tale, but the look o' the man told me different; he couldnae look me in the eye, but I knew yae were safe, wherever yae were. So that's how I wa' involved really laddie, by no' pursuing what I knew tae be the truth o' the matter an' by turning a blind eye an' throwing a deaf 'ear."

Robbie pondered this new perspective for few moments. The thought that a policeman, an official like that, had *turned a blind eye,* should have shocked him really, but it didn't. It just seemed to reinforce the general consensus that his father was considered to be such a danger to him that local people, including a copper, were willing to risk doing time to help get him out and to a place of safety, to Annie.

"Were yae abroad then?" Gregor asked him. "Is that how yer aunty kept yae safe?"

Robbie half smiled. "Not unless y' count England as abroad."

Gregor looked troubled. "But I don't get it Michael; I don't get how such a wee boy as yae were back then wouldnae let it slip somewhere down the line?"

Robbie looked at the old man in silence for a while, trying to decide if he should be telling him anything. He concluded that as he'd said nothing for thirty-five years already it was likely testament to his probable trustworthiness. Besides, didn't he deserve to know? All the unanswered questions he must've had throughout those thirty-five or so years. The questions he must've had to answer himself at the time. He was after all the local police constable; he would've had to lie, or at the very least, 'neglect to mention' things that he really should have done.

"I don't really remember Mr Scoular," Robbie began. "But I'm told that I really did fall overboard that night. Jock an' Jamie rescued me, put me an' Annie down at Ku-koo-bree, which wa' planned all along. An' I don't really know, but I must've been in shock, or traumatised or summat, but my mum said, I mean Annie, she said that my memories had got all muddled up anyway wi' all that'd happened, an' that it wa' fairly easy t' convince me that I were Robert McAndrew an' not Michael Whithorn. I was a kiddie an' I just accepted it apparently.

"We moved away from where she'd lived before; where folk knew her baby had died, the real Robert. An' it wa' just accepted that I were her son. I don't think I would've known any different t' be honest."

The old man listened quietly, readjusting his hat again. "So yae really don't remember anything o' yaer life here in the Isle at all son?" he seemed confused if not a little disheartened by the prospect.

Robbie felt disheartened too. "Bits, I suppose. I've had dreams or odd memories that I've put down t' be just dreams or nightmares all my life. Summat happened recently though; I had a pretty bad head injury, nearly died apparently." He explained in a tone that tried to make light of it. "I had amnesia for a bit, but had all these weird visions about being a kid, being scared, being near the sea, all sorts. Then I wa' convinced I were called Michael; even told the doctors at the hospital that I thought I wa' Michael. I'd no identification on me y' see, when I were found, so they didn't know *who* I was. My family had reported me missing, but they'd reported Robert McAndrew as missing an' I wa' telling' people I were Michael, so it took a day or so before the police made the connection.

"Anyway, it didn't take long for me t' remember my girlfriend an' family, my work etcetera. I just couldn't shake all the Michael stuff either. I think that's why mum decided she had t' tell me. Said she'd wanted t' years ago, but didn't know how."

Gregor drew in a long, deep breath and raised his eyebrows. "I bet she didn't. Must o' been hell for her all those years living wi' a secret like that. Not some'ing yae can just drop intae the conversation o'er yer Sunday roast is it?"

"I don't suppose it is Mr Scoular," Robbie agreed.

"Call me Gregor, or Dredger," he laughed. "Everyone calls me Dredger. My old nickname from when I wa' a copper; *dredging* up information on stolen goods or naughty bairns. Some o' the kids round here used tae think it wa' my real name; PC Dredger instead o' PC Scoular."

"Did I call y' that?" Robbie wondered.

Gregor smiled to himself. "No laddie. You always called me PC Scoular; yae'd o' been too afraid o' yer da' tae get it wrong. Besides, there wa' a tele programme on back then, "Garnock Way" I think it was. There wa' a bobby in that called PC Scoular too; you bairns thought it wa' very funny that yae'd got yer very own PC Scoular here in the Isle."

Robbie could sense the conversation was coming to a close for the moment. "You erm...ya'll not say anything will ya? I mean, I'm sure you understand. It's just that the whole world thinks I'm Robbie McAndrew, an' it might cause trouble for Annie if it got out. I wanted t' come here t' try an' remember my real mum. I went to her grave before, in Stennoch. She seemed more real there instead o' just Annie's descriptions, *I actually remembered* for myself. It's important."

The old man stood up and turned to face the other side of the harbour. "Son, I've said nothing in all o' this time. An' I've done so in the knowledge that Annie's a wonderful woman, just as Mona was. Right or wrong I was just as eager tae see yae away from that man as much as they were." He raised his arm and pointed across the water. "I live o'er there, on the Brae. Y'ask anyone where Dredger Scoular lives an' they'll point yae in the right direction laddie. You tell yer aunt, yer ma, that yae've spoken tae me tonight. An' when the times right for yae, yae come an' speak tae me again okay?"

Robbie agreed and the two men shook hands as they parted, separated by a generation but united by a common knowledge. Strange how the oddest things would pop into his mind at the most unexpected times though.

As he watched Dredger shuffle off into the darkness, Robbie suddenly found himself thinking about an old television programme that he'd long since forgotten about, "Take the High Road", the same actor who'd played PC Scoular had been in that too. Why on earth would that spring to mind when more important memories were eluding him?

# Chapter Twenty-Seven

"Dredger Scoular?" Annie repeated at breakfast the next morning. "Aye, I remember him, but I never would've recognised him if ya hadn't told me Robbie," her meaning didn't quite match up with the sound of her words, but he paid little heed. "Still, it's been a very long time I suppose an' yer probably right, or he is should I say. If he were wearing his police uniform I'd have likely known him straight away."

"Is he alright?" Clive asked, concerned. "I mean will he say owt? He won't drop yer in it will he love?"

Annie smiled, "No, the Dredger I remember won't. A decent sort he was. He knew the truth of it back then, tried tae help my sister countless times. I'm told Eban was a bit scared o' him; him an' Jock Maguire were the only men that Eban struggled tae make eye contact with. No nonsense kind o' men they were. Eban was always very pleasant tae people whenever one or the other o' them was within earshot."

"Should we pay him a visit then Annie?" Lynsey asked.

Annie thought about it for a moment before answering. "Yes, yes we should, but not yet eh? I think me an' Robbie should go an' see Joe today."

Robbie was tired; he'd not slept at all well. In fact he'd spent half the night sitting by the bedroom window, looking out over the harbour. It had been a crystal clear night and the amount of stars visible in the sky had been phenomenal. He'd never seen such a vision before, or if he had, as a child maybe, then he couldn't remember it. The whole place seemed so tranquil, so peaceful. It was hard to envisage just what had gone on behind that closed door of what had once been the Manse, the place as a small boy, he'd called home. Someone else was now living there, happily unaware of its history.

*** 

Joe was sitting in the conservatory of his daughter's house in Cutreach, a few miles up the coast from the Isle of Stennoch. He'd moved in with her and her family five years previously, after Izzy's death. He stood up as his grandson showed Annie and Robbie into him. He smiled as he extended his hand out to Robbie, examining his face for signs of the boy he'd once been.

"Oh laddie, yer a sight for these sore eyes so y'are," Joe grinned. "Och I wish my Izzy wa' here tae see yae now Michael. I'm sorry it's Robert yae prefer now so I believe?"

"Robbie," he corrected. "I'm really pleased t' meet ya. I've heard all about you and Izzy an' how y' both helped, thank you. I'm sorry not to have had the chance t' thank her in person too though."

Annie looked away, another wave of guilt washing over her. If only she'd have told him sooner, if only he'd have known, if only this, if only that. She tried not to dwell on things, what was done was done, but it didn't stop her regretting the way things were done, in part at any rate.

"He's a fine man Annie," Joe continued. "Mona'd be so proud, I'm sure of it. My Izzy always knew we'd done the right thing. Robbie, d'ya remember her, my Izzy? She was yer teacher yae know son."

Robbie smiled, thinking back to the class photo that had been in the bag Annie had given him. "Yes I do," he said. "I didn't before I saw a school photo she were in. I recognised her straight away then; she was mum's friend wasn't she? She'd come to our house sometimes."

Joe was pleased that Robbie could remember his wife because he adored and missed her terribly still. Even after five long years without her, life just wasn't the same. "Aye, she'd sneak in the back door like a thief in the night. Eban didn't allow yer mammy any visitors, so it wa' the only way. An' it were the only way the two sisters could keep contact too, through my Izzy. Marvellous woman she was son," he looked sad. "I so wish she could o' seen yae son. She'd be so, so pleased how yae turned out."

Robbie thanked him as he sat in the chair beside him. "You's sit yerselves down. I'm just away tae the other room.

There's some'ing I have for yae Robbie." Joe headed off into the living room and over to a chest of drawers. He called through to his grandson to put the kettle on while he rummaged through one of the drawers. He came back a short while later with a cream coloured envelope in his hand.

Passing it to Robbie he explained that Izzy had written him a letter. "Her memory wa' failing her in those last few years yae see," he said sadly. "She knew she'd forget eventually, so while she still had it all she wanted tae write it down for yae. For the day yae'd come looking, 'cause she knew ya would, one day."

Robbie looked at the envelope in his hand, *For Michael's eyes only* it read. Joe put a hand on his forearm. "Open it later son," he said. "I already know what she wrote, so you open it later eh?"

"Dredger Scoular spoke tae Robbie yesterday Joe." Annie mentioned.

Joe raised his eyebrows before shifting his gaze from Annie to Robbie. "Did he now son? An' did he know who ya'are?"

Robbie smiled as if the thought of concealing his true identity from the former PC Scoular would be a truly futile exercise. "Yes, yes he did. As soon as he laid eyes on me apparently," he explained.

Joe laughed out loud. "Och I'm sorry Annie," he said. "I know it's no laughing matter, but that old coffin dodger's still got it don't yae think?"

Annie smiled in response and looked away. Robbie's brow furrowed in puzzlement at this apparent private joke, which didn't go unnoticed. "The thing is son," Joe continued, "yae never could o' got a thing past Dredger, he bloody knew everything so it seemed, an' the more ancient the old duffer gets, the sharper his mind seems tae be. Memory like a bloody elephant that man."

"He told me that he always knew I wasn't dead. Did he?" Robbie asked.

Joe tensed his mouth and rubbed his hand across his chin. "Aye, he did. None of us ever told him anything in an official capacity y'understand, but he's a gift for reading folk so he has. He knew."

"How d'ya mean...reading folk?" Robbie was curious.

"Well I suppose what I mean is that he was like a bloody human lie-detector. God knows how the man ne'er became a chief inspector or some'ing. Think he wa' just happy wi' his lot, but he could o' gone higher in the force I'm sure of it. He always had that 'knowing' look about him, like Father Christmas would know the truth of it despite the naughty wee boy swearing blind he'd been good, yae know what I mean Robbie?"

Robbie smiled in acknowledgement. He'd only met Dredger the once, but even he knew exactly the look that Joe was referring to. It was the same look that had met his own eyes, the one that silently told him: *there's no point lying to me boy, I know exactly who you are.* He did have an uncanny way about him, an air of calm confidence that made you trust him, the kind of character that would've done well whichever side of the law he'd chosen to make his career in. Luckily he'd chosen the right one, though maybe he'd have been richer on the other side of the fence so to speak.

"Now then," Joe continued, "what can I help yae wi' Robbie? Whatever yae want tae ask I'll answer if I can."

Robbie thought about it for a moment before deciding what he wanted to know the most, though he was aware of Annie's presence in the room and didn't want her to feel hurt or insulted by anything he might talk about. The fact was, Joe was an impartial bystander at the time, so his view of things mattered greatly to Robbie. "How well do y' remember me as a boy Joe, back then I mean? Do ya remember a lot of it? Was it like they say? Was Eban the kinda man I've been told he was? An' my mum, Mona? I really wish I could remember more about her, but it's still so sketchy."

Joe nodded his head a little in concentrated effort. "Aye Robbie, I remember yae very well. Knew the sisters for most o' their lives." Smiling he looked towards Annie. "Lovely girls the both o' them. An' as for Eban; aye, he was everything yae've been told he was, and more; the devil in a dog-collar no doubt about it son. Wi' the way things are nowadays though, there'd probably be some kinda name for his sort, some kinda mental illness, a label tae excuse the behaviour, but there is no excuse laddie, not for him nor the complicit bastards that let it continue. Pardon my French son, but it makes me angry even now, after all this time, tae think that everything that took place since, could'ae been prevented. Yae could'ae grown up there in the Isle where yae should'ae, taking yer own wee bairns round tae see their granny for Sunday lunch an' the like. God rest that poor woman's soul. She didnae deserve tae live like that an' as for the way she left this Earth, well..." He shook his head in retrospective despair, taking note of Annie who was sitting silently listening, just staring out of the window. Joe knew the pain she'd suffered, the sacrifices she'd made. He knew there was more, things she was still to disclose, though whether she ever would...? He maintained his gaze on her while he addressed his words to Robbie. "There's no' really any words I can say laddie, tae describe the way it was in the way I want tae. The turmoil, the tragedy...an' then there was your very own saviour, your auntie Annie; she took on the dragon for *you* son."

Annie could feel his gaze, while she began to shake with emotion. Joe knew she was suffering still but he wanted Robbie to know, to see for himself. "That dragon left some deep, deep scars on *you* Annie, the kindae wounds that'll ne'er heal, no matter how much time passes. It breathed its fire an' burned away half o' yer soul lassie, I can see that. But yae've won. Look at what yae've done," he indicated towards Robbie. "Look at the man here, who'dae ne'er o' made it this far without yae."

Robbie got up from his chair and knelt before Annie's, his eyes wet and ready to spill at any time. "I love y' mum, an' I'm so sorry," he whispered. Annie's cheeks were pink and wet; she looked so weary and weak as she turned to face him.

"Every time you've uttered those words to me '*I love you mum*', every time I've heard you call me mum I've felt like I was cheating you, like I was cheating my sister an' my baby. I gave you the love that your own mother should've been able to give you; I gave you the love that I should've been able tae give tae my own baby boy. But life intervened Robbie, an' we were both in the most vile and intolerable of circumstances. You, too young an' too damaged to be able to deal with it, an' *you* being the only thing I had left, my only reason for living. You were my sister's life, her angel, you were the promise I'd made tae her son..."

Robbie placed his hand on her arm. He smiled. "It's okay mum, I understand now. I know why y' did the things y' did. I know that Mona's my real mum and I love her, but I love you too, you're my mum too. I don't think she'd mind that so much d'you?"

Joe's grandson brought in a tray with three mugs of tea, a jug of milk, a sugar bowl and a plate of bourbons on it. He placed it on the coffee table by Joe and one of the mugs splashed a little of its contents over as he did so. "Sorry Grandae," he said smiling.

Joe just shrugged off the minor indiscretion as he wiped up the spillage with some tissues. Then he, Annie and Robbie made themselves comfortable as they continued a while.

## Chapter Twenty-Eight

Robbie wanted to be alone when he read Izzy McStay's letter to him, to Michael. No-one had questioned him or tried to enforce their company on him. He'd left it in his jacket pocket ever since Joe had handed it to him that morning, but now that he'd taken himself off a way down the Cairn and taken a seat on one of the benches there, he reached inside for the envelope and took it out.

It was a fine evening, a bit chilly, but the evening sun felt warm between the gusts of sea breeze. He had the Solway to three sides of him and out into the distance straight in front he could clearly make out the hilly silhouette of the Isle of Mann. Just to his left there was an old rusted anchor bedded into concrete, put there as a testament to the lives of some local fishermen who were lost at sea off the Mann coast over a decade ago. So much history was here in the Isle. His history had started here too, as had his mother's and the lives of many others long since dead. How many testaments to these people could this small Cairn bear he wondered.

Looking down at the smart, cream coloured envelope in his hands, he thought for a moment about how well kept it had been, considering that it had been a fair few years since its contents had been sealed there within. How much Joe must've loved his wife to have kept it safe on her behalf for all of this time. He wondered if he and Lynsey would still feel so much for each other in their own grey years. Biting the bullet, he pushed his thumb into the top corner of the envelope and began to gently break its seal bit by tentative bit until it was open, like Pandora's box, never to be re-sealed again.

*"My Dearest Michael*

*"I hope that you've a memory of me love. I know that if you're reading this letter that you are alive, and well I hope. I know that by now you'll be a man and no longer the child who I remember sitting quietly and fearfully at the back of my classroom.*

*"Please understand that this is a very difficult letter for me to write to you and will more than likely be a very painful letter for you to read, but it's important that I do this now sweet child. You see, I'm not very well now, my body is failing me and so is my mind. I don't know how much longer I have, but I really don't mind as I'm very tired most of the time now. Joe said that I don't need to do this, write to you I mean, but I think I've been needing to do this for so many years now and never known how to start. My memory's getting muddled love. Vascular Dementia they call it, so it's important that I write this all down for you while I've still got the capacity to do so. So here goes:*

*"Though we all grew up in and around the Isle, I didn't really get to know Annie and Mona until I was in my teens. I used to mind them sometimes, take them to the shops with me, the park, that sort of thing. Happy girls they were, always smiling and full of life.*

"We remained close as they grew up. I stayed in touch with them while I was away in Stirling at the university, training to be a teacher, and they each grew into the beautiful young ladies I remember, ready to embark on their own lives.

"Annie was just in the early flutters of courtship with Peter McAndrew by the time I returned from Stirling and Mona was having aspirations to follow in my footsteps when she was old enough. I'm not sure she wanted to be a teacher, but she'd mentioned on many occasions that she wanted to go to university like I had. She was a good student and she'd studied hard, I'm certain that she would have been accepted at any of the universities she cared to apply for.

"But before she'd even finished her schooling here in the Isle, Eban arrived and her head was turned by him. He was a bit of an enigma at that time. The tall, dark, handsome stranger arriving in town, all he was missing was the horse to ride in on. I suppose the dog-collar around his neck only aided in boosting his appeal to the young ladies of the village back then. Several of them cast an eager eye in his direction, but he showed no interest.

"Don't get me wrong, if I hadn't have already been settled with my Joe, I might have been tempted to cast a glance in his direction myself. There was something about the man which was interpreted by the most of us girls as 'the strong, silent type', a little

259

*mysterious, someone new, though I think there must have always been those among us that saw through him, even in those early days.*

*"Anyway, Mona seemed to be the only girl he'd set his cap to. He was the perfect gentleman, she was too young for him to start with and so he waited for her to come of an age where it would be considered decent. He endeared himself to the Cummings family. They all loved him, thought of him as the perfect catch for the younger of their daughters; a Minister's wife, what an honour.*

*"It seemed the perfect marriage at the start too. The problem for Eban was that he'd been living a lie and as we all know, to do such a thing is unsustainable. I'm sure he tried, but his dark side refused to remain hidden for very long. I suppose that back then Mona facilitated his behaviour through ignorance. She didn't know any different and felt it to be her duty as his wife no doubt but he just got worse, especially after Mr and Mrs Cummings had died. Mona only had her sister left then and Annie had a family of her own. I suppose this only served to isolate her even more.*

*"Eventually his drinking became such that he wouldn't even bother to make attempts at hiding his deplorable behaviour towards his wife and son. He once took you away from the house to punish her. He locked her in and took you to the cave a way up the coast. He left you there and returned to the village. Your mother saw him through the window without you and began banging on the glass in panic.*

*"Dredger Scoular saw her and went to help. Jock gave that man such a beating that night, but he was just too drunk to be able to say where he'd left you. Every man, woman and child who was old enough turned out that evening to search for you. You weren't found until daybreak though, tired, cold and hungry, but most of all you were absolutely terrified. Eban had terrorised you by telling you that if you set foot outside of the cave that the Lord would beckon up a swell big enough to carry you away to sea, never to be seen again. He'd said that you'd be eaten alive by sharks and sea monsters and that your mother would be struck down by a lightning bolt in punishment for your disobedience. I don't know if you'll remember that Michael, but we all did. It was nothing less than chilling for a grown man to do such a thing to any child, let alone his own son. You had nightmares for months afterwards and would wet yourself at the raising of a man's voice, especially your father's. The things he did were despicable Michael; he was nothing short of evil.*

*"Eventually your mother found the strength to get herself and you away from him; it was all planned very carefully over a few months. It's almost funny to think of it now, if it wasn't so bloody tragic that is. We were like a war committee, meeting in secret at every opportunity, planning, organising. We had secret codes and looks that helped to bring things to a head.*

*"I don't know how, but Eban must've found out what Mona was planning to do. She was last seen in the late afternoon, bringing in her washing from the line. The weather was turning as the year*

*grew older, but we'd had a couple of good days in amongst it and like the rest of us, she'd taken advantage of the drying weather. No-one saw her after that; not until the next morning when her broken body was found washed up in the rocks below Burrow Head. You were home alone and Eban was found still drunk in the Kirk, on the floor between two of the pews. He claimed to have been there since the Harvester had locked him out the night before, but according to them, he'd left earlier. He'd been seen at some point in the Queens Arms but only for the one drink apparently. No-one recalled seeing him anywhere else and he claimed to know nothing about what had happened to his wife or how she'd ended her days in such a way. To this day Michael, nothing will convince me otherwise that he not only knew what had happened to Mona, but that he was solely responsible for it too. He was emotionless, even at her funeral he stood by her coffin like she were just another of his parishioners. He didn't want to speak of her, or to say a word about her that day, just stood there while one of his colleagues conducted proceedings.*

*"You clung onto Annie for grim death, pale and fearful. I can remember the dark red rings beneath your eyes even now as I think back. You were so young and frail, but your eyes were those of an old man who'd suffered many torturous trials in his life. I know it sounds awful to say, but I remember thinking to myself how you'd the look of the terminal about you, like a cancer patient with only a few weeks left of his life, you were a heartbreaking sight. That's when we knew we couldn't leave you with him for too much longer;*

*he was killing you from the inside out. So we agreed between us that it was only right that Mona's wishes for you, for your safety, be carried out. The rest I'm sure, you know by now.*

*"Eban accepted news of your "death" in much the same way as he had that of Mona's: silently and with no emotion. There was one evening a few weeks later when Mrs McGuffie told us that he'd screeched at her to get out of his Kirk when she'd caught him on his knees begging forgiveness and sobbing. He just seemed to lose his mind rapidly thereafter.*

*"The Bishop brought his replacement about six months later and no-one saw Eban again. We were told that his so called tragedies had left him feeble minded and he'd been taken to the Church of Scotland infirmary in Glasgow to be looked after. It was a lunatic asylum, we all knew that, but they'd never tell us such. Closed ranks around him as they had always done, probably to cover their own failings rather than to protect him. The last I heard he'd had a couple of strokes and was on his last legs, but that was a couple of years ago now and by the time you read this Michael, the man could well be dead and buried. And God forgive me, but that would surely be a blessing.*

*"Well that's about it son, there's probably not much more I could tell you, even if I could remember. Just remember this Michael if nothing else. What we did, we did for love of Mona and out of genuine fear for you. I know what a good woman Annie is,*

*just like Mona was. I know that she will have kept you safe and cherished you in the name of her sister and if anyone could give you that chance in life that you so deserved, then Annie could. I'm proud to have called your mother my friend Michael; I'm proud to have had her grace my life and I miss her every day but most of all, rightly or wrongly, I'm proud to have been a part of rescuing her precious child from the miserable and doomed existence laid out before him.*

*"I hope you've had a happy and successful life son and I really hope that you've been free of fear. I don't know if I will ever see you again, but if I do, and I don't recognise you anymore, then please forgive me my failing mind, but know that you have always been in my heart, kept safe there with Mona.*

*"All my heartfelt love, Izzy."*

Izzy had been right; that had been a difficult read. Robbie felt true grief that he hadn't seen Izzy before she'd died, while she'd still have known him. To think that these people who'd made such sacrifices and taken such risks on his behalf unbeknown to him, had continued to live their lives and keep his secret safe for decades was more than he could contemplate. He felt detached, as if he were outside of himself looking in. He thought back to his nightmares in the hospital, the terrors he'd felt and the cave, that cave with the rising tide. How terrified it had made him feel as an adult's nightmare and yet, as a child's reality it must've been unbearable.

One thing he did know was that he needed to find Eban, if he was still alive that was.

# Chapter Twenty-Nine

Annie felt quite sweaty and feverish as she came out of the en-suite bathroom, she looked tired. "I'm fine Clive." She insisted. "Please don't look at me like that."

"Like what?" Clive asked.

"All pitying, and worried, like I'm about tae pass out or something," Annie snapped.

Clive sighed, knowing he'd been caught out again. "Well I'm sorry love, but I *am* worried. Whatever this bloody chest infection is, y' just don't seem t' be able t' shake it off. It's been weeks now Annie an' yer still not right."

Annie sat on the edge of the bed, weary. "I know," she replied. "I know you're right an' I'm sorry. But Robbie needs me right now, an' I need tae be here for him. It's important Clive, surely y'understand that?"

"O' course I do lovey, but Robbie knows yer not well y' know. He's not stupid an' I'm certain he'd rather y' got yerself right than ran around after him..." A knock at the door interrupted Clive's flow; it was Lynsey.

"Morning, we were just wondering if ya'd both be down for breakfast?" she asked, before her cheery look altered to one of concern when she saw Annie. "Oh Annie, y' don't look too good, y' look so pale, is it yer chest still?"

Clive answered for her. "Yes it is. We were just discussing it. I want t' take her home an' get her right, but she wants t' stay here."

"Oh Clive stop fussing for Christ sake!" Annie snapped at him again.

Lynsey wasn't convinced by her protests though. "Look Annie, I don't mean to interfere or anything, but y' really don't look so well. I think Clive's right; y' don't need t' be coping with all this that's going on. Robbie'd hit the roof if he thought y' were making yerself worse by trying t' soldier on."

Annie turned away from her. She knew she was right, she knew they both were and if she were honest with herself, she knew she had neither the energy nor the inclination to argue about it with them. But she also had an overwhelming desire to support her Robbie, to be there for him. The thought that she might be letting him down in some way made her want to cry to the point where she could feel her eyes prickling as the tears built up, though she was fighting hard to maintain her composure in front of them, in part because she felt too exhausted to weep.

Lynsey came and knelt in front of her, taking her hand with both of hers. As the two women's eyes met, Annie knew that she was defeated. "Annie," Lynsey began. "I know you're worrying yerself about Robbie, but y' really don't need to, honest. An' I realise that's easier said than done; but he's a grown man, an' I'm here. I'll stay with him for as long as it takes. *You* know what'll happen if he sees y' like this, he'll want t' take y' home himself an' then how'll y' feel?"

"Rotten," Annie replied. "I'll feel rotten. I know...I know you're both right, an' I know Robbie'll be fine. He's strong, like Mona was."

"He's strong like you are too!" Clive corrected her. "An' he'll be furious if he thinks ya've been trying t' tough it out for him. Lynsey's right love. We don't want him worrying about you while he's getting his head round everything else do we? Let's go home Annie, please?"

*** 

Robbie and Lynsey had gone to see Joe again and Clive had taken advantage of his absence to sneak Annie away. It had been agreed that Lynsey would tell him that Clive had spoken to Rich who was having child care issues, so Annie had wanted to go back to help out. Robbie was so distracted anyway that he'd barely questioned anything.

As Clive closed the boot of his car on their suitcase, Annie noticed that Dredger was watching from the pier. She indicated to Clive to wait as she made her way down Harbour Row towards the old stalwart who was resting his bones on a bench there.

"D'ya see this seat here Annie?" Dredger said as she approached him.

"Aye, I do," Annie replied.

He pointed to the dedication plaque in the centre. "He's a good friend o' mine Tam, so he is. Lost tae the sea like so many afore him eh? D'ya remember Tam lassie?"

Annie looked closer at the name on the plaque: *Albert Thomas Stebbings, Son of the Isle, Taken by the Sea, RIP dear friend.* "Tam Stebbings; Aye, I remember Tam," she said. "What happened?"

"Bloody impatience is what happened lassie. Would'nae wait for a calmer water. Wanted tae get them damn lobster pots landed so he did, said he'dae customer for 'em, nor would he wait for a mate tae help, said he could d'it himself an' off he went alone. Done it a thousand times afore, but he was'nae as young as he used tae be, like us all. When they found him, he'dae rope from a creel caught around his left ankle, reckon he'd lost his balance trying tae get it off an' gone over the side. All battered an' bloated he was when the coastguard brought him home. Been dead hours they reckoned, most likely since no' long after he'd set out, daft old bugger. Always thought he knew best Tam did. Ne'er listened."

"Ya trying tae tell me something Dredger?" Annie asked as she sat down beside him.

"Just that sometimes lassie," he paused in thought for a moment, "sometimes yae just need tae take a step back an' let someone else take the lead d'ya no' think? Just like I did thirty-odd years ago despite the unfinished business 'tween us. Folk manage well if left tae'it; they find their way. Mona's boy, he'll find his way d'yae ken Annie lass?"

Annie smiled nervously. "I know. He's so like her in so many ways."

"He's so like the both o' yae Annie." Dredger nodded towards Clive. "He's a good man that, like Peter was a good man. He did'nae deserve..." he suddenly stopped himself and sighed heavily. "Shame Mona ne'er had yer seeing for folk but that's the way of it. Harsh I know, but there's no changing the past."

Annie looked out to the harboured boats. "I know that," she said, knowing exactly what he'd meant by it.

"Then yae need tae let it go lassie." Dredger was nothing if not to the point. "Stop re-living it. It's done. Gone. They're all gone now. Mona's dead but her son's alive. Yae did that right

Annie. Good people will live on through their sons thanks tae you; Peter McAndrew, Mona Cummings. Take solace there. Yae've given the boy the tools; now let him forge for himself, his own way. Some'ing tells me yae've a need tae be taking care o' yerself now Annie."

Annie smiled. "Yae never did miss a thing did yae PC Scoular? Aye, I'm no' so well. Clive's taking me home today."

Dredger drew in a deep breath before standing and offering his hand to help Annie up. "There wae'a time I could'ae walked yae home from here lass, no trouble, taken care o' yae. But that was a long time ago now, an' home's a long way away for you now too."

As they walked slowly towards Clive and the car they reminisced briefly about days gone by and the people who'd come and gone in the Isle's long history. Annie had loved this far flung place at one time, fishing off the Cairn with her sister as children, lifting tatties with her classmates, but it was no longer home, it no longer offered that comfort and sanctuary it once had. All the people she'd loved here had gone. Oh there were happy memories here that made her smile to herself, but there were dark and painful ones too.

Dredger took both of her hands in his as they reached the car. He looked old now as Annie searched his watery, weary eyes. His weathered face telling the tale of his life in each furrow and wrinkle; a deep, deep soul he was. "I know yae'll ne'er come back here Annie." He startled her with this prediction. He smiled and

271

squeezed her fingers gently as he reassured. "Come now lassie, yae'll no' lay eyes on this place again an' who'd blame yae. But ne'er forget it. An' ne'er forget this too Annie: yer loved here an' always will be, yer a daughter o' this Isle an' nothing' or no-one can e'er change that. Yae'll live among the memories an' be sure o' this too lassie; you an' me, we'll be seeing each other again yae mark my words."

Annie didn't feel the need to question his meaning; she knew what he'd meant and it calmed her. He tipped his hat to Clive as he walked on towards the Main Street while Annie took a last, long look around the unchanged harbour before getting into the car. They drove slowly out of the village, past the Kirk and the old Manse with its new and hopefully happy occupants. With one last glance back over the sunlit, glistening water in the harbour, they drove away. Annie knew Dredger was right, she knew she'd never look out over this scene again; it saddened her a little, like the closing of a book.

# Chapter Thirty

"So what did Joe have tae say t'yae son?" Dredger asked Robbie as the two men sat opposite each other over a pint in the Harvester.

Robbie was feeling fired up. The more he learned about his past, the more he wanted to know. "He said that he thinks Eban's in a home near Stranraer. He's disabled now or summat. I wanna try an' find out which one he's in. Would y' know how t' go about it Mr Scoular? Do I need t' go through the Church people?"

"Why d'ya wan'nae know where he is laddie? What purpose'll it serve yae? An' its Dredger son, no' Mr bloody Scoular. Yer no' my bank manager are yae?"

Robbie shrugged, a little embarrassed. "Dredger; sorry, yeah," he relented. "I want the chance t' go an' see him, before it's too late I mean. If he's as ill as Joe says he is, then he might not have too long left."

Dredger took his hat off and placed it in his lap. He rubbed his finger and thumb up and down either side of his chin a few times while he considered Robbie's response. "D'yae think it wise tae seek him out? He'll no' be able tae tell y'anything."

This puzzled Robbie. The old man continued. "He's no' spoken t'anyone in years son. He can't. Strokes yae see Robbie; he's very sick. Don't get me wrong, I know where yae're coming from, but I'm no' even sure the man'll understand yer questions, an' he'll definitely be in no position tae provide yae wi' the answers yae're wanting. I'd just hate for yae tae be getting yer hopes up where he's concerned laddie. I fear yae'll come away wi' more questions an' still no answers is all."

Robbie was taking mental note of everything Dredger Scoular was saying, but an increasing sense of realisation was growing too. This old man knew far more about Eban Whithorn than he'd let on before and he was being evasive. Why?

"*You* know where he is don't y' Dredger? Are y' gonna tell me then or shall I just make my own enquiries?" Robbie was determined.

Dredger laughed out loud. "Yae'd o' made a fine bobby laddie, done well in the po'liss maybe." He lowered his tone again in case anyone was within earshot. "Okay, I'll tell yae where yae can find him if yae promise me yae'll no' be doing anything stupid now. D'yae hear me laddie?" Robbie nodded his agreement and so Dredger continued.

He explained to Robbie that though Eban *had* been in a retirement home near to Stranraer, after a further stroke some years ago, his condition had worsened and so he'd been moved to a proper nursing home on the Ayrshire coast, St Ninian's on the Coalpots Road, in a place called Girvan, where they were better equipped to look after him. It was owned by the Free Church of Scotland and run by a man called Dieter Richter, a German, though he'd been nursing in Scotland most of his adult life.

Further to Robbie's surprise, Dredger explained that he'd been there, several times. "Why? I don't understand."

"Because in a wee sick way, it gives me a little pleasure tae see the man in the state he's in. They always say the Devil'll come for his own an' by God the man's a wreck now; it's pitiful really I s'pose." Dredger's expression never changed; he really did have no sympathy at all for Eban. "When he looks at me I've only my instincts tae tell me that he knows exactly who I am. It's in his black eyes, I'm sure of it. It's that self same look he'd have each time I had him by the throat when he'd done something dire tae yer mammy or you: fear, not knowing what I would do. But a look that told me he'd known exactly what it was that he'd done. Bastard!"

There was a look of disgust on Dredger's face as he spoke about Eban. "D'yae know it's him that has the flowers sent tae yer mammy's grave? Has done for years. Started about twelve or thirteen years ago, just out of the blue the bloody hypocrite! I don't know how he's the nerve son."

"How? If he can't talk or anything...I mean, I don't get it," Robbie puzzled.

"The Kirk folk, that's how," Dredger answered. "Seems he got them tae start back when he was in th'other home. Kirk elders encourage the old Ministers tae say what things they'd want for themselves should they become incapacitated through illness, write it down, yae ken? That's one o' the things Eban wanted and so the Kirk honour it on his behalf. I've ne'er been able tae work out whether he does it out of some deep seated regret for Mona, or if it's a way in his pathetic, sick mind of letting her know he's still around, controlling her. D'ya get my meaning laddie?"

Robbie nodded silently, expressionless, but far from being put off seeing Eban, it had just fired him up more. He wanted to look his father in the eye. He wanted to try and see into his soul for himself, daft as that might sound, but the hunger he felt to do so was becoming unbearable.

***

Lynsey was reading Izzy's letter as Robbie entered their room. She wiped her eyes as she heard him come in. "He's sick; he must've been sick, Robbie. It's not normal t' be like that."

Robbie partially smiled as she handed the letter to him. "Funny, that's pretty much what Joe said; that they'd have some fancy name these days for whatever made him like he is. Don't think Dredger'd agree though, he just thinks my father's an evil bastard, thinks he knew exactly what he wa' doing. Calculating."

Lynsey put her arm around Robbie's waist as she joined him by the window. They both gazed out over the harbour. "He's in Girvan, Eban, I mean. Dredger told me where he is. The old git knew all along; he's just told me. I wanna go there, first thing tomorrow okay?"

Lynsey was naturally apprehensive, but she knew there'd be no point trying to talk him out of it. He wasn't normally a reactionary and so she hoped that he'd stay true to that, but these weren't normal circumstances. Would he go in guns blazing? She didn't think so, that wouldn't be how he'd usually react, but she didn't feel a hundred percent about it now. Rich yeah, Rich would go in fists first, but not Robbie, not normally.

***

The waitress handed Robbie a hand-written note when he went to the bar. "This man phoned for yae Mr McAndrew; said he'd tried yer mobile but couldnae get through. I told him it was most likely the bad reception round these parts. Anyways, he said it's urgent. We've a phone in the office if yae'd like some privacy?"

"Thank you," Robbie said as he followed her to the office while opening the note to read.

*"Call Bash, urgent,"* it read, with a landline number written beneath.

Robbie lifted the grubby cream coloured receiver as he began to dial. He'd forgotten all about Bash and the fact his assault was still an open case. The very thing that had brought all of these current circumstances about and he'd forgotten about it. He'd been sidetracked to distraction.

"Sajid Bashir!" the disembodied voice announced on answering.

"Bash; it's Robbie, Robbie McAndrew. I got a message t' call ya." For a fleeting moment Robbie felt a sudden wave of paranoia. Did he know? Had it come out? Had someone let it slip maybe? But those thoughts were quickly dispelled as Bash began to explain.

"Ah Robbie. How y' doing' fella? Your stepdad told me where t' find ya. I hope y' don't mind me disturbing yer holiday?"

Robbie was relieved. "No, no that's fine; don't worry about it. Message I got said it were urgent though. Has summat happened?"

"Gareth Dalby an' Dale Price. Either o' those names mean owt t ya Robbie?" Bash asked.

They didn't, but there was still the occasional thing that caught Robbie off guard. His memory was pretty much as good as it was before, his *Robbie* memory that is, but he couldn't recall hearing those names before.

Bash continued. "We arrested Dale Price day before yesterday for a number o' things. While the usual questions were being asked in interview, his Brief asked for some other stuff t' be taken into account, one o' which was the assault an' robbery on you Robbie. He grassed his mate up in a heartbeat an' forensics puts them both there. So we've got 'em! Thought ya'd like t' know. Not collared as fast as we'd have liked I know, but they're banged t' rights now Robbie...You okay fella?" Robbie's silence concerned Bash for a moment.

"Yeh," Robbie finally spoke. "Yeh I'm good, honest; I just...I dunno...Does my mum know?"

"She does," Bash confirmed. "I couldn't get hold o' you or Lynsey on yer mobiles, so I called the Wilkinson house. I hope that's okay?"

Robbie felt numb. So much had happened since he'd been attacked and so much of it because he'd been attacked. He didn't really know how he felt, or should feel. "No, no that's fine Bash, honest. I'm sorry, I know I must sound like a right dick. I'm just...I dunno. I wasn't expecting it, that's all. But I'm glad, an' thanks, thanks so much. I know ya've worked really hard on this."

"Scum like this deserve everything that's coming their way Robbie. If I've played any part in 'em getting what they deserve then I don't need thanking fella," Bash explained. "But it's nice t' know we're appreciated. You enjoy the rest of yer holiday Robbie; I'll keep you informed."

After hanging up, Robbie paused for a few seconds before lifting the receiver again and dialling. "Hiya Clive. It's me; is mum there?"

Annie sounded wheezy and tired, but happy to be speaking to him. She was overjoyed that someone would finally be held accountable for what they'd done to her Robbie. She played down how ill she was feeling for fear of worrying him too much and it was for the same reasons that Robbie had neglected to tell her what he knew about Eban's whereabouts, not to mention his plans to go there the next morning.

Lynsey had been given a lift to Cutreach, where they'd been told by the landlord, a farmer would hire out his car for the week if the price was right. She'd be back soon and he couldn't even remember the names of the guys that Bash had just told him: Dale somebody and another guy. How ridiculous that he couldn't remember. Who they were was of vital importance, or it should be, but Robbie just couldn't muster the energy to feel much of anything where they were concerned. He'd got far bigger fish to fry and the biggest of all was Eban, who'd become nothing if not an obsession for him.

# Chapter Thirty-One

"Who'd o' thought Coalpots road would be this bloody long?" Lynsey growled, frustrated that they seemed to be heading out of the other side of Girvan but hadn't found the nursing home as yet. "What was it that manager said on the phone? Something about a roundabout?"

"Er...yeh, Shallochpark Roundabout," Robbie replied as he tried to find it on the crumpled map he was holding. He checked the equally crumpled piece of note paper too, where he'd written the details that Dieter Richter had given him over the phone.

"Drive into town on the A714," he recited from the note. "On the left, just before Shallochpark Roundabout." He looked up in time to see a sign for Victory Park. "That's not mentioned Lyns; think we've come too far. We must o' past it somehow, love."

Lynsey pulled to the side of the road just past the park's sign and leant over to look at the map. She ran her finger along the line that represented the A714 road. "Well if we've come in this way," she said, "then we really have come too far. Look; that's the only roundabout I can see. I don't remember driving round it but I s'pose we must o' done, Robbie. Right; I'll turn us round. Make sure y' keep yer eyes peeled this time, an' if we're going back the other way, then it's gonna be just after the roundabout an' on the right, not left, ok?" she was a little curt. "We're already gonna be later than we said."

Robbie felt like she was trying to teach him to suck eggs, but he remained silent. She was tired, worried about him meeting Eban and a little bit pissed off. It wasn't worth causing an argument at this point, so he left her to rant for a moment or two as they set back off the way they'd come.

The tense mood was broken however as they approached Shellochpark roundabout with its big, red stone monument in the shape of a ship right in the middle of it. How the hell had they managed not to notice that? They quickly glanced at each other before bursting out laughing at the large words inscribed into the side of it. *"Whit's Yer Hurry?"* it read. How appropriate. The people of this town clearly had a sense of humour. They both realised how ridiculous it was to get worked up about it, so they were a bit late, so what. It wasn't really that important.

Not important and not even noticed as they entered the lobby of the large, old Victorian style manor house, no longer the home of landed gentry, but still as magnificent with its original mosaic floor and wood panelling on the walls with a wide, sweeping staircase which split into two halfway up and went either side to the floor above. It was like being in a scene from Downton Abbey.

A small, grey-haired woman wearing a floral, yellow pinny and maroon beret approached them from the room just to the left of the foot of that magnificent staircase. "Helloo there," she beamed as she shuffled towards them, her hand outstretched in greeting. "I'm Mrs Maynard. Are yae tae visit someone hen? Only I'm no' familiar wi' yer faces an' I know most o' the folk that frequent here about so I do."

As she looked up from one face to the other waiting for an answer, a tall, dark haired man in his mid-forties followed her out from the same room. "It's okay Martha; these people are here tae see me I think." Though his accent was of a well spoken Scotsman, there was just the hint of the Germanic stubbornly hanging on too. This must be Dieter Richter. "Remember? I told you Reverend Whithorn was tae have a visit today?" he prompted her.

"Och, so yae did, aye, I remember now," she grinned. She began to shuffle back towards the room she'd just left, waving her left hand in the air as she turned her back. "Yae know where I am if yae need me then," she called as she disappeared round the corner without a second glance.

Dieter held out his hand to shake first Robbie's, then Lynsey's in turn. "Dieter Richter," he introduced himself. "And you must be Robert, Reverend Whithorn's nephew. Is that right?"

Robbie smiled. "Yes, I'm Robbie and this is Lynsey, my girlfriend."

"Well I'm very pleased tae meet you both," Dieter continued. "You must excuse Martha I'm afraid. Her husband, Reverend Maynard, was a resident here until he passed away two years ago. She used tae come in and help out, bake cakes for us, that sort of thing; liked tae feel useful I think. When the Reverend passed, we none of us had the heart tae stop her coming in. She's a little muddled these days, but she means well bless her.

"I must confess tae being more than a little curious as tae your visit today. He only ever sees Kirk men as a rule. He used tae get a visit from an old friend from his former parish I think, but no' for a while now. Over a year I think." He must've been referring to Dredger's visits. Though old friend he was not.

For a nanosecond, Robbie's mind went blank and he didn't know how to reply. Luckily for him, Lynsey did. "Well, we've been living down south for a while. London. We're back up in Leeds now. An' well...y' see Robbie an' his brother, Rich, Richard, have been looking into their family tree. They didn't know that Eban, I mean Reverend Whithorn, was still alive until they'd made quite a few enquiries. Robbie's not seen him since he was very young y' see. But since we were in this part of Scotland on holiday, he thought he should at least visit...if that's okay?" She sounded a little nervous, but convincing. Robbie was impressed.

285

"Really?" Robbie asked. "No-one else visits? Ever?"

Dieter puzzled for a moment. "Well his brother came once, from Ireland. Another Reverend Whithorn. Jacob, I think his name was. But that was just after the Reverend arrived here himself, tae settle some affairs as I recall. But he's not been back. I got the impression they were not so very close. A busy man himself though, I suppose. Would he be your uncle too then?"

The question threw Robbie. He'd forgotten that Eban had a brother. Annie had mentioned a brother who'd attended Eban and Mona's wedding; he'd never returned after that either. "Erm, no...No. I'm Eban's nephew through marriage. He was married t' my mum's sister, Aunty Mona." Robbie hated the deceit, but couldn't think to play it any other way.

"Oh I see," Dieter said. "Well, I suppose I should show you tae his room then if you'd both like tae follow me?"

Lynsey had been gently holding Robbie's hand, but let go suddenly. "Erm, I think it might be a bit much for him if we both suddenly invade his space, like that," she lied. "He's never met me; he might feel awkward about it." She didn't look too long at Robbie. She didn't want to let him down, but nor could she face seeing the man that had been so cruel to Robbie when he was too little to have defended himself. She felt a little bit nauseated and hoped that Robbie would cope without her being there.

He didn't need to question her reasons. He loved her and felt so much pride and sympathy for what she'd had to go through too. After all it hadn't just been his world that had been turned upside-down and thrown in a blender. This had had a massive effect on them all as a family, and Lynsey, well she didn't have to endure it, she could've walked away at any point, but she hadn't. She'd stood by him, fought his corner, comforted him and cried for him. He'd walk over hot coals a million times for her and it still wouldn't be enough to pay her back for all she'd done for him.

He kissed her cheek and smiled, just so that she'd know it was okay with him. He winked briefly as she looked at him before turning back to Dieter. "Lead the way," he smiled. "Lynsey's always been the considerate one. It wouldn't have occurred t' me t' think we might overcrowd him."

Dieter nodded his approval as he headed towards the stairs with Robbie close behind him. "I'm sure Martha will sort you out with a cup o' tea Lynsey. Just go through." He gesticulated towards the room he'd earlier vacated as the two men climbed the vast stairs.

"Thanks," Lynsey smiled. She was actually gasping for a cuppa and would've been happy to take up the offer, but before she got too far she could feel her mobile phone vibrating in her coat pocket. She walked slowly towards the front door to take the call first.

***

"How much of your uncle's condition do you know?" Dieter asked Robbie.

"Well," he paused, "only that he's disabled I think. Didn't he have a stroke or something?"

"Correct. Several strokes in fact," Dieter explained. "Each one taking away a little more of him. It's tragic really. He's totally paralyzed down his right side and very weakened down his left. He doesn't speak at all, I don't think he can, but he's not backward in coming forward when he doesn't like something, let me tell you," he laughed. "Aye, he's quick enough with the disapproving grunts if he's disturbed in the wrong way. Other than that he doesn't really react at all." Dieter stopped in his tracks on the corridor that had led off from the left staircase. He turned to Robbie. "Just so you're not expecting too much, that's all. I told him last night that he'd be having a family visit today; he never flinched. He sits by the window most of the day; doesn't seem tae notice if he's got company or not."

"What's his mental state like? Does he have dementia then?" Robbie didn't want to be confronted by someone with no memory of him. He wanted Eban to know, to remember him. Oh he didn't quite know what he wanted. Answers, though he knew he'd never get them and that was frustrating enough.

Dieter drew in a deep breath while he considered Robbie's question. "He seems tae understand, but without his cooperation it's not easy tae say if his mental function has been impaired. Though vascular dementia due to the number of strokes he's had is entirely possible," he explained. "Put it this way, he's never been diagnosed with any kind of mental dysfunction as far as I'm aware, but that's not tae say there isn't any. Just see how you go I suppose Robbie."

They came to a stop at the dark oak, panelled door with the name plate on which read *Reverend Eban Whithorn*. Robbie had been calmer than he'd expected to be previous to this. Now however, now he was about to see his father for the first time and his heart began to pound. He could feel himself shaking *like a shite'ing dog* to paraphrase his brother. He hoped it wasn't too noticeable to Dieter. He couldn't understand why, why would he feel fear at this big old door opening? He already knew that whoever was on the other side was in no way a threat to him, but he couldn't stop this cauldron of mixed emotions that was stirring a part of him to want to turn on his heels and run. He'd come this far though. This is what it had all been building up to and he was determined to see it through.

# Chapter Thirty-Two

As the oak door swung open, Robbie took in the sight of the large room before him, still with the sound of his heart pounding in his ears. The floorboards were bare and polished and creaked a little as Dieter took a step forward. They were of a dark oak like the door, with a big, deep green rug covering a large proportion of them. The walls were cream, with various framed prints strewn about them, seascapes mostly. Immediately to the left of the door was an en suite bathroom and beyond that, an electronic, hospital bed where a hoist rested to one side. On the opposite side were some bookshelves and a small television on a stand.

A large bay window dominated the room, a moderate table and a couple of chairs at its foot, and, to the left of the table sitting in a wheelchair, staring diagonally out of the right side of the window, across a couple of fields and to the sea beyond, was the room's resident. The man himself. The Reverend Eban Whithorn.

"Reverend, your visitor's here." Dieter gestured for Robbie to sit at the table opposite Eban; he did so though his father made no effort to look at him. "Reverend, this is your nephew sir; this is Robbie, Robert McAndrew. Do you remember Robert here?"

Though Eban looked at neither of them, his deep eyes suddenly widened before he held them shut; he drew in a long deep breath.

Dieter smiled sympathetically at Robbie, as if by way of saying "*Didn't I warn you not to expect too much?*" "I...er, I'll leave you tae it if that's alright with you, Robbie. I'll be downstairs if yae need anything, okay?"

Robbie nodded and followed with his eyes as Dieter vacated the room, only to be confronted with Eban staring straight at him as he looked back in that direction. He had a brief sensation of fear; it was that same feeling that had haunted his nightmares, the fear that had stalked a defenceless little boy being terrorised; it was Michael's fear. But Michael wasn't that boy anymore, he was a man, and battered and broken though his body may have been, it was healing and he was far more a man than the pathetic looking creature sat before him.

Robbie maintained his gaze with Eban as he leant back in his chair, folding his arms in front of him. He cocked his head to the right a little as he watched the old man visually examining his face. Robbie looked Eban up and down too. Not a word had been spoken as yet. He noticed a bulge beneath Eban's lower right trouser leg; just beneath the hemline the tip of a white pipe was visible. Eban must be catheterised; that was a urine bag.

"So...Uncle Eban," Robbie finally broke the silence, "do y' remember me then? Remember holding me in yer arms as a baby do ya?"

Eban grunted and turned away, uncomfortable with what was going on, but powerless to prevent it. He threw an angered stare back at Robbie as his breathing rate increased. *Wow!* Robbie thought to himself. It seems Dredger had been right about the cold, black eyes. The longer he looked his father in the eye, the more he remembered of the fear he'd once felt, of the sickness in the very pit of his guts. He remembered the feel of his mother as he'd clung to her and she'd wrapped her arms around him for comfort.

Robbie continued his minor torment. "...or maybe it's that y' remember attending my funeral is that it?" Eban's shaky left hand lifted a white handkerchief to his face as he attempted to wipe away a couple of beads of sweat from his forehead. "Or perhaps the penny's dropped now...Dad?" Robbie leant forward, resting his elbows on the table while staring straight at Eban.

Even the old man's breath was shaking now, he looked towards the door as if willing help to arrive. It didn't.

"Do I look like her?" Robbie was on a roll. "My mother I mean, do I? Do I look like Mona?" Unable to decide if it was a look of despair in Eban's eye, or one of blind fury, Robbie didn't much care. "Wee Michael; that's me. Michael Whithorn, son of the very lovely Mona Cummings and that nasty bastard, Eban Whithorn: bully, terroriser of women and children and a now pathetic piece of scum who can't even piss for himself. How things have changed Dad, don't y' think?

"This must be the look that old Dredger told me he gets from ya. The *Oh shit what's he gonna do* look." Robbie stood up and walked round to look out of the bay window. "Ya've a nice view here Dad, haven't ya?" He looked back at Eban. "But that's all ya've got.

"So, wadda y' think? About yer son here I mean? Think I've turned out well do ya? Down t' good mothering that is Dad. Annie took over where Mona left off, so I've been really lucky y' see. Two mothers, an' the both of 'em the best in the world at it.

"D'ya know summat Dad? Damn near the whole village were in on it that night when I wa' *Lost tae the sea*." He parodied his best Scottish accent for those last four words. "What does that tell y' eh? What a bastard they all thought y' were, that's what. And...if y' think about it, it also goes t' show just how fucking stupid y' were, how easily y' were manipulated into fucking off t' the pub while a load o' folk went into yer house an' took yer kid. Ha, what a dickhead!" Robbie looked with disgust at Eban.

"Dredger told me that the Devil will always come for his own, an' that he's coming for you bit by bit. I hope it's just yer body he's fucked wi' for now; I think it is. 'Cos to have an active, sane mind trapped inside that pathetic shell must be complete torture for ya, hopefully."

There was a knock at the door as it opened and one of Eban's carers popped her head round. "Is everything okay?" she asked. "Dieter thought yae might like a coffee or tea."

Robbie was relishing this opportunity, to have Eban as a captive audience was satisfying beyond words. He'd thought he might feel a little too cruel, but every flare of Eban's nostrils told him this man deserved the lot, and more. "I'd love a cup of tea, thank you," he said. "I don't know about Uncle Eban though."

"Och he's generally partial tae a cuppa. He's a special cup I'll need tae put it in though, it's a lid on so'as he does'nae spill it on himself  He's no' much strength in his arm, yae see," the young girl said as she opened a cupboard and took out a blue, plastic feeder cup. "I'll be back in a wee while wi' yer drinks." She smiled as she closed the door behind her.

Laughing mockingly, Robbie turned to Eban. "That's a fucking baby's cup. It's like the one our Rich uses for his kid. Does yours have a picture of Thomas the Tank Engine on it too?

"I thought ya'd sounded like a pathetic excuse for a human being when everyone told me about ya, but by Christ I wish they could all see this. I would really, really like t' think that my mother is looking down on you now an' laughing her socks off at the disgusting, pathetic sight of ya. Do y' shit yerself too Dad? Does that poor lass have t' wipe yer arse for ya? Haha, for fuck sake; ya'd be better off taken t' the local vets an' put down. That's what they'd do if y' were a dog. But then dogs deserve a kindness when their suffering gets too much," Robbie spat. "You fucking don't; you just deserve t' suffer more."

He leant right in beside him, his face only about a centimetre from Eban's right cheek. "I hope with all my heart that your *nasty* fucking mind remains intact until the day you die, in agony with a bit o' luck. I'd hate t' think that you were ever granted the solace of dementia. I don't want you t' be able t' drift away wi' the fairies to a field full o' daisies or anything. I want t' know that you're constantly tortured by your lot."

The door opened again as the young woman entered carrying a tray with a china cup for Robbie and Eban's 'baby cup'. There was a small plate of biscuits on there too. "Thank you very much," Robbie smiled. "That's very kind of you, isn't it Uncle Eban?" He glanced at him.

"Och yer welcome. I hope it's okay?" she replied.

"I'm sure me and Uncle Eban will like it; I know I will anyway, thank you." Robbie was surprising himself at his ability to...well...bully.

He sat back down, Eban's dark eyes still firmly fixed on him. He took a slurp from his cup then placed Eban's in front of him. "Don't y' want yours then Dad?

"Well, back t' me then," he continued. "You'd be a proud father, if y' were capable that is, t' know that your young Michael's grown up t' be very happy an' successful. I've grown up with a loving family, Annie an' Clive, my second Mum an' Dad. I've a younger brother too, Richard, though I suppose he's technically my cousin, but let's not split hairs, eh? I've a wonderful woman in my life who loves me very much, Lynsey. I'm gonna marry her one day. Oh I haven't actually asked her yet, but I will, an' I'll keep on asking 'til she says yes.

"D'ya know summat, Dad, I could never imagine hurting my Lynsey the way you did my mum. She wa' your wife for fuck sake, why on earth would y' want t' hurt her; how...could y' hurt her?" Robbie considered for a moment before he continued. "Why would you do that to another human being let alone your own wife?" He fixed his gaze firmly on Eban before delivering his next accusatory question. "*Why would you kill her*? Why would any man kill the woman he swore t' love an' protect, the mother of his only child? Only living child that is as it seems any siblings I could've had died at your hands too you fucking psychopath! What vile and nasty kind of low life are ya? Really?" He remained staring at Eban as if anticipating that he'd answer, though he knew he couldn't, or wouldn't.

He noticed that Eban's gaze kept flitting past him towards the bookshelf. Looking round he noticed a small, framed, black and white photograph sitting on the bookshelf. Walking over to it he picked it up. It was of Mona holding a baby, holding him. His first instinct was to rip it out of the frame. Why should that bastard be allowed to keep a photograph of Mona? Who the fuck did he think he was? But then he thought better of it.

"Does it fuck with your head to have my mother looking at you every day in this pathetic, twisted body ya've been left wi'? Do y' feel her glee as she watches y' piss an' shit yerself? I'm not religious myself, but if there is a God up there, then he took my mother into his embrace a long time ago. Where exactly d'ya think he'll be sending you then, eh? When your time comes t' finally shuffle the fuck off this mortal coil; who exactly d'ya think'll be waiting for you then...Daddy?"

There was another photograph beside that of him and Mona, an even older one. It was a family portrait; a mother, father, two boys and a girl. Robbie studied it closely. The father was wearing a dog collar, a Minister of some kind; he was smiling warmly, as was the mother. The older boy and the little girl were smiling too, but not the middle child, the younger boy whose face appeared quite stern, put out at having to stand still for his picture taking perhaps. It dawned on Robbie that the stern little face was the very same one that was glaring at him now.

"These must be my grandparents?" he asked rhetorically. "No-one ever knew them it would seem. Not even my mother. This must be Jacob?" Robbie pointed to the older boy in the picture, aware he was having the conversation with himself by this point but working things out in his head. The fact that he was still in the room with Eban had become, very briefly, irrelevant. "This must be your little sister then? I didn't know you had a sister too. How strange. No-one ever mentioned a sister, not even Annie. Didn't she know?"

Taking the photo back to the table with him, Robbie placed it in position facing Eban before sitting back down in his chair. "They were ashamed o' you weren't they?" He pursued the point.

Eban's nostrils flared out again as he gulped in air and grizzled. He tried to reach for the photograph, but his clumsy, uncoordinated grasp only managed to nudge it further from him. Robbie watched in amazement.

"Well, well," he snorted. "That wa' quite a reaction wasn't it? Black sheep o' the family were ya? I bet they all pretended ya'd died years ago. Lied an' told folk ya'd been mauled by a lion in Borneo or summat, just so they didn't have to have owt t' do wi' ya. Always been an evil little bastard then have ya?" He picked up the picture again and studied the, all but one, happy faces there.

The brothers were very similar to look at and the woman, Robbie's grandmother, looked lovely: a short, roundish woman, but warm and, well, motherly looking. It was difficult to see how, had they still been alive that is, how they wouldn't have ever visited him when he was little; he was their grandson after all. He remembered Annie mentioning that Eban's parents had been missionaries, but she'd not given the impression that they were dead, nor had she mentioned that he had a sister. Dredger had been right; he was finding that if anything his mind was filling with more and more questions that he knew he wasn't going to get any answers to, not at the moment anyway.

"Do y' think yer Dad's looking down on y' wi' sympathy then...Eban?" Robbie couldn't help himself. "Do y' think he's looking at y' wi' pride? Do y' think he ever looked at y' wi' pride then?" Robbie snorted with disgust. "I doubt it, don't you? I bet that if they'd o' known what y' were gonna become, I think they'd o' held a pillow over y' face when ya were born. I bet y' were the kinda kid that pulled the wings off o' butterflies an' tortured small animals weren't ya?" He stood up as he slurped the last few dregs from his cup. Once he'd placed it back down, he walked round the table to Eban; again leaning down with his face millimetres from his father's.

"You'd better hope you're visited by the Grim Reaper before you're visited by me again...Daddy!" he spat in a lowered tone.

"'Cos let's face it Dad; you're just not gonna know when I next fancy another little family get-together are ya? I could get used t' these little visits. Lot of catching up t' be done don't y' think, eh?" He patted Eban patronisingly on the back. Then added. "Do y' know? You even smell like piss close up."

With that he headed towards the door. He didn't really feel the need, nor have any intention of ever seeing this miserable twat again, but he didn't want him to know that. There was nothing more to be gained from seeing Eban. He'd faced his demon and thoroughly beaten it. There were no answers for Robbie here, and his retribution was the knowledge that his father would be forever tormented after seeing him.

\*\*\*

As Robbie headed down the last of the stairs to where Lynsey was waiting for him, he felt purged. In part he wondered if he'd gone too far with Eban, if he'd been cruel. It wasn't like him to behave that way; it was out of character, which made him worry that maybe he had more of Eban running through his veins than he'd like to think he had. But it was done, at least in part.

Dieter asked if he'd be visiting again. "I'm sure I will," Robbie lied. "I'm not sure when though."

"Not tae worry," Dieter said. "Just give us a call anytime, I'm sure we'll be able tae accommodate you."

"Thank you," Robbie said. "I was wondering if you'd be able t' help with something Dieter?"

"Oh?" Dieter was curious.

"Jacob. Uncle Eban's brother. Would you know how t' get hold of him at all?"

"Oh I'm afraid not, sorry," Dieter shook his head. "He isn't even named as Reverend Whithorn's next of kin; that's the Bishop. Any decisions on your uncle's care etcetera have tae go through him and him alone. I'm afraid there's never been any family involvement in that as far as I'm aware. I suppose you could write tae the Bishop yourself and ask; he might know about your uncle's family. I'm sorry."

"That's fine." Robbie thanked him. They shook hands and Robbie walked across the lobby to join Lynsey, who stood up as he approached her, a worried look in her eye.

Robbie smiled. "Its okay love, I'm fine," he reassured her.

"Good," she said anxiously. "That's good, but it's not that Robbie. Just after you went upstairs I got a call from Rich. It's yer mum Robbie, she's been rushed into hospital this morning…she wa' struggling t' breathe apparently."

Robbie got a cold chill down his spine at this news. "What? Why the fuck didn't y' come an' get me? Oh Lyns!"

She put her hand on his forearm. "She's okay now. She's still poorly but she's stable, comfortable Rich said. They're keeping her in an' doing some tests. She didn't want anyone t' tell ya, wanted y' ta have chance t' finish things here first."

"How are we gonna get home? Her an' Clive took the car," Robbie worried.

"Like I said; she's comfortable, she's not going anywhere. Clive's already been in touch wi' Joe McStay. If we go back t' the village tonight, then Joe'll sort someone to drive us t' the station in Stranraer in the morning. He's sorting tickets an' everything, it's all in hand."

Robbie ran his hand through his hair as they headed outside. "In the morning? We can't wait 'til morning Lyns; we need t' be off now."

"If we go now, then by the time we get home it'll be about half eleven tonight. They won't let y' see yer mum at that time Robbie," she argued. "We need t' be sensible. If we go in the morning, we'll be home just after five an' Rich can pick us up from the station, take us straight to the hospital if y' like."

She was right of course, but he couldn't help realising just how far away they were. Eban had paled into insignificance for the time being as he worried about Annie. As Lynsey drove them back down the A714 in their hired car, a worried Robbie phoned his brother.

# Chapter Thirty-Three

*It's pounding down with rain, it's dark and Robbie can hear an old, but familiar song playing, coming from somewhere in the distance; Thunder in my heart by Leo Sayer. He feels confused.* A sudden jolt focuses him. He must've been asleep, exhausted after seeing Eban.

"Sorry," Lynsey says. "It was a fox I think, just ran out. You okay? Ya've been asleep for ages. We've just passed Wigtown. Not far now love. Are you alright?" Golden Oldies hour was playing on the car radio and that Leo Sayer song was just coming to an end. Robbie felt very strange, detached almost.

He readjusted his position; his leg was aching and he'd got a crick in his neck. Rubbing his eyes he looked out onto the road ahead. "Yeah, yeh. I'm fine," he said. "Must've been dreaming. How long was I asleep?"

"Since not long after y' finished talking t' your Rich about yer mum," Lynsey explained. "Y' must o' been exhausted; ya've been catching flies most o' the way back," she laughed. "I'll drop you at the pub when we get back an' take the car back t' Cutreach, okay? That way y' can get most of our stuff packed before I get back, so we can just get off in the morning and not have t' worry about it."

That old song kept going round and round in Robbie's head the rest of the way back; he even seemed to strangely know most of the words.

It was mid afternoon as Lynsey dropped Robbie outside the Solway Harvester, saying that she'd not be too long. He stood, watching her drive away, half in a daze. He switched his gaze to the other side of the harbour, towards the Brae. He wanted to see Dredger. He wasn't sure why, but it just felt right. He'd only known the old fella for a few days, but he felt a connection with him; he felt that he needed some kind of confirmation from him regarding the day's events. He set off to walk round there.

Sitting at Dredger's kitchen table and looking out of the tiny window across the harbour, with a hot mug of coffee in his hands, Robbie pondered on things for a while.

"Well laddie?" Dredger prompted. "Yae've nae come here tae admire the sea view now have yae? Spit it out for Christ sake; yae've seen him then?"

"Yeh," was all Robbie could think to say.

"Yeh, bloody yeh?" Dredger repeated. "Is that all yae've tae say on the matter?"

Robbie shook his head. "Sorry, yeh, I've seen him, an' y' wa' right: there wa' no answers for me there, just more questions.

I'm glad I went though. It sounds a bit warped but I'm glad I saw him like that, like the sad old bastard he is. An' I'm glad that he knows I've seen him like that. I made it clear who I was...who I am. He knew, I could tell he understood."

"Och aye he'd bloody know alright," Dredger insisted. "How wae he? How'd he look?"

"Tortured," Robbie answered.

"Aye?" the old copper quipped. "An' good enough for him it is. No man deserves tae feel that way more 'an himself does, I can tell yae." He seemed satisfied by Robbie's answer.

Would Dredger know more about Eban's family? Robbie thought for a moment or so before asking. "Did you happen t' notice an old photo in his room when you went there Dredger?"

The old man rubbed his finger and thumb up either side of his jaw line, the way he always seemed to do when he was in deep thought. "Was it by the one o' you an' yer mammy?" he asked. "Old black an' white one? Eban as a bairn I thought. Is that the one?"

Nodding, Robbie continued, wanting to find out as much as he could about his paternal family before he left in the morning. "That's the one, yeh," he said. "What d'ya know about 'em? If anything? Only...I vaguely remember my mum mentioning that he'd a brother, 'cos he'd attended my parents' wedding I think. An' that manager at the Home, Dieter, he said that a brother called Jacob had once visited but never been back. D'ya remember this Jacob, Dredger?"

"Aye, now yae mention it son, I think I do. I remember him being there at the wedding. He'd no' stayed very long though as I recall. Can'nae remember if he wa' at the reception. A Minister I think, like Eban. Ne'er seen him speaking' tae anyone I don't think, just kinda breezed in an' back out again by all accounts. Why d'y'ask about him son?"

"Curiosity I suppose," Robbie answered. "Seems odd that no-one knows owt about Eban's background, his family an' that. They're my family too, but I don't think they ever saw me. I don't even know if they knew I existed. Don't y' think that's odd Dredger?

"I'm thinking' o' writing t' Eban's Bishop; see if I can't get some more info on 'em. Everything about my father has t' go through him apparently," he explained.

"I see," Dredger puzzled. He got up to go and rinse his cup at the sink. "I tell yae what son; leave it wi' me. I've still a pal or two in the po'liss. I'll see what I can dig up for yae. Yae're away in the morning I understand?"

Robbie had to think for a minute.  He didn't remember mentioning that yet.  "Yeh, that's right," he said, "but how did y' know?"

Dredger chuckled to himself.  "Och laddie, 'tis a small, wee world yae ken an' news flies fast around it.  Joe telephoned me this morning.  It's yer mam, she's no' s'well as I understand it."

"That's right," Robbie confirmed.  "It's her chest; she's been bad with it for a while.  It doesn't seem t' be getting any better.  She took a turn for the worse early this morning according t' my brother."

"Yae must be worried son," the old fella consoled.  "She's tough yae know?  Tougher than she looks.  She's a daughter o' this Isle yae ken.  They're bred tae fight in these parts laddie."  He smiled a wrinkled smile through his stubbly jowls.  He meant well.

Robbie stood up and passed his empty cup to Dredger.  "I need t' be getting off now Dredger.  Lyns'll probably be back from Cutreach by now.  She'll be wondering what's happened ta me."

"Aye," Dredger said.  "Well, I hope now yae know where yae started yer life, that yae'll be back here Robbie...some day."  He held his hand out to shake.

"I'll be back Dredger," Robbie announced.  "After all; I'm a son o' the Isle aren't I?"  He smiled as he took the old man's hand in his. On compulsion he then lunged forward and put his arms around old Dredger, patting him on the back. "Thank you, for everything ya've done. I mean it."

Dredger was taken aback and touched by Robbie's gesture. "Nay laddie, I've done nothing but fill a few gaps for yae."

"Oh I think ya've been helping me all my life Dredger, not just recently, an' I want y' t' know that I appreciate everything. I really do mean it."

Dredger smiled as he looked away, a little embarrassed maybe. "You give my love tae Annie son; tell her she's in my thoughts, always has been. An' yae take good care o' yerself too. Yer right, yer a son o' this Isle right enough."

Robbie walked towards the door. He was apprehensive to leave though he didn't know why. He was desperate to see Annie and the rest of his family, which was where his heart lay and where he felt safe. The place he knew he'd be welcome, no matter what. But Dredger and the Isle of Stennoch mattered too now. Now that he was due to leave he could feel the pull. He knew he'd be back soon.

# Chapter Thirty-Four

It had taken about six hours or so from Stranraer to get to Leeds. They'd had to change trains twice: first at Ayr, then at Glasgow. At least everything had run to time.

It was nearly ten past five by the time they'd made their way through the turnstiles past all the shops and towards the exit. They were both tired and stressed. Much of the latter part of their journey had been in silence as neither of them had felt much like talking.

As promised Rich was there to meet them. Sitting in the cab of his Warrior, totally oblivious to the fact that he was pissing off the local taxi drivers again by taking up one and a half of their designated waiting spaces. A transport police officer was heading towards him just as Robbie and Lynsey threw their bags onto the back seat and got in. He must've thought better of it as he let them go with a stern, disapproving shake of his head.

"You okay bro?" Rich asked him. His voice was solemn, not his usual chirpy manner.

"Am good yeh," Robbie replied. "How's mum? Is she any better?"

Rich shrugged. "She's not as bad as she wa' yesterday morning, but I wouldn't say she's better either."

"Have her test results come back?" Lynsey asked concerned. Maybe it was just a *woman's intuition* thing, but she'd picked up on the change in Rich's demeanour, she didn't want to push it though.

"Some have," Rich answered. "Still waiting for others. Listen. If y' give me yer keys, I'll drop yer bags round at home for you after I've dropped y' both at the hospital. Clive's there; he's gonna meet y' at the entrance, so ya'll know which ward t' go to. I've got to go pick Jodie an' the kids up from her mum's, but I'll come back after, okay?"

"Er...yeh, okay," Robbie answered.

"So ya've met yer dad then?" Rich tried to show interest. "Wanker?"

"Yeh; wanker," Robbie confirmed.

Lynsey could feel a tight knot forming in her stomach. Something was wrong. She glanced at Robbie to see if he'd picked up on it too, but she couldn't tell. There was so much strain telling on his face of late that he was getting harder and harder to read.

Rich pulled up outside the Chancellor Wing entrance of the hospital where Clive was waiting. "Right," Rich said, "I'll drop yer stuff off like I said an' I'll be back in about an hour or two, okay?"

"Yeah, thanks," Lynsey said as she handed her keys to him before getting out of the car.

Robbie was looking more concerned now. He'd seen Clive's sullen expression and it was worrying him. "I'm just tired son." Clive tried to reassure him as they headed round to the right to where the lifts were.

"Is she any better then?" Robbie pressed for some kind of positive news, anything.

"Erm; a bit I s'pose. She's more comfortable now certainly," he explained. "Ya'll be able t' see for yerself in a minute anyway," he smiled unconvincingly. "How was yer journey? Did Joe sort out getting y' both t' the station in Stranraer okay?"

"Yes he did," Robbie answered. "His son-in-law came for us. Good of him wasn't it?"

The knot in Lynsey's stomach was tightening. She couldn't swear to it, but Clive's eyes looked a little puffy and pink, more than just being tired. He looked like he'd been crying. Something was very wrong. She squeezed Robbie's hand in hers as they were buzzed into the ward via the intercom.

Clive nodded to the Sister as they passed by the nurses' station, down the corridor, past three bays containing four beds a piece and into a side room to the left.

Annie was propped up in bed with a nasal catheter blowing oxygen up her nose, a green cannula cap poking through a small bandage on the back of her left hand. Her breathing was a little laboured and she looked pale, very pale as she turned to look as the door opened and her Robbie came and sat beside her.

"Robbie," she smiled; she seemed delighted to see him. "Oh its good tae see ya son. How was it? Did yae see Eban? Are yae okay?" She was full of questions. All questions that Robbie couldn't face answering at the moment. She looked awful and all he could think of was her. What was wrong? Why did she look so ill? And how could she have gone downhill in just the few short days since he'd last seen her?

He ignored them all. "Mum! What's going on? Y' don't look at all well. What is it? This is more than that chest infection isn't it? Is it pneumonia? Is it serious?" He was sounding quite desperate now.

She took his hand and smiled. "I'm just a wee bit off colour son that's all...."

"Oh for God sake stop it!" Clive exclaimed in despair. "This just won't do, Annie. Just tell him, just bloody tell him." Annie sighed and looked from Clive back to Robbie, then back to Clive again.

Lynsey could feel her eyes welling up as Clive took over the mantle. "They think it might be cancer, on her lungs they think."

Annie shook her head before calmly correcting him. "No they don't Clive; they know it's lung cancer, they just don't know what type it is yet. I've had an x-ray and scans yesterday Robbie, amongst countless other prodding and poking. I'm fed up of it all tae be honest son."

Clive fought to maintain his composure; he took in a deep breath. "Yes, okay yes," he half whispered. "The consultant from oncology came round this afternoon. He's having yer mother moved t' the Bexley Wing in the morning when they've a bed. That's the cancer unit."

Robbie couldn't speak. He felt like he'd just been shot out of a cannon and was flying through the air, waiting to hit the ground in flames. Lynsey was shaking and clinging to his arm in tears. "How...how serious d' they think it is Annie? I mean...have they said?"

Annie seemed remarkably composed, far more so than the rest of them. "No love they haven't. I suppose a lot depends on what type they're dealing with, how treatable it is I mean."

"What if they're wrong mum?" Robbie grasped at straws. "Have you had a second opinion or owt?"

"Robbie, look at me sweetheart," Annie pleaded cautiously. "*Do you* really think they've got it wrong?  D'ya think these cancer specialists don't know a ravaged lung when they see one?"

Robbie couldn't stop shaking his head in bewildered disbelief.  "But y' never even smoked or anything; I don't get it. How can someone like you get lung cancer?  It must be something else mum…it must be."

"Look," Annie reassured.  "I know it's hard," she looked to her husband, "for all of yae.  But until we know exactly where we go from here I don't want any more doom an' gloom okay?  Now son, tell me about what yae found in Girvan, I've been waiting tae hear."

***

Rich and Jodie arrived at about seven-thirty.  Jodie rushed straight to Annie and tearfully threw her arms around her.  "Oh Annie I'm so sorry," she exclaimed.

Robbie looked to his brother almost accusingly.  "You knew didn't ya?  When y' met us at the station; you already knew?"  Rich nodded silently, expressionless.  "Why didn't y' say then?  I don't get it."

Clive intervened to explain how they'd decided that Robbie should be told by him and Annie themselves. They'd made Rich promise not to say anything until they'd had the chance to see him face to face. "Don't turn on yer brother Robbie; he only did what we asked of him. We'd o' done the same wi' you if he'd o' been the one away from home at the time, son."

Annie was struggling to stay awake by this point. "I love my boys, equally," she emphasized. "I love you all, but I've no' the energy tae be strong for y' all. I need ya tae be strong for each other now...and for me too. I don't want tae have tae be worrying about you lot. I know it's been a hell of a shock, I appreciate that. But it's a fact, an' whether yae like it or not, yer all going tae have tae learn tae deal with it, an' stick together. Okay, lecture over, now away with the lot o' yae. I need my sleep. Think it's all this medication."

"I'm going nowhere!" Clive insisted.

"Clive I'm tired. Please," Annie said.

"I said I'm going nowhere love. You're my wife in sickness an' health. That's what I swore an' I'm staying right here, wi' you." He was adamant.

Annie relented, seeing his determination, but insisted the others go home, have a meal, cry all their tears, have a good night's sleep and come back the next day refreshed.

# Chapter Thirty-Five

As soon as visiting started the next morning, the boys were there together. "I'm sick o' fucking hospitals," Rich said despondently. "First you an' now mum, it's depressing."

"Neither of us chose t' need t' be in one y' know," Robbie retaliated.

Sighing, Rich nodded without making eye contact. He was just venting his frustration at the circumstances that was all. He knew full well that Robbie was right. He just hated the fact that events were beyond his control again; and he was scared, more scared than he'd ever been, they both were. Annie meant the world to them and the thought that they could be losing her was silently terrifying them.

"Oh, Annie Wilkinson?" the nurse checked. "Yes, she was moved to the Bexley wing about an hour ago. D'ya know yer way there?" After getting instructions to the fairly new built Bexley wing, the boys set off down one corridor after another.

Several wrong turns later, they eventually followed a kindly old porter who showed them to the right place. He pointed towards the lifts. "Y' want floor five, right at the top," he explained with a smile.

"Thank you," Robbie called after him as he set off back out of the doors.

Rich was looking around in amazement. "It looks like a fucking airport departure lounge," he finally said. He wasn't wrong; it did look like an airport departure lounge. There was a big reception area, a shop, a Costa coffee bar and a large seating area. There were some sculptures dotted around and several large canvas paintings of wildlife, a chimp, a tiger cub, that sort of thing. It was quite impressive, but nothing like the rest of the hospital, nothing like a hospital at all really.

Stepping out of the lift on the top floor, Annie's new ward was just in front of them. A male nurse was just leaving as they arrived and held the door open for them. "Cheers mate," Robbie said as they passed each other.

They were shown into a room where Annie was in bed, with Clive in the chair beside her, holding her hand. A big window looked out across the city and there was a flat screen television on the wall. It even had its own en suite wet room and there were tea and coffee making facilities for the patient's visitors on top of the cabinet by the window. It was unreal. If it wasn't for the hospital bed and the many plug sockets on the wall with the oxygen feed attached to Annie, it could've passed for a room at the Holiday Inn.

Annie held her hand out to them as they entered. "Yae found me then? How are ya both?" she asked with a sympathetic smile. "Have ya had chance tae absorb things yet?"

Rich shook his head but didn't speak, the slight wobble of his chin betraying the turmoil he felt. "Don't know that we'll ever quite get our heads round it t' be honest wi' y' mum," Robbie answered for the both of them. He looked at Clive. "You been here all night Clive?" he asked him.

"I went home for a couple of hours, but yeh, pretty much son." He sounded weary, and he looked like shit, a cold, half-drunk cup of tea beside him. "Sorry, I would o' let y' both know they'd moved her, but it wasn't that long ago, an' I...well, I just hadn't got round to it yet, sorry." He was clearly exhausted.

"It's okay," Rich placated him. "We're here now aren't we? It's a lot nicer than the other ward was though isn't it mum?"

Annie nodded. "The nurses were lovely there though. I hope they're just as nice here too."

"I'm sure they are," Robbie smiled. "How are y' feeling today mum? Any better? Lynsey sends her love by the way. She's had t' go into work, what with having all this time off recently, but she'll be here later." Annie smiled in acknowledgement as Robbie was reminded of Dredger's parting words. "Oh mum; that reminds me," he said. "Old Dredger said t' send you his love. I forgot t' tell y' yesterday, sorry. He said t' say that yer always in his thoughts, an' summat about being tough, 'cos yer a daughter o' the Isle of Stennoch."

"Bless him," Annie whispered. "He's a strange one that man, but a heart o' gold. Would give yae the shirt from his back if ya' asked him for it. He's seen life an' suffered it too. I wish I…"

A nurse came in to check Annie's obs. As she was attaching the blood pressure cuff, a tall thin man of about sixty walked in followed by a younger man and woman.

"Morning Mr Pennington," the nurse acknowledged him as she finished writing the obs down on Annie's chart.

"Morning," he replied. Then turning to Annie, "Mrs Wilkinson. Good morning. How are you feeling today?"

"Much the same I think," Annie said. "Certainly no worse."

"That's good," Mr Pennington smiled warmly. "Now I've already met Mr Wilkinson, but are these the two sons you've told me about?" Annie nodded. Turning to acknowledge his two subordinates, he continued. "These are my registrars Doctors Emma Quinlan and Damian Partington." They greeted one another.

"And this is my eldest, Robbie and his brother Rich," Annie said.

Clive, though the epitome of good manners on most occasions, was just too tired and stressed to show much patience for pleasantries at this point. "I'm sorry," he said, "but we just want t' know...what's t' do? D'ya have them results yet? So we can get cracking an' start getting my wife better."

Mr Pennington sighed and glanced at Dr Quinlan as he made his way to the foot of Annie's bed. He looked from Annie to Clive and the boys, as if wondering whether it was okay to talk in front of them all.

"We're not leaving," Robbie insisted. "Mum, there's been enough deceit, whatever the intentions. No more; we're not leaving. I want to hear this too...for myself."

Annie nodded before taking a tighter hold of her husband's hand and squeezing it hard.

Mr Pennington took his lead from her. "Right," he said, "okay, well here's where we're at." He paused to choose his words carefully. "The test results *did* come back and they show that you've got something called Metastatic Lung Cancer and a Renal Adenocarcinoma."

"What does that mean in English?" Clive demanded to know. "How long will it take t' treat? An' when will my wife be well enough t' go home?"

"I'm afraid it's not as simple as that Mr Wilkinson; and it means that apart from a tumour in Annie's lung, there's also one on her kidney," the Consultant explained as best he could. "The problem is; they're both secondary cancers."

Clive pulled a face in puzzlement. Annie pulled his hand closer to her chest. "He means that if they're secondary cancers Clive, then there must be a primary somewhere. Isn't that right Mr Pennington?"

"I'm afraid so Annie. Those extra tests I asked for last night have shown that you have a grade three Glioma - that's a cancerous brain tumour Annie, I'm so sorry."

Annie drew in a sharp, shaky breath as tears began to fall freely down her ashen cheeks. Clive gasped and began to cry and Rich punched the wall and rushed out of the room. There was only Robbie still in his seat, breathing deeply through his gaping mouth, his whole world crashing down around him.

"No, no, no, no, no, no......" Clive kept on repeating. "It can't be right. This can't be right; this is *my wife* don't you people understand that? She's my..." Sobs of despair prevented his further outrage.

Annie looked pleadingly to Mr Pennington. "I don't understand. Brain tumour? I've not had any problems with my head. It's been my chest, this cough and the episodes of breathlessness, yes; but no headaches. Nothing out of the ordinary anyway. How can that be so?" Reading the expression on his face Annie drew a long, shaky breath in. "I'll no' be going home will I? I'll no' be coming back from this?"

The consultant walked around to where Rich's chair had been left vacant and sat himself down beside her. "I'm afraid cancer doesn't always follow the logical path Annie. There *are* several treatment avenues we can explore; but in the long term..." He paused for thought. "In the long term I'm afraid that *it is* terminal. The tumours in your lungs are already quite well established and advanced; and the one in your brain is unfortunately in a non-operable region. I apologise if this all sounds a bit blunt, but experience teaches us to be direct with information like this. That way there's no room for misinterpretation. I really am so very sorry the news wasn't more positive for you.

"I think for the moment, you and your family need some time to get things into perspective. We can discuss those treatment options later; and I'm sure that if you feel you'd be more comfortable at home, then it can be arranged that way for you in due course. In the immediate, how's your pain this morning? Are we on top of it for the time being?"

Annie nodded. *Pain?* Robbie hadn't even known his mum had been in any pain. She'd not said; he felt awful. He just sat there, silently shaking with tears streaming down his face while he stared at her. He couldn't bring himself to look anywhere else, just at her.

"One of us will call back later Annie, when you've had some time with your family." With that the medics said goodbye and left the room.

Robbie lunged forward and took a hold of Annie's other hand, scarcely able to breathe. "Oh mum," he cried.

She squeezed his hand from side to side and tried to smile. "Please go an' find yer brother?" she asked. "Don't leave him alone, please find him for me?"

Robbie was desperate to stay with her, but he knew how worried about Rich she'd be if he didn't go and find him. So reluctantly he let go of her hand, still shaking, and walked slowly to the door. He glanced back over his shoulder as he left. As he did so, he saw his beloved mum burst into tears and throw her arms around Clive. The sight of the two of them sobbing uncontrollably in each other's arms was more than he could bear. He turned away and left to look for Rich.

He didn't have far to go; the nurse had headed him off as he'd run out and very sensibly taken him to the relatives room where she was sitting with him as he sobbed. As Robbie stood in the doorway looking at his normally tough little brother, he couldn't help but feel anger. Why Annie? This was so, so cruel when scum like Eban Whithorn are still allowed to breathe along with decent people.

Rich stood up and headed towards Robbie with the most pleading, desperate look on his face that the older brother had ever seen on anyone. "I can't do this Robbie," he sobbed. "I can't take this in; I'm not gonna cope. How're we meant t' cope?" he sobbed.

Robbie could barely make him out through his own tears. "We can; an' we will," he stated. "Because we have to, she's our mum an' we just *have to*."

# Chapter Thirty-Six

Mark Pallister had become the go-between for Robbie and his work. Luckily Dave Smith, their immediate boss had been extremely understanding of the dire, intolerability of Robbie's recent and current circumstances. Dave had visited when he'd found out about Annie's terminal prognosis. Robbie had been due to start back at work on a phased return the Monday after getting back from Scotland; that had been the original plan anyway. Now of course, things had changed.

Dave had suggested that Robbie work from home and that Pally spend half his time working in the office and half working at Robbie's. That way, projects could continue to be worked on and contracts with clients fulfilled. For the most part meetings could be dealt with by conference call or video link and though occasionally Robbie would need to attend in person, but those times could be kept to a minimum. It meant that Robbie could work to his own timetable for the most part and could be free to be with his mum as often as he needed.

Lynsey's sister, Natalie, was around to help more too. Things between her and Pally were going well, so that helped. But it meant that she could also help to take the pressure off Lynsey to some degree.

The brothers were now spending much of their days at the Bexley wing with Annie. Clive had pretty much taken up residence there, going home only occasionally; and only then because Annie would make him. "You need a break," she'd insist. "Get some fresh air Clive." She loved him to bits, but watching him suffer her decline was breaking her heart.

Annie had had a couple of treatments, some chemotherapy, but it had made her so ill that she'd refused anything further. Clive and the boys had been mortified by her decision but she wouldn't budge. Her body and voice were now markedly weakened, but her mind and her resolve were strong, remarkably strong. "None o' this is going tae stop me from dying. I want tae die on my own terms an' there's an end tae it," she'd battled them.

It had broken their hearts to back down, but seeing how weak and exhausted she'd become they'd decided between themselves, and between their endless tears, that they would respect her wishes, that they would all make a conscious effort to do their best to remain positive around her. In private they could fall apart, but for her they were to put on their brave faces.

Annie was on oxygen all the time now. She slept much of the time due to the powerful medications she was on. Sometimes when she first woke up, she wouldn't remember where she was; she'd mention conversations that hadn't happened, talk about seeing the neighbours gardening in the rain, daft stuff, things that didn't always make sense to anyone but her. It could take ten or fifteen minutes before she became re-orientated sometimes.

She'd started to have seizures too. Turns out she'd been having them for quite some time, but nobody had realised, not even Annie herself. They were what the consultant had described as *vacant episodes.* She'd appear to just be daydreaming, to just be staring off into space or something, sometimes lasting moments and sometimes a couple of minutes at a time. One seizure, three days previously, had developed and Annie had become rigid, shaking and twitching violently; a generalised grand mal seizure, the doctor had explained, not unexpected apparently and possibly the first of more to come. It had terrified poor Clive, who'd been the only family member there at the time it happened. So despite what she'd thought, Annie *was* having symptoms due to her brain tumour after all.

Clive felt terrible as she'd had a handful of these vacant episodes before anyone had known she'd been ill. He hadn't thought anything of it at the time, just thought she'd stopped listening to him, or was away in deep thought. He felt as though he should've known back then; that things would be different if he had and that they wouldn't be facing this terrible and inevitable tragedy.

One of the registrars, Dr Quinlan, had been brilliant with him. She'd told him that even if he had have noticed, that by that time the tumour had already taken a hold and that the secondary cancers would have been well established too. There was nothing he could've done and no way of knowing and that to blame himself was about as logical as blaming a number thirty-two bus. "That doesn't make bloody sense," Clive had protested.

"Exactly," Emma Quinlan had stated. "And that's my point."

***

Robbie was sitting with his mum and they were alone for the moment as Clive and Rich had gone to the canteen for some breakfast.

"Have yae done anything else about Eban?" Annie whispered. "Have yae heard anymore?"

"T' be honest Mum, I've not given him that much thought. I refuse t' waste my mental energy on him; he's scum an' I don't care about him. I wish it was him an' not you in this bed I really do," Robbie sighed. "Sounds bad I know Mum, but I'd give anything for it not t' be you."

Annie smiled and stroked his face. "I've been so very proud of you Robbie yae know that don't ya son? I love yae so very much."

He gulped back the potential of a sob as he squeezed her hand. "An' I love you Mum. Ya've always been my world; y' do know that, don't ya?"

She smiled softly as she placed her hand back to her own chest. "Ya've got Lynsey. She's gold dust that one; I hope yae appreciate her son."

Robbie nodded as he thought back to what he'd said to Eban about Lynsey. "You know what Mum, I kinda decided a while ago that I wa' gonna ask her t' marry me."

"And have yae?" Annie pushed him.

"No, didn't seem right somehow. Not at the minute." *Not while his beloved mum was dying,* is what he'd meant. He wasn't sure he could face a potential rejection under the current circumstances, not that he thought Lynsey would say no. He knew that she loved him; but how could he make a romantic proposal like this?

Annie studied him intently. "Tell me son; did yae decide ya wanted her for yer wife before or after yae knew I was ill?"

"Oh before, a long time before," Robbie duly answered. "I suppose I've known how I felt for ages really."

"Then ask her Robbie," Annie said. "Don't wait; just do it love. Life's too short an' it's easy tae think back with hindsight an' tell yerself: *Och yae know what, I wish I'd married that girl when I'd the chance.* When yer dad, I mean Peter, sorry…well when he proposed tae me it was over fish an' chips out on the Cairn an' tae me it was the most romantic thing I'd ever known." A slight wetness in her eyes told of her emotion at this precious memory. "I can still remember it as if it were just last week," she smiled lovingly. "I can remember what he was wearing; the smell of his aftershave and the feel of his arms around me when I said yes. I love Clive very dearly, but *he* was the love of my life...my Peter, just like you're the love of hers. Don't waste time love," she paused. "Besides I want tae know what she says. Ask her soon son."

Robbie instinctively knew what she'd meant by that; she wanted it done soon so that she could rest in the knowledge that he'd have someone to love him, that he wouldn't be alone.

There was a soft tapping on the door and a slim woman in her late thirties with long, blond hair tied back in a loose bun walked in. She wasn't in any kind of uniform like a nurse, but she did have an ID badge hanging from a lanyard around her neck. *McMillan Nurse* it read, with a small photo of her and her name beneath it: *Emily Bennett.*

"Annie Wilkinson?" she clarified before venturing any further. "Hello Annie. I'm Emily from the Palliative Care Team; we'll be looking after you once you get home. I just wanted to introduce myself and explain a little about our role. I can come back later if you'd prefer?"

Palliative Care Team. Those words screamed at Robbie. He knew his mum was dying, but to be faced with someone from Palliative care, a McMillan Nurse just made it all the more real in his mind.

"No," Annie said. "I've been expecting you. You stay love." She looked at Robbie as if to say *It's time to go son, I want some privacy.* He took the hint and got up from his chair, leaning over to kiss her as he did so. He was relieved in part, he didn't want to listen to them discussing his mum's descent into the abyss; it was coming, he knew, but to openly discuss it, to him, felt like an acceptance of it, and he wasn't ready to accept it. He couldn't.

He found Clive and Rich in the canteen. They'd just finished eating and had been about to go back upstairs. "McMillan nurse is there," Robbie told them. "I think Mum wanted to be on her own with her." Clive agreed and suggested they all get another cuppa and sit for a while.

"Have y' spoken t' Joe McStay yet Robbie?" Clive asked. "I've had a couple o' messages on the answer phone from him."

Robbie shook his head. "Yeah me too, but I just can't face talking to him at the moment. I can't really do wi' talking to anyone; they always ask about Mum. I know they mean well, but how many times can y' tell the same story to a million different people? I just feel talked out."

Rich was quietly nodding his agreement. He knew that feeling so well too. Having to explain and then re-explain, time and time again was exhausting. When your fuel tank feels empty and your engine's running on fumes, it forces you to focus on one journey only, with nothing in the reserve tanks for anything more.

"I'll ring him later," Clive said reluctantly. "I think he'd like t' talk t' you though son, but he'll understand I'm sure."

***

Emily Bennett was still there when the three men re-entered Annie's room. Surprisingly, Annie looked quite cheerful; her and Emily had obviously hit it off. It lifted Robbie's heart to see his mum laugh again. Emily stood up as they approached the bed.

"Are we interrupting ya?" Clive asked.

The two women looked at each other briefly, Annie nodded to Emily. "Yae go ahead love. Can *you* tell them about it? I'm too tired."

"What's this then?" Rich joked. "You planning a party? Are we invited?"

"Not quite," Emily explained apprehensively. "Me and your mum have been discussing what she'd like for when she comes home, that sort of thing. I've already made a couple of phone calls and got the ball rolling." She looked to Clive. "Will you be able to sort out a downstairs room by tomorrow Mr Wilkinson? Annie seems to think your dining room would do. Only if you can; I can arrange for a hospital bed to be delivered in the morning. Then if everyone's happy, we should be able to get your wife back home with you by tea time."

"Yeah," Rich interrupted, "me an' our Robbie can sort that out, can't we bro?"

Robbie was worried. "But is it safe? I mean what about all her tablets an' stuff? What if she needs a doctor?"

Emily smiled sympathetically. "I understand your concerns," she said. "But there's nothing your mum's on that either myself or a colleague can't administer. Annie would go home with the full complement of medications that she's on now, plus some more that might prove useful if needed.

"We're there for all of you, to help ease the burden of illness. Myself and a colleague will be calling in several times a day anyway. We can stay, sometimes all night if that's what it takes, or we can leave you in peace after a visit if you're happier that way. We're used to this, and there's nothing we can't deal with. If we feel that Annie needs a doctor, or to be re-hospitalised, then we can arrange it quickly.

"If you want me to call outside of a usual visit, then you've only to ring me. I've got some information leaflets for you all and my phone number's on the front. One of us will always be available for you," she finished.

Clive walked over to Annie and took her hand. "Seems you've been busy while we were out," he smiled.

"There's one more thing," Emily said uneasily. She sucked in her lips, unsure of their reactions. "Annie's informed me that she would like a doctor to authorise a DNACPR form." The look of puzzlement on their faces told her that she needed to explain further. "That stands for erm...'Do Not Attempt Cardio Pulmonary Resuscitation'; it's quite common under these circumstances."

"No! You've talked her into that," Rich accused her.

"I asked her," Annie whispered. "Not the other way round. It's what I want son. I'm tired; I've had enough."

"I know it's not easy to talk about," Emily empathised, "but it doesn't mean that your mum isn't going to be looked after, she will, of course she will. If she has any pain, or feels sick, or anything else, anything at all, then she'll be treat and looked after just as you or I would be. All it means is that if and when she stops breathing or her heart stops beating, then she doesn't want any intervention. She's expressed a wish to be allowed to slip away peacefully."

Clive squeezed her hand, a tear in his eye. Annie stared back at him, pleadingly. "It's what I want Clive. I know how yae feel love, I really do. It's not me giving up ya' understand. I'm being realistic. This is a fight I can't possibly win, an' I'm tired. I don't want tae have tae go down fighting knowing that I never stood a chance; I just want tae go tae sleep. Please understand love?"

Clive nodded his acceptance. "If it's what you want my lovely," he wept.

"Boys?" Annie searched their faces for acceptance.

Rich couldn't bring himself to look her in the eye, so he stared out of the window by way of distraction, his chin shuddering. "Okay Mum," he sputtered.

"Yeh, okay Mum," Robbie reluctantly agreed.

# Chapter Thirty-Seven

"Where are we going?" Lynsey was puzzled at Robbie's insistence that she ask no questions and just drive, following his instructions.

"If I was allowed t' drive my-bloody-self, then I'd just not tell ya, an' ya'd just have t' come along for the ride wouldn't ya? Now stop asking," Robbie joked.

Lynsey felt a little sorry for him. "Ya'll get yer licence back soon hun. It's just procedure after what happened."

"Yeah I know. It's just frustrating, that's all," he replied. "Do a left at these next lights Lyns."

He got her to pull over outside a parade of shops while he went in for something. She still didn't know where they were going as the car door opened again and Robbie got back in with a bulging, white plastic bag.

"Can I smell fish an' chips?" Lynsey asked. "Good. I'm starving, but we could o' just gone for a pub tea," she protested.

"Just keep driving up this hill," Robbie insisted. "Go straight on at the little roundabout when y' get to it."

Lynsey pulled a face. "Now y' know what happens when us two tackle roundabouts don't ya?" she laughed. "Remember Girvan?"

*"Whit's yer hurry?"* Robbie parodied with a smile. "Yeh, that was funny."

The car rattled over a cattle grid in the road as they continued onto the moors. "Just up there on the right Lyns; see where that ice cream van's parked? Pull in just there."

Lynsey followed his instructions and parked the car at the other end of the lay-by from the Mr Whippy van; she parked so they could both look out over the valley below. "Okay," she said, as if expecting the explanation. "What now? Why've y' brought me here?"

Robbie opened the carrier bag. "To eat fish an' chips," he said as he unwrapped them and gave Lynsey hers.

"We could've had fish an' chips back at home." She wasn't giving up. "Why've y' brought me miles away just to eat fish an' chips in the car?"

Robbie shovelled four chips into his mouth at once and gazed out across the Aire Valley. "Nice up here isn't it?" His rhetoric hadn't gone unnoticed. "We came here wi' mum a lot as kids. She used t' work down in the village there; it's where she met Clive. We used t' play on these rocks me an' our Rich. Used t' give mum a heart attack sometimes, scrambling round 'em like lunatics, playing cops an' robbers."

Lynsey smiled at the thought of the two brothers as little boys. It seemed sweet, the days of innocence. "This place is special to ya then love," she said.

"It is." Robbie shuffled round in his seat to face her. "An' I want it t' be special t' you too."

"It is," Lynsey reassured. "If it's special t' you then that's good enough for me."

Robbie rested his head sideways against the headrest of the passenger seat. "That's not what I mean," he said. "I want it t' be special t' you for yer own reasons; and I want it t' be more special t' me too."

Narrowing her eyes, Lynsey was lost if not confused. "I don't get it Robbie. What are y' talking about?"

He took a deep breath as he looked out over the view and then back to Lynsey. He held his hand out for her to take. "I want it t' be more special t' me, because I want to always remember this as being the place where I proposed to my wife."

Lynsey laughed briefly, followed by stunned silence as she looked at him in disbelief while the penny began to drop.

"Lynsey Lewis." Robbie was grinning at her. "I love *you* more than life itself. Will you do me the very great honour of becoming my wife?"

Shaking uncontrollably, Lynsey burst into tears. Holding her free hand over her mouth she nodded, sobbing with happiness.

"I can't hear ya," Robbie teased her. "What was that?"

She flung her arms around his neck. "It was a big, fat yes, you idiot!" she sniffed. "I love you so much, Robbie McAndrew."

They both laughed as they realised there were chips all over their laps and the car seats. "I haven't got you a ring yet. I'm sorry it wasn't more romantic," Robbie smiled softly.

She held his face in her hands and smiled back. "It was perfect Robbie; just so perfect, thank you."

***

Clive and Jodie had stayed behind to oversee the delivery of Annie's hospital bed, while Rich, Robbie and Lynsey went to the hospital. Dr Partington was just leaving her room as they arrived.

"Ah," he said when he saw them, "I'm glad I've caught you. Your mum's just had another seizure. Everything's settled down again now but she's still a little post-ictal, confused. It's perfectly normal after a seizure, so don't be worried by it. She should be back to normal soon okay?"

"Will she still be alright to come home today?" Rich was worried.

"There's no reason why not," Dr Partington explained. "If she has one at home, it's nothing that the palliative nurses can't deal with. Mr Pennington will want to see her himself at some point this afternoon. If he's happy, he'll discharge her then." With that he smiled and left them to go on to the nurses' station and complete his notes.

There were two nurses with Annie when the boys and Lynsey entered her room. One of them was plumping the pillows around her while the other was taking a set of obs.

"Hi," the first nurse greeted them. "I heard the doctor explaining what's happened. She's still away with the fairies a little, but she'll be okay soon. If y' want to ask anything or ya've any worries, y' know where we are okay?"

"Mum," Robbie said softly. "It's me an' Rich. How y' doing Mum? Had another funny turn have ya?"

Annie turned to face him, silently examining his face with her eyes. She almost looked drunk. After what seemed like forever, she finally smiled. Robbie felt a wave of relief as she looked at him.

"Hello Michael, I was just chatting wi' Dredger about you love." She looked away as if trying to recall the conversation. Robbie was taken aback by what she'd called him. Lynsey put a reassuring hand on his shoulder. "Ya've done well for yerself he says, Mona's so proud." She drifted for a moment before looking round at them all again. "Och, my boys," she smiled. She sounded more Scottish than they were used to hearing. "Ma' Robbie an' Richard. All grown up. Dredger's been wanting tae see yae Robbie, he says..." She drifted off a little briefly. "It wae nice o' him tae visit wasnae it? It's a long way for him yae know." She looked round the room, searching. "Yae mustae missed him. Said he wants tae see yae afore he goes. He no' be far," she seemed upset.

. As always, Lynsey rescued the moment. "Don't worry Annie," she reassured. "We've just seen him; he's just gone for a coffee." It might have been a lie, but it worked. Annie settled back down and drifted back off to sleep for half an hour or so.

She woke, still with her boys by her side. "How long have you two been here?" she asked. "I didn't hear ya come in." She'd no memory of what had happened on their arrival and they'd no wish to recount it.

"We didn't want t' wake y' Mum," Rich told her, though he still felt a little disturbed by what he'd witnessed.

342

She smiled and looked round at Lynsey. "Hello love," she said to her.

"Mum," Robbie grinned while taking Lynsey's hand. "I'd like y' t' meet the soon t' be Mrs Lynsey McAndrew," he stated with pride.

A tear ran down Annie's cheek. "Oh, oh yae did it, oh I'm so pleased. He only told me this morning that he wanted tae ask ya love. Oh I'm so very pleased for the both of yae."

"That wa' yesterday Mum, its morning now," Robbie corrected her.

"Was it? Oh right, of course," Annie conceded. "Oh I'm so happy. Does Clive know? Did yae tell Clive yet?" She didn't wait for an answer as she held her other hand out to Lynsey. "Was it nice an' romantic love? Did he push the boat out?"

Lynsey began to laugh. "He took me for fish an' chips on the moors," she chirped.

Annie looked to Robbie and winked at him. "Did he now?" She raised a weary eyebrow. "Sounds perfect."

"Oh it was," Lynsey said. "It really was perfect."

***

Clive had arrived at about eleven so the others decided to leave them to it and come back later, to make sure the consultant was happy and it was all still going ahead. Before they left the room, Clive pulled Robbie to one side. "I've had a call from Joe this morning son. Bad news I'm afraid. Mr Scoular, Dredger, passed away last night, in his sleep by all accounts. He wa' found by his neighbour at about eight this morning. He was in his arm chair; looked like he'd been there all night apparently. I'm sorry son; I know y' took a shine to him." Robbie's jaw fell open in disbelief as he looked at Lynsey. What Annie had said earlier about Dredger visiting her had just become all the more poignant. "I don't want your mother knowing," Clive warned. "Don't tell her, will ya?"

They agreed not to risk upsetting Annie with the news. Robbie felt his heart sink, but his grieving for the old man would have to wait. He needed to keep things together for now.

They took the opportunity of a few hours away from the hospital as they wanted to get the house ready properly for Annie's return, get some shopping in for them. The girls had wanted to put a few balloons up, to welcome Annie home again. So they'd all hugged and kissed as the nurse had explained that Annie would be taken home by ambulance once the consultant had been round. She'd told them he usually came at around half past two, so three o' clock onwards would be the best time to come back.

They'd planned that Jodie and the kids were going to wait at Clive and Annie's house for them, while the boys and Lynsey would go back to the hospital. Lynsey had pointed out that Clive might want to travel in the ambulance with Annie, so if they all went in one car, then Rich could drive Clive's car back home while Lyns and Robbie followed in hers. That was the plan anyway.

***

It was ten past three as they made their way back through the main entrance of the Bexley wing. They'd noticed a couple of ambulances parked outside and wondered between them if one of them was there to take Annie home.

Robbie and Lynsey were holding hands as they stepped out of the lift. A student nurse they recognised was just about to exit the ward when she saw them; she smiled uncomfortably then turned round and went back in. Rich stepped forward. "Summat's not right," he said. "Did y' see that? I'm telling y' Robbie; summat's happened, I know it has."

He was right. As they made their way onto the ward, Mr Pennington, Dr Quinlan and a sullen faced nurse were heading towards them. "Can we just step in here please?" The nurse ushered them cautiously towards the relatives' room as the two groups met. "We just need t' speak t' you."

Robbie felt himself being taken over by a cold sweat and a deep sense of foreboding; Rich had turned drip white.

"Please take a seat," Mr Pennington began. "It's never an easy thing to do and I'm so very sorry..."

"No...." Lynsey's wail interrupted him.

"What?" Rich demanded. "She's not dead! She's not. She's coming home today. We've got everything ready for her."

Robbie began to shake uncontrollably as tears ploughed down his cheeks. "We only saw her a few hours ago. What happened? How can she be..." He couldn't bring himself to say the word: *dead.*

Mr Pennington sat down opposite them. "I really am very sorry, but it could've happened at any point. Your mum, Annie, went into another seizure. I'm afraid this time it didn't stop, a Status Epilepticus. Nothing we did was bringing her out of it and after twenty-five minutes of trying, I'm afraid her heart just gave up. She died at two-thirty-nine. I'm so sorry."

The two brothers couldn't speak through their sobs of despair. Lynsey, though grieving herself wanted to comfort them, but Robbie didn't even know she was there, locked in his own turmoil and Rich, snotty and tearstained was pacing round the room repeating; "No, no, no, no, no...." He finally fell to his knees with his face in his hands and bawled like a small child. Like the little boy he'd briefly become again who needed the comfort of his mother. But she'd gone, and she wasn't coming back.

About ten minutes later they were led round to Annie's room by the nurse. The door, which had previously always been propped open, was now closed, quietly protecting the dignity of its occupant and the private grief inside.

Annie was laid down flat in bed, the sheets clean and neat around her. Her eyes were closed as if asleep and the oxygen feed that had been there for so many weeks was now gone. She was free of the tubes and cannulas and monitors; she looked peaceful as if she were taking a long deserved rest. On a chair beside her, his head in his hands was Clive; he was weeping and rocking gently back and forth.

Robbie walked around to him and put his arms around the poor man. Clive buried his head into Robbie's stomach and sobbed. "I loved her so, so much y' know," he wailed. "I never thought...How am I t' go on without her? I can't..."

Rich, still sobbing, walked slowly up to the side of his mother's bed, her death bed as it had become. He stroked her fringe back up her forehead and bent down to kiss her. "She looks so peaceful. I hadn't noticed all the pain in her face 'til it's gone," he said. He was right; it was so plain to see that all the pain had gone.

His tears fell onto her sleeve as he spoke, "She's beautiful isn't she, my mum?" his voice trailing off to something between a croak and a whisper. "No more pain now, Sunshine."

# Chapter Thirty-Eight

Robbie discreetly pocketed a letter he'd just read. Then he opened a more official looking one in the kitchen of his mother's house while Lynsey straightened her cream blouse and put on her black jacket, the matching piece to the demure black skirt she was wearing for Annie's funeral. "How y' doing love?" she asked him, concerned. "Who's the letter from?"

After glancing over it, he folded it back up and replaced it into the envelope. He handed it to her. "Can y' keep it in yer bag love? It's just summat about me being awarded criminal damages for the assault. I haven't really read it; can't be arsed with it today."

"Of course," she replied as she took it from him. "Let's just get today out o' the way; let's say goodbye t' yer mum properly before we try dealing with anything else love. Have y' seen Clive? He went up t' get changed ages ago."

"I'll go up an' see if he's alright," Robbie suggested as he kissed Lynsey's forehead and turned to leave the kitchen.

Upstairs, Robbie could hear Clive softly talking. He approached the partly open bedroom door and looked in. Clive was sitting on the edge of the bed facing the window. He was clutching a framed photograph of Annie and himself, taken the previous year when they'd been on holiday.  They were standing with an arm around each other, half laughing it looked like.  Robbie remembered seeing those pictures when they'd returned from that holiday.  They'd had a really good time; they'd gone with friends to celebrate the retirement of one of them.

Clive wiped his eyes as he spoke in a quiet, soft voice. "I never thought I'd have t' face this day my lovely," he said to Annie's picture. "I never thought I'd be wi'out y' so soon." He smiled through his tears. "D'ya remember George taking this one?  He belched really loudly an' that's why you were laughing so much in this picture.  He caught y' so well in this love.  You look so beautiful.  You are so beautiful." He crumpled into tears.  Robbie decided to leave him alone to mourn and crept off back downstairs.

Annie had wanted to have a lot of input for her funeral.  "*It's my party*", she'd told Clive.  She didn't want to be buried, she wanted to be cremated and then, when the time felt right for them all, she wanted them to scatter her ashes, with baby Robert in Stennoch and with Mona and her parents too.

"But what about me?"  Clive had asked her at the time. "What if I want t' be with ya when my time comes?  Y' know, laid t' rest beside ya." He'd been more upset than he wanted to let on about it, but she'd reassured him as she always did.

*"You'll always be with me Clive,"* she'd told him, *"an' I'll never leave you…Always there."*

She'd left instructions for her funeral service too. *"Definitely not religious,"* she'd insisted. That hadn't surprised Robbie at all. Any faith she may have held as a child had been well and truly ripped from her very being, along with the pieces of her heart that had gone with each and every tragedy she'd had to endure.

Annie even wanted a say in the music. She'd asked that her coffin be carried in to the song 'Martha's Harbour' by All About Eve; said it always reminded her of going home. She'd asked that three more songs be chosen, one each to be chosen by Clive and the boys: *"Nothing too depressing"*.

Robbie had chosen 'Run' by Snow Patrol and Rich had chosen 'Carry You Home' by James Blunt. Clive however had struggled deeply; he couldn't think of any particular song that encapsulated just what his beloved wife had meant to him. In the end, Jodie had sat with him a while and talked about the happy times. She'd made some suggestions and eventually, with her help, Clive had decided on 'Kiss from a Rose' by Seal. The final song had been Annie's choice too; 'There You'll Be' by Faith Hill; it was the one she'd wanted everyone to be leaving to.

Some friends of Clive and Annie ran the local working man's club and had insisted that they be allowed the honour of organising the Wake. So they had: the function room, the food, the bar. They wanted to do it all *"for our lovely Annie"* they'd told Clive. He'd tried to offer them money, but they wouldn't hear of it. They wanted to give her a proper send off. Clive was very touched by their kind gesture and to be honest, it had come as a blessed relief, one less thing to worry about.

The door to the living room opened and Jodie walked in. "They're here," she said quietly. "The hearse; Annie's here now."

***

The brothers, though tearful, walked tall into the chapel behind their mother's coffin, a weeping Clive walking between them to the sound of Annie's first song choice playing softly in the background. Lynsey and Jodie were immediately behind. Through his wet, bleary eyes, Robbie looked around him as they made their way through. His gaze was drawn to the sight of a police uniform. He looked closer and realised it was Sergeant Bashir come to pay his respects in full uniform with his cap in his hands. He nodded to Robbie as he passed by. How nice of him it was, Annie would've appreciated that.

Two rows in front of him were Joe McStay and his daughter, Marie. Robbie felt so touched that they'd made such a long journey to pay their respects to Annie, especially seeing as the poor man had also just attended Dredger Scoular's funeral only two days previously. Marie was passing her dad a white handkerchief that he used to dab his eyes with; he raised it a little in acknowledgement when he saw Robbie walking past him.

A little further on the same row was Robbie's boss, Dave Smith, sitting beside Pally and Natalie. Clive and the brothers hadn't realised just how well liked and respected Annie had been. There were so many faces filling the room, it was standing room only as more people shuffled into spaces at the back. Emily Bennett and two of the nurses from the ward at the Bexley wing were there too. Friends past and present; faces young and old, many of whom Robbie didn't know. Some seemed familiar to him though their names were lost. He nudged Clive. "Look at how well thought of she is," he whispered. It was comforting to know that Annie had touched so many people and that they'd all felt the need to come and say goodbye to her.

The funeral Officiant opened proceedings by thanking everyone for their welcome attendance. He talked about Annie and the family briefly, but not for long as Annie had also stipulated that she didn't want someone who hadn't known her waffling on about her, when the room would be full of people who knew her better.

The Officiant introduced George, Clive and Annie's friend who'd taken that photo of them, the one in their bedroom. As he spoke about Annie and his and his wife's memories of her, Robbie couldn't help but recall hearing Clive say how George had belched loudly while taking the picture. It made him smile as he listened to the chubby little man recounting tales and fond memories of Annie.

Rich's song was played and then the Officiant invited him to speak. He was really struggling and so Jodie accompanied him to the lectern. As he began, the only words he managed were "My mum..." Emotion overtook him and so Jodie, fighting desperately for her own composure while supporting her husband, took his piece of paper from him and began to read his words out loud, her voice shaky and her tone lowered to a barely audible quiver.

"...My mum," she repeated, "never let me down. Never gave up on me. Never turned her back on me or my brother. She worked hard all her life and she had...so much love to give. Not just to us as a family either. She was one of the most caring people that I or any of you are ever likely to meet. She was soft and she was gentle, but she was also very tough and very strong because she'd had to be." Rich by this point had his face in his left hand, sobbing unashamedly, while his right hand remained firmly clasped around his wife's waist for support.

Jodie held him just as tightly as she continued to read. When she'd finished Rich turned to look at his mother's coffin. "I love you Mum!" he declared as he walked to place a single white rose on the casket.

The Officiant respectfully bowed his head as they passed him to take their seats again as Robbie's song choice began to play. Then it was his turn. He was determined to get his words out despite his grief. Lynsey stood beside him, as she always had.

"When my mum became ill," he began, "it was like the biggest kick in the guts that I'd ever experienced. Like my brother said, she was always the one who was there for us, always strong. To see her deteriorating before our very eyes was the worst of any tortures imaginable. But she was brave, always brave and always strong. She was still the one holding the rest of us together; wasn't she?" He looked to Clive and Rich for confirmation; they were nodding their agreement back to him.

"Our mum is my hero; she's my inspiration and I love her so very, very..." His voice trailed off as he fought to maintain control.

Then, looking at Clive. "Y' know what Clive? You've been the best of dad's t' me an' our Rich; an' the best of husband's to our mother." Clive drew in a sharp breath as his tears spilled over. Robbie continued, "She once told me that you saved her. She called you her knight in shining armour. Said that you were the man brave enough t' take on a broken woman an' t' fix her; an' that ya'd devoted the rest of yer life holding her up, holding her together if y' like."

He looked out on the many faces that were looking back at him, the majority of whom were crying openly. "It's so hard t' find the right words..." he stumbled. "Or even t' find any words that are appropriate for something like this. My lovely, beautiful Mum has died an' we're all heartbroken..." He bowed his head crying. Picking up his white rose, he placed it onto Annie's coffin, kissing it as he did so with his shoulders shaking, giving away his despair.

As he made his way back to his seat, his brother stood to embrace him and Clive's song choice began to play.

Clive proved to be the bravest of the three of them. He thanked Robbie for his kind words and returned the compliment. He then talked about how he and Annie had met; how he'd fancied her for ages before plucking up the courage to ask her out on a date. He recounted the day he'd first met the boys; how he'd tried to impress Annie by spoiling them with sweets and a toy each and how Annie had laughed when Richard had thrown up on him because he'd eaten too much.

There was gentle laughter in the room as Clive told everyone about his happy memories and then more tears, as he told of his grief at losing the only reason he had for waking up each morning. He told the boys how proud of them she was and of how much she loved them. He talked about her joy at Richard and Jodie's wedding and at becoming a grandmother; and then he told of the day that she died.

"She was happy," he explained, "before we lost her. Our Robbie had just told her that him an' Lynsey were gonna get married." There were a few gasps of approval from various people around the room. "Y' know son; she told me that I had t' make y' promise t' be married before the year's out. Said that if ya'd promised it, then ya'd do it, 'cos yer a man o' yer word." He smiled as he looked to Robbie for an answer. "You have t' promise son, let's have summat nice come out o' today lad eh?"

Robbie looked to Lynsey who, through her own tears, was smiling back at him. "I will if you will," she said softly.

Robbie looked up at Clive who was still waiting. "We will," he said. "We promise that we'll honour my mum by making' sure we've tied the knot before the end o' this year; okay?" Everyone in the room began to clap and a few cheers went up before Clive finished by promising Annie that he'd always be there for her boys in her name.

The Officiant again thanked everyone for coming and informed them that they were all welcome to go to the Wake and raise a glass with the family in memory of Annie, should they choose to do so. Annie's final song choice began to play as he invited first the family, and then anyone else to come to the coffin and say their goodbyes to Annie before guiding them out of the two available exits at the back of the room.

Clive, both hands resting on the foot of Annie's coffin with his forehead pressed against them, was sobbing wholeheartedly as one after another, people passed by to pay their respects. Endless pats on the back and words of comfort tried to reassure him that he'd be okay, that he'd get through it. He'd lived long enough to know that in time he'd learn to live without her, but for now it was just too much of a prospect to face. At that moment, he didn't want to live without her.

***

Groups of people were gathered round with their glasses of wine in one hand and plates of sandwiches and chicken drumsticks in the other, as they recounted their own memories of Annie. Former work colleagues, neighbours, friends from the club. There were happy tales of his mother being told in various corners of the club as Robbie made his way round, thanking people for coming. He'd lost count of how many times people had told him how sorry they were for his loss, but it didn't matter. It all felt somewhat surreal to him as women he couldn't remember would recount how Annie had taken him into work with her when he was a little boy, in his Nativity costume; how cute he'd been and how proud of him she'd been. He couldn't remember much of it, but it was nice to hear the fond memories her friends had of her.

He spotted Marie at the bar. "Where's yer dad Marie? I've been looking for him," he asked her.

"Over there." She pointed to a table about twenty yards away to the left. "Here." She pushed a full pint glass into his hand. "Will yae take it tae him please Robbie? I need the loo."

As Robbie sat down with Joe he placed the pint glass in front of him. "I can't believe y' made the journey all the way down here, Joe. Thank you, it means a lot."

"Wouldnae o' dreamed o' no' coming." Joe smiled as he reached for his drink and took a slurp. "Says I can only have a couple an' no more; my Marie does." He rested back in his seat. "A big turnout isn't it Robbie? Annie would'ae been made up tae see 'em all there for her. A fine woman that, they both were; her an' Mona the both o' them the finest so they were laddie."

Robbie smiled; it was hard to know how to respond. "Will y' come to my wedding Joe?" he asked. "I know mum would've liked y' to." He looked a little pensive again for a moment, remembering the letter in his pocket before continuing. "It would o' been nice t' be able to invite old Dredger too. I feel so bad that I didn't see him before...I mean, I know he...an' I didn't return your phone calls either Joe; I'm sorry."

Joe patted his forearm. "D'nae worry about that son. I understand how bad things were for yae, an' so did Dredger. He wouldn't o' expected yae tae leave Annie's side for him. Yae've really nothing t'apologise for laddie."

Robbie told Joe about the last time he'd seen his mum; how she'd been convinced that Dredger had been there. That he'd visited her and they'd had a conversation. "It was so strange at the time Joe."

Joe pulled his mouth down at the sides and shrugged his shoulders. "Whose tae know," he said. "Who of us can be arrogant enough tae dismiss it as hallucination. After all, of all the times Annie could'ae said he'd been; it was'nae 'til the morning after he'd died that she seen him. Maybe it's coincidence son; or maybe it's no', but I tell yae some'ing for nothing; there was'nae a thing old Dredger Scoular could'ae done that would'ae surprised me laddie. There was far more tae that man than any o' us could'ae fathomed that's for sure."

He leant in towards Robbie and rested his elbows on the table. "I've some'ing for yae son, from Dredger." Robbie was puzzled as Joe continued. "I realise that now might no' be the best time for yae, but he wanted yae tae have it; said it was important."

Shrugging his shoulders and looking at Joe's hands for something that wasn't there, Robbie asked: "What is it? What did he want me t' have?"

"Information," Joe replied. "He was tae find some information for yae the last time yae saw him; is that right son?"

Robbie suddenly realised what it was that Joe was talking about and why Dredger had been asking to speak to him; he'd forgotten all about it since Annie had been ill, but he remembered now. "Jacob Whithorn," he said to Joe. "Dredger was gonna put some feelers out about Eban's brother Jacob. I'm sorry, I should o' known. I've just not thought much about it recently."

"O' course yae haven't laddie," Joe said. "That's understandable son."

"What did he tell ya?" Robbie asked suspiciously, suddenly questioning his memory of the letter he'd read that morning. Did Joe know too?

"Och, there's a file full o' information that he got for yae Robbie. I brought it wi' me. When Marie gets back I'll give it tae yae son. It's in her bloody bag."

Robbie, though interested, was struggling to concentrate. "I don't know..." he stuttered.

Joe smiled at him reassuringly. "In yer own time son," he said. "There's grieving tae be done first. But one day, when yae feel yer ready, then yae'll have all that Dredger dug up there for yae if yae decide yae want it." He faltered a little. "There was a letter wi' yer address on it on old Dredger's table when he wa' found laddie. I posted it. Thought that'd be his wishes. Did yae get it son?"

"I did, yeah. Thanks," Robbie replied. He didn't want to hold Joe's gaze too long. He didn't want to know if he knew the contents or not. He wasn't ready to deal with any more just yet.

As Marie sat back down beside them, Joe asked her to give the information to Robbie. She reached down to her bag and pulled out a slightly crumpled and stuffed foolscap envelope and passed it to him; it was quite heavy.

"Bloody hell!" There looked to be more information in there than Robbie had expected to see. "He found out about Jacob then?"

"Aye," Joe smirked. "That he did. Jacob Whithorn; Elizabeth an' Martin Whithorn too; an' one or two others."

"Elizabeth an' Martin?" Robbie repeated. "Eban's parents I take it; my grandparents?"

Marie smiled and shook her head as Joe leant further forward. "No son, Eban's children," he said in a whispered tone. "Yer sister an' brother; seems Eban wae' married 'afore he came tae the Isle Robbie. Seems that Mona was'nae his first wife but n'body knew. It's all in there for yae when an' if yae want it."

Robbie could feel his chin hanging down in disbelief as he sat staring at Joe. He felt numb. He didn't know what to say.

Marie was the one to retrieve him from his stunned silence. "Yae've a lot going on at the minute Robbie. I think what my Da's saying is that if yae want tae know about it at some point in the future, yae know, when things have settled down, then the information yae'll need is there for yae."

Joe nodded his agreement. "Aye laddie, that's it. But one thing I will say's this. When things have settled down an' yae feel yerself in a better position to decide..." there was an air of cautious warning in his voice. "Then yae need tae decide if yae really want tae know; if yae're really s'bothered tae know, 'cause yae'll be opening a can o' worms if yae do son. I'm just saying is all."

Lynsey came over to join them. Robbie briefly explained what Dredger had passed on. "I've got an older half sister an' brother Lyns."

Lynsey spun to look at him. "You've *what...?*" she was stunned.

Robbie passed the large envelope to her. "You keep it. I don't want owt t' do with it at the minute. When we get home I want y' t' put it somewhere safe for me please love," he said as he smiled and leant over to kiss her. "I'm not interested in it for now; I've a promise t' keep an' a wedding t' plan for."

He stood up from his seat. "Back in a minute love," he appeared a little distracted as he headed away through the groups of people.

Lynsey turned to face Joe and Marie. "I think he just needs a few minutes," she explained. "It's been a long an' difficult day."

"Aye," Joe agreed. Though his eyes followed closely as he watched Robbie head outside.

# Epilogue

Leaning against the wall around the back of the club house, Robbie looked out across the field. There was a stiff breeze and the long meadow grasses were bending with it. It was still daylight, but the Starlings were beginning to flock. They were looking for somewhere to roost for the night, going through their usual 'end of the day' routine. Great numbers of them forming living clouds in the sky; and the noise. The noise they made easily penetrated the sound coming from the nearby road. They were in competition with the traffic and they were winning.

Robbie took in a deep breath as he took the folded letter out of his inner breast pocket; removing it from the envelope. He wondered how long the old man had deliberated whether to post it to him or not, or if he ever would've done at all. If he hadn't have died, would this letter have ended up on his fire, never to be seen? He began to read Dredger's words for the second time that day. Just to be sure he'd not imagined those words he'd seen that morning; he needed to have another look.

*"Robbie. I should've been a little braver I think. There's something I wanted to tell you when you were here, but I couldn't think how to. And there was Annie to consider. Poor Annie. She's*

*carried all this guilt around with her for years. She must feel like she's being punished all the time; her whole life.*

*The thing is, I feel that I'm responsible for much of what happened back then son, and for the way things turned out. Eban you see, he found out something that he used against me. And what he found out was what closed him down to Annie. He stopped the sisters from seeing each other or even speaking. He took mine and Annie's sin out on your poor mother, Mona.*

*The thing is Robbie, and please don't blame Annie for this. She's never known about Eban finding out you see. But the thing is, I'd always had a soft spot for Annie, I was sweet on her you could say. We all got drunk one night after she'd married Peter and I slept with her. Don't ask me how it came about and I know it was wrong, but it happened.*

*She always declared her baby to be Peter's, but he wasn't, he was my son. Wee Robert was my baby boy, not Peter's. I've a birth mark on the inside of my upper right arm. Robert had the exact same mark, there was no mistaking it. Peter never knew, God bless the man. Just me and Annie. I wanted them both to be with me, but she'd have none of it. Told me she loved Peter and that what had happened between us that night had been a mistake. I knew that she'd never forgive me if I told Peter the truth, and so I kept my silence. Kept our secret. Watched from a distance while another man held my boy in his arms and called him son. But then Eban found out.*

*It was after my boy died. I couldn't go to the funeral, she didn't want me there. Said that if folk had seen the grief-stricken state I was in that they'd be suspicious. She was sobbing alone out on the Cairn the night he'd been buried. I'd got there before her, she didn't expect to see me. But when she did, we just fell into each other's arms and cried our hearts out for our baby boy. I was telling her how hard it was to pretend everything was alright when my soul felt so crushed. That I'd lost my son too.*

*We parted and she left me alone there. It was dark and as I'd watched her pass the pier I became aware of him, Eban. He was standing behind the white tower, he'd been there all along in the darkness, heard everything. He glared at me. I told him that whatever he thought of me, he needed to put Peter and Annie first, that he'd to understand their grief, let them be. I was no shrinking violet and I'd made it clear that I expected his silence.*

*That's when I did some digging around in his past. I wanted something I could threaten him with if I needed to. That's when I found out about his first wife, Sofie, she was called. They had two children. She was still alive and I couldn't find any record of a divorce. I couldn't prove it Robbie, but I think he was married to your mother bigamously.*

*It wasn't long after that, that Peter and Annie left for England. Almost as soon as they'd gone, Eban took steps to cut the sisters off from one another. He referred to Annie as a whore and said that Mona must be too as they were cut from the same cloth. He began to question your paternity and when Mona had any further pregnancies, he refused to believe they were his.*

*I spent a long time believing that Mona had begun paying for my crimes then, but I found out that he'd been a bastard to her for quite a while before that. That things had just intensified with his new knowledge. Each time I tried to intervene he'd bring it up.*

*I made it clear to him what I knew. I had the man pinned to the floor once for what I'd seen him do to your mother with my own eyes too. Jock was behind me and Mona was nearby crying. Eban glared at me and smiled. "Go on," he said to me. "Go on, you do your worst and I'll do mine shall I, Daddy?"*

*I knew then that we had an ungodly agreement between us to keep each other's sins hidden. The others were within earshot. I was afraid for what it might do to Annie and Peter's marriage if I let him tell, and to Mona's reputation too. Not to mention my job. In those days I could've lost my job for the sin of fathering a child to another man's wife. Conduct unbecoming; and all that.*

*I couldn't keep my hands off him time and time again for what he was putting your mother and you through. Yet time and time again I stopped short for fear of what he might say to the wrong people.*

*I can't tell you Robbie how much I've regretted my weakness back then. If I'd have done what I should've done, the right thing. Then there's no doubt in my mind that your mother would still be here. I could've stopped him before it had gone that far, but I didn't.*

*Annie never knew that Eban had found out about Robert, but I think he'd told Mona. I think it was just another stick to beat her with as far as he was concerned. She was always a little afraid of me after that. Not that she thought I'd hurt her, I'd never do that. But I think that she was afraid to be seen around me. I think he'd banned her from speaking to me too, though she did sometimes, but she was always on edge.*

*I can't even find the words I need to tell you how sorry I am Robbie, for the part I played in Mona's death. I feel so certain that I could've prevented it if I'd known, if I'd acted differently. If I'd been a better man.*

*Please forgive me, Gregor.*

\*\*\*

The birds were all resting in nearby trees now, though they were still vocalising their presence loudly to one another as Robbie folded the letter back into its envelope, carefully replacing it in his pocket. Would this nightmare ever end? He felt numb as he slowly made his way back inside. His head so full that he thought he might pass out.

Feeling light-headed, he took the first empty seat that he came to as he re-entered the building. A hand came to rest on his shoulder. It was Clive.

"Robbie. Are y' alright son? Y' look a bit pasty," he noted.

"I'm just tired Clive. It's been a long day. I'm fine though, don't worry," Robbie reassured him. He rested his hand across his chest where he could just feel the letter in his pocket crinkle a little. Just to prove to himself that he hadn't imagined it. Unfortunately it was all too real.

***

**The End**

## Author's Note

Thank you for reading this far. I hope you enjoyed the story. Please keep your eyes peeled for what happens to Robbie next and where things take him in his search for the history of his father's family. What made the Reverend Eban Whithorn into the man he turned out to be, and was he truly a bigamist?

***

There's a wee, small corner of Scotland that has become my sanctuary when I need a little peace and quiet. This is where I've based Robbie/Michael's origin. A beautiful fishing village where I've been much inspired. I've drawn on the local history there and used some of it in my work here. There are many examples of which I could give you, but I wanted to pay particular tribute to The Solway Harvester.

In this story, this is what I've chosen to call the local pub. In reality the pub is called The Steampacket Inn, a great little pub with good food and a fine beer selection. The Solway Harvester was the name of a Scallop Dredger that sank off the coast of the Isle of Man on 11th January 2000 during a force nine gale. All seven lives were tragically lost that night and all hands were from this village or its surrounding area. Memorials of this tragic event are evident on the Cairn at the far end of the village. Rest in Peace to those young men and all others taken by the sea.

Some of the family names I've used are also historic to the village, as I'm sure local people will confirm if you should ever find yourself there, and I highly recommend a visit.

The original Wicker Man movie really was filmed in and around this area and much of the knowledge I gained here was from my friend and local artist, Amanda Sunderland. She has a working studio that's worth a visit too.

Cutreach and Stennoch are really farms in the local area; and though I've changed things around a little, the village itself is based on the Isle of Whithorn (d'ya see what I did there?). The name of the Harbour Master's boat in this story, The Charlie Peake, was in fact the name of the village's first ever life boat in 1869.

Finally, I would also like to pay tribute to my colleagues. Guys; I have nothing but fondness and the deepest of respect for you. I hope you don't mind me playing around with your names in here but I needed something to help counter my infamous thirty second memory. Much love to you all. P.x

Printed in Great Britain
by Amazon.co.uk, Ltd.,
Marston Gate.